Peking University Linguistics Research

Volume 1

Peking University Linguistics Research (PKULR) is a cooperation project between Springer Nature and Peking University Press. This series presents the latest discoveries and developments of significance in linguistic research conducted by famous Chinese scholars. Titles in this series are carefully evaluated, examined and selected by Peking University (which ranks No. 10 in the world and No. 1 in China in the QS World University Rankings-Linguistics 2016) and Peking University Press (which was honored as the most influential publisher in linguistics according to Chinese Book Citation Index, 2016), covering all major aspects of linguistics—phonetics, phonology, pragmatics, semantics, morphology, syntax, theoretical linguistics, applied linguistics and inter-disciplinary studies. PKULR aims to provide an invaluable guide to the very nature of language. On the one hand, it tries to offer a thorough grounding in the fundamental concepts of linguistics; on the other hand, it also attaches great importance to the practical application of these concepts, esp. in Chinese context.

More information about this series at http://www.springer.com/series/15701

Ping Ke

Contrastive Linguistics

Ping Ke
Department of English
Nanjing University
Nanjing, Jiangsu, China

ISSN 2524-6119   ISSN 2524-6127 (electronic)
Peking University Linguistics Research
ISBN 978-981-13-1384-4   ISBN 978-981-13-1385-1 (eBook)
https://doi.org/10.1007/978-981-13-1385-1

Jointly published with Peking University Press, Beijing, China

The printed edition is not for sale in the Mainland of China. Customers from the Mainland of China please order the print book from Peking University Press.

Library of Congress Control Number: 2018950194

This Springer imprint is published by the registered company Springer Nature Singapore Pte Ltd.
The registered company address is: 152 Beach Road, #21-01/04 Gateway East, Singapore 189721, Singapore

Preface

The first edition of this book was published under the heading of *Contrastive Linguistics* in 1999 and has since then been used by many colleges and universities in China as a coursebook or listed as a major reading item for graduate students of English who took the course Contrastive Linguistics. This new edition was revised and slightly enlarged to accommodate the needs of students studying languages or other subjects in the humanities or social sciences. It may be used as an introductory reader of contrastive linguistics for learners who have little knowledge of linguistics but are interested in such disciplines as Contrastive Linguistics, Applied Linguistics, Translation Studies, Second Language Teaching, Chinese as a Foreign Language, Communication, or other subjects of study which involve the use of a second language.

The work grew out of an attempt to rethink my introductory course offered for years to graduate students enrolled in programs of Linguistics, Translation Studies, or Bilingual Lexicography at Nanjing University and, in the past academic year, to the undergraduate students of Translation at the University of Macau as well. It is written with a one-semester course in mind although, with the addition of some supplementary materials, it could be used for two semesters.

Although many tertiary institutions in China and other countries or areas of the world have included Contrastive Linguistics in their postgraduate or undergraduate curricula for a long time, the subject of the course remains indeterminate to some extent and many explorations made in this field are still somewhat tentative. While researching and writing this book, I kept reminding myself that a work providing merely a general survey of the "state of the art" of this particular branch of linguistics and its general, "standard" theories would not be of much help to the students: contrast and comparison are not ends in themselves; they should serve some meaningful purposes. The important point is that the contrastive analysis made should lend us useful insights into some real problems in areas of language use and study. In my opinion, these areas should include, among others, the theory and practice of translation, second language teaching and learning, bilingual lexicography, and general linguistics. Based on this understanding, this work places somewhat greater emphasis on what contrastive linguistics has to offer to related fields of linguistic studies and practice than on the discipline of contrastive linguistics itself.

For the convenience of readers, key terms are usually printed in boldface type, especially when they are newly introduced into the text. Each chapter concludes with a "Questions for Discussion and Research" section, in which are presented some questions and issues related to what is dealt with in the chapter. By trying to respond to them, students can not only test their understanding of the content of the chapter but also learn to apply what they have learned in the course to the analysis of interlingual problems in the real world.

A book of this kind no doubt draws on a wide variety of sources. I owe a lot to the authors of the sources as listed in the References and wish to express my deep appreciation to all of them for the valuable information and inspiration their work has benefited me with. I am also very grateful to my students at Nanjing University and the University of Macau, whose questions, comments, suggestions, and keen interest in the book itself have been the chief driving force behind the revision of this work one decade after the publication of its first edition.

Macau, China   Ping Ke
June 2014   Department of English (Nanjing University), FAH
                                              University of Macau (Visiting Professor)

Contents

List of Figures

List of Tables

Chapter 1
Introduction

This book was written in a plain and direct style. It consists of seven chapters. In the first two chapters, we discuss the name, nature, classification, and history of **contrastive linguistics** (对比语言学), as well as the general principles of and procedures for contrastive analysis. By doing that we get some basic ideas about the subject of our study: its status, its theoretical background and assumptions as well as its methodology.

The remaining chapters, which make up the main body of this book, will be devoted to contrastive analysis at various linguistic levels. We shall first take a "classic" contrastive look at languages, concentrating on **lexis** (the total stock of words in a language 词汇) and **grammar** (语法); and then assume a macrolinguistic approach to **contrastive linguistics** (对比语言学), treating language as function in context, and looking into such topics as **contrastive text linguistics** and **pragmatics** (语用学). The emphasis of these chapters will be placed on the contributions contrastive linguistics can make to fields as diverse as translation studies, language learning and teaching, writing, and general linguistic theory.

1.1 What Is Contrastive Linguistics?

When we take up any subject for study, we usually start by investigating its nature, its relevance to us, and the way to study it. In other words, we ask three basic questions: **(a)** what it is, **(b)** why it is needed or important, and **(c)** how we are to do it. In this section we shall try to answer these three basic questions about **contrastive linguistics** (对比语言学).

© Peking University Press and Springer Nature Singapore Pte Ltd. 2019
P. Ke, *Contrastive Linguistics*, Peking University Linguistics Research 1,
https://doi.org/10.1007/978-981-13-1385-1_1

1.1.1 The Name and Nature of Contrastive Linguistics

1.1.1.1 Linguistics

Apparently **contrastive linguistics** (对比语言学) is something related to or subsumed under linguistics. So let us, as the saying goes, begin from the very beginning and start with an examination of the name and nature of linguistics.

Language is used by us every day. It is a reality, that is, it is something actually observed or experienced by us. Generally speaking, we can distinguish three modes or aspects of reality—physical, social, and psychological—and at least five modes of knowing or approaches to the understanding of reality, that is, **philosophical, mathematical, theological, hermeneutic,** and **scientific.** Researchers in various disciplines, depending on the specific mode(s) or aspect(s) of reality they are concerned about, approach their objects of study largely from one of these five perspectives.

We may consider the following facts about language and possible ways of understanding the reality of language before we characterize the nature of **linguistics** (语言学).

(1) As structured (linguistic) use of the auditory-vocal mode of patterned human communication, language is **physically real.** Created by, acquired and used in the human society, language is a social phenomenon and obviously has **social reality,** too.

(2) As human behavior, language is **psychologically real.** Two major linguistic schools that evolved in the 20th century were **structural linguistics** (结构语言学) and **generative linguistics** (生成语言学). Both structural linguists and generative linguists analyze language in terms of human behavior (that is, "verbal behavior"—in fact a book American behaviorist and structural linguist B. F. Skinner [1904–1990] wrote in 1857 takes that very title).

Structural linguistics (结构语言学) adopts a behavioristic approach towards language, treating it as a product of the **stimulus-response** (刺激-反应) mechanism of the humankind. This approach has been proved to interpret the nature of the phenomenon of language in an inaccurate or inadequate way. The limitations of behaviorism as a method of explanation of human behavior have been severely criticized by the generative schools of linguistics led by Noam Chomsky.

Chomsky argues that the basic mistake of behaviorists is that they do not postulate any mental mechanism underlying organized human behavior, linguistic behavior included. The transformational theory of language assumes the existence of such an underlying mental structure which, it asserts, is common to all people. The study of language makes access to this mental reality possible. Thus, the linguistic theory is supposed to contribute to the general knowledge about the mental capacities of man rather than to the knowledge of his linguistic behavior.

Although structural and generative linguists hold different assumptions about the nature of the mental mechanism operating under observable language behavior, it is not difficult to see that they all regard language as something related to human mind and treat language as a psychological reality.

(3) Language is not usually considered to be related to the nature of God and religious beliefs, so the study of language is rarely, if ever, approached from the **theological** perspective. Neither is language per se about the nature of knowledge, reality, and existence (as philosophy is), or about the numbers, quantities, or shapes used to calculate, represent, or describe things (as mathematics is). Therefore, the **philosophical** and **mathematical approaches** to the study of language are relevant only in limited ways.

(4) The **hermeneutic approach**, which was developed in the 19th century by German Protestant theologians (Rudolf Bultmann [1884–1976], Friedrich Schleiermacher [1768–1834], etc.) and German philosophers (Wilhelm Dilthey [1833–1911], Martin Heidegger [1889–1976], Hans-Georg Gadamer [1900–2002], etc.) and which has been influential in many realms of humanistic inquiry for more than a century, is however not typically employed in modern studies of language. The **hermeneutic approach** (阐释学路径) lays emphasis on the individual characteristics. The typical method it employs is known as *verstehen* ("understand [from within]" [设身处地地去理解领悟 (对象)]), which is a term used in Germany from the late 19th century on to denote the understanding of a subject of study from within, by means of empathy, intuition, or imagination, as opposed to getting to know it from without, by means of observation or calculation. The hermeneutic approach was thought by some to be characteristic of history, literature, and the social sciences as opposed to the natural sciences, and by others to be characteristic of history and literature as opposed to the social sciences.

Most present-day researchers of language, however, do not approach language as hermeneuticians would do: basically they do not focus on the individualistic traits as seen in the use of language, but on all the properties which are common to all the users of a given language, and further, on all the properties which define the notion of human language as such; neither do they rely on the *verstehen* method in their study of language, because that method is based on a belief that is hard to verify (in the sense of establishing a belief or proposition as true), i.e. we can understand the behavior of human beings by being able to share their "state of mind." According to the logical positivists, if a proposition is to be significant, it has to be verifiable by sense-experience, or by attention to the meaning of the words that express it, or, indirectly, by induction or demonstration. The *verstehen* method is certainly not a method of verification and can hardly be used as a scientific tool.

(5) What is most widely followed in contemporary language studies community is the **scientific approach**. Modern language study (**linguistics** [语言学]) claims to be an empirical science and as such aims at producing true (in the sense of "**verifiable**" and "**falsifiable**") statements by means of formulating **testable hypotheses**.

Based on the essential characteristics of language and the relevant approaches to the study of language as elaborated above, we may depict the nature of linguistics as follows:

Linguistics (语言学) is the scientific study of human language, which exists primarily as physical, social and psychological realities.

1.1.1.2 Contrastive Linguistics (Contrastive Analysis)

What, then, is contrastive linguistics? Apparently, **contrastive linguistics** (对比语言学) is a kind of or a branch of linguistics. As its name suggests, contrastive linguistics involves **contrast** or **comparison**. Comparison is one of the basic ways by which we study and get to know things, just as the saying goes, "only by comparison can one distinguish."

The method of comparison is widely used in linguistics. Almost all the branches of linguistics involve comparison of one kind or another, since to identify and elaborate on a particular feature of the human language, linguists usually have to make explicit or implicit comparative or **contrastive analyses** (对比分析) (**CA**) of the various forms which the feature finds expression in and the parallels of these forms in other comparable or related systems. For instance, to establish the grammatical feature of the **plural**, linguists have to compare different languages to find out the various possible forms with which it can be actualized, like inflection (such as *cats* [/kæts/] and *dogs* [/dɒgz/], and *classes* [/klɑ:sɪz/] in English), and lexical means (such as **haoxie** *maogou* [好些猫狗] and **duoge** *banji* [多个班级] in Chinese).

We may come to a better understanding of the nature of **contrastive linguistics** (对比语言学) by putting it in the perspective of a general framework of comparisons within and between languages.

Comparison may be conducted intralingually or interlingually, on a synchronic basis or on a diachronic basis. So four types of comparison may be distinguished (Table 1.1):

(1) **Synchronic intralingual comparison** (共时语内比较). This is the comparison of the constituent forms of the phonetic, phonological, lexical, grammatical and other linguistic systems within a particular language during a specific period of its evolution. For instance, to identify and describe the phonetic system of a

Table 1.1 Types of comparison within and between languages

	Synchronic	Diachronic
Intralingual	(1) Synchronic intralingual comparison	(2) Diachronic intralingual comparison
Interlingual	(4) Synchronic interlingual comparison	(3) Diachronic interlingual comparison

particular language, linguists need to compare all its **phonemes** (音位) with regard to their **places of articulation** (发音位置) (e.g. front as /iː/ in *beat*, back as /oʊ/ in *boat*, high as /ʊ/ in *put*, low as /ɒ/ in *pot*) and **manners of articulation** (发音方法) (e.g. unrounded as /e/ in *bait*, rounded as /uː/ in *shoe*, voiced as /d/ in *den*, stopped as /t/ in *team*), their acoustic qualities as well as their **distributions** (分布) in the syllables of the language.

(2) **Diachronic intralingual comparison** (历时语内比较). This kind of comparison would be made in the study of a given language's history. A diachronic comparison of English, for instance, reveals that the language has undergone four stages of evolution: Old English (mid-5th century to 1150), Middle English (1150–1500), Early Modern English (1500–1700) and Late Modern English (1700 onwards), with its grammar becoming increasingly analytic, that is, the number of inflected word endings (词尾部分) drastically decreased and **grammatical meanings** (语法意义) were increasingly expressed by **word order** and function words (such as prepositions). Diachronic intralingual comparison is the principal method used by researchers of language history, etymology and other related branches of linguistic study.

(3) **Diachronic interlingual comparison** (历时语际比较). When comparison is made across language borders, we get a very important branch of linguistics that emerged in modern times. This is the so-called **(comparative) historical linguistics** (比较历史语言学) (also known as **philology** (语文学)) which started in the late 18th century and evolved into a dominant branch of linguistic study in the 19th century. The (comparative) historical linguists (or philologists), such as Karl Verner (1846–1896), Rasmus Rask (1787–1832), Franz Bopp (1791–1867), and August Schleicher (1821–1868), were concerned with **linguistic genealogy** (语言系谱学), or the establishment of genetic "families" of language-groups. They achieved the objective through a comparison of the linguistic systems of different but usually related (**cognate** [同源]) languages in their various stages of historical development. By means of comparing historically related forms in different languages, they tried to postulate or *reconstruct* the **proto-language** (原始母语) of a group of related languages.

For instance, the English orientalist Sir William Jones (1746–1794) compared **Sanskrit** (梵文) with **Greek** (希腊语) and **Latin** (拉丁语) and pointed out in 1786 that the former bore a strong affinity to the Latin (/p/ in Sanskrit, e.g. is found to be systematically related to /f/ in English, as *pita* "father" and *father*). Based on the findings of Jones, some German scholars, notably Schleicher (who used the term "**comparative grammar** (比较语法)" first), reconstructed the **Proto-Indo-European** (原始印欧语) (also called "**Indo-Aryan** [印度雅利安语]" or "**Indo-Germanic** [印度日耳曼语]") language (**PIE**).

About half the world's population speaks one language in the Indo-European family as their mother tongue. These languages are classified as Indo-European because they are sufficiently similar to each other in vocabulary and grammar to form one major linguistic division. These similarities led Schleicher and other scholars to postulate that all Indo-European languages are descended from one prehistoric parent language, known as "**Proto-Indo-European**" (原始印欧语)" (**PIE**). PIE is generally believed to have been originated in the Pontic-Caspian steppe of Eastern Europe and Western Asia and spoken as a single language (before divergence began) some time before 4000 B.C., perhaps before 8000 B.C. or earlier. Since there are no written records of Proto-Indo-European, it apparently was in use before writing was known to its speakers. As the ancient speakers of PIE moved away from each other and migrated over the greater part of Europe and into Asia as far as northern India, their language broke up into a number of daughter languages, which later split up still further and eventually gave rise to the many modern Indo-European languages.

The reconstruction of **PIE** is one of the most prominent achievements of (-**comparative**) **historical linguistics** (比较历史语言学). In this case the comparative method helped linguists to find out a probable and perhaps the only really satisfactory explanation of the common features shared by Indo-European languages used either in Europe or India, i.e. these apparently different tongues have one and the same common **ancestor language** (始祖语)—**PIE**.

(4) **Synchronic interlingual comparison** (共时语际比较). According to the purpose of comparison, three kinds of synchronic interlingual comparison are distinguished:

(a) The first kind of **synchronic interlingual comparison** (共时语际比较) is carried out with a view to finding out the common features of or common patterns underlying the structures of all the languages of the world. The goal of the comparison, as generative schools of linguists headed by **Transformational Grammarians** (转换语法研究者) have been concerned about, is to discover such "**language universals** (语言普遍项)" or "**linguistic universals** (语言普遍项)" as subject, predicate, object or first, second and third pronouns, which are present in all languages and which ultimately derive from our psychological make-up and our perception of the world. Some currently unsolved problems in linguistics are indeed about such universals, e.g.

- Is there a universal definition of **word**?
- Is there a universal definition of **sentence**?
- Are there any universal **grammatical categories** (语法范畴)?

(b) The second kind of **synchronic interlingual comparison** (共时语际比较) is conducted for the purpose of finding out the typical differences between different languages of the world in their structure so that these languages can be classified according to their formal features. This approach, called "**linguistic typology** (语言类型学)," has established a classificatory system for the languages of the world into which individual languages can be slotted according to their preferred grammatical devices: so now we can talk about "**synthetic**," "**analytic**," "**inflectional**," "**agglutinating**," and "**tone**" languages:

"**Synthetic language** (综合语)" is a cover term for agglutinating and inflectional languages.

An "**analytic language** (分析语)," also known as "**isolating language** (孤立语)," is a language in which word forms do not change, and in which **grammatical functions** (语法功能) are shown by **word order** and the use of function words. Chinese and Vietnamese, e.g. are highly analytic languages.

An "**inflectional language** (屈折语)" or "**inflecting language** (屈折语)" is one in which the form of a word changes to show a change in meaning or **grammatical functions** (语法功能), e.g. *mice* (= *mouse* + plural) and *came* (= *come* + past tense) in English. **Greek** (希腊语) and **Latin** (拉丁语) are typical inflectional languages.

An "**agglutinating language** (粘着语)," also known as "**agglutinative language** (粘着语)," is a language in which various **affixes** (词缀) may be attached to the **stem** (词干) of a word (that part of a word to which an **inflectional affix** [屈折词缀] is or can be added) to add to its meaning or show its **grammatical functions** (语法功能). For example, in Swahili *wametulipa* "they have paid us" consists of:

wa	*me*		*tu*	*lipa*
they +	perfective marker	+	us +	pay

Languages which are highly agglutinating include Finnish, Hungarian, Turkish, etc.

There is no clear-cut distinction between **analytic languages** (分析语), **inflectional languages** (屈折语), and **agglutinating languages**, e.g. English is more analytic than French, German, Russian and many other European languages, but obviously less so (or more inflectional) than Chinese.

A "**tone language** (声调语言)" is a language in which the meaning of a word depends on the tone used when pronouncing it. Chinese, e.g. is a typical tone language, in which four different **tones** (声调) are employed to distinguish between different meanings:

dā (high level tone)	搭 ("put up")
dá (high rising tone)	达 ("reach")
dǎ (fall-rise tone)	打 ("beat")
dà (high falling tone)	大 ("big")

The approach adopted in this kind of comparison is synchronic in that languages are typologically grouped according to their present-day characteristics, no reference being made to their histories, not even to their historical relatedness: thus it might happen that two languages, such as Swahili and Hungarian, which could not possibly have ever been related genetically, turn out to belong typologically to the same grouping (both being a so-called "**agglutinating language** [粘着语].").

(c) The third kind of **synchronic interlingual comparison** (共时语际比较) is conducted within the scope of usually two languages, although more languages may be involved. The aim of this kind of comparison is to find out the discrepancies and, to a lesser degree, the similarities in the structures of the languages being compared. This is exactly what contrastive linguistics is about (Based on Xu, 1992, pp. 3–4).

We may, therefore, define **contrastive linguistics** (对比语言学) as:

- **a branch of linguistics which studies two or more languages synchronically, with the aim of discovering their differences and similarities (especially the former) and applying these findings to related areas of language study or practice.**

Contrastive linguistics (对比语言学) is also known as "**contrastive analysis** (对比分析)" (**CA**) or "**contrastive studies** (对比研究)." These three terms are largely interchangeable. In the United Kingdom and the United States, "contrastive analysis" is a regular term, but in Eastern Europe, China and some other parts of the world, the name "contrastive linguistics" is preferred, perhaps because the term "contrastive analysis" or "contrastive studies" may give one an impression that they refer to approaches to specific problems in a field instead of being a field of study in itself, while the term "contrastive linguistics" sounds more like a discipline in its own right, as it really is.

In this book, the terms "**contrastive linguistics**" (对比语言学) and "**contrastive analysis** (对比分析)" (shortened to "**CA**") will be used synonymously most of the time.

1.1.2 Micro-Contrastive Linguistics and Macro-Contrastive Linguistics

Having identified the nature of contrastive linguistics as well as the status it keeps in the broad area of linguistic studies, it is appropriate now for us to take a look at the make-up of this branch of linguistics. Broadly speaking, **contrastive linguistics** (对比语言学) can be classified into **micro-contrastive linguistics** (微观对比语言学) and **macro-contrastive linguistics** (宏观对比语言学).

As we know too well, a linguistic system is made up of many layers or levels. These layers or levels are often considered to form a scale or hierarchy from lower levels containing the smallest linguistic units to higher levels containing larger functional segments. So we have phonetic, phonological, morphemic, lexical, syntactic, textual, and pragmatic levels of linguistic structure or description. According to the levels on which it is enacted, **contrastive linguistics** (对比语言学) may be roughly divided into two branches, i.e. micro-contrastive linguistics and macro-contrastive linguistics.

Table 1.2 The differentiation between micro-contrastive linguistics and macro-contrastive linguistics

	Micro-CA	Macro-CA
Major concern	Language structure	Language use
Performed on levels of language	Phonology, lexis, grammar	Text, pragmatics

Micro-contrastive linguistics (微观对比语言学) is the "classic," traditional mode of contrastive linguistics. It is "**code-oriented** (面向语码的)," that is, oriented towards *langue* (语言系统) (which, in Saussurian linguist theory, means the system of language) or "**Competence** (语言能力)" (which, in **Transformational Grammar** [转换语法], refers to a person's internalized **grammar** [语法] or ability to create and understand sentences, including sentences that they have never heard or read before). The goal of micro-contrastive linguistics is to compare the universal as well as particular structural properties of human languages. Specifically, it concentrates on four structural levels of linguistics: **phonetics** (语音学), **phonology** (音系学), **lexis** (词汇), and grammar.

Macro-contrastive linguistics (宏观对比语言学) represents a broader perspective of linguistic analysis and offers considerable scope for new work in contrastive linguistics. The goal of **macro-contrastive linguistics** (宏观对比语言学) is to compare and understand how people use different languages to communicate with each other. Specifically, it addresses problems on two higher levels—the textual and the pragmatic levels—of linguistic description (James, 1980, p. 61).

The differentiation between **micro-contrastive linguistics** (微观对比语言学) and **macro-contrastive linguistics** (宏观对比语言学) may be summarized as follows (Table 1.2).

In this book we are dealing with issues in both micro-and macro-contrastive linguistics. Whenever possible, we shall also pay as much attention as possible to the practical side of any given topic that is being addressed.

Since text is coming increasingly to the fore in contemporary linguistic and translation studies, we shall give ample space to its discussion, in the belief that this will serve to heighten our readers' awareness of textual organization, thereby substantially improving their proficiency in both second language writing and linguistic translation.

1.2 Why Contrastive Linguistics?

Having answered the question of "what," we are now in the position to take up the question of "why." Why do we need **contrastive linguistics** (对比语言学)? The short answer to the question is that we need it for at least two reasons: one theoretical, and the other practical.

1.2.1   The Theoretical Need for Contrastive Linguistics

Viewed from a theoretical perspective, **contrastive linguistics** (对比语言学) is indispensable to the development of general linguistics.

Different models of language can describe different features of language with varying degrees of success. **Transformational Grammar** (转换语法), a major theory of generative linguistics, e.g. can effectively account for native English speakers' intuition that certain types of construction (e.g. active and passive sentences) are somehow related (cf. *Tommy opened the door* and *The door was opened by Tommy*) and that certain others are ambiguous (e.g. *Flying planes can be dangerous*). On the other hand, **Case Grammar** (格语法), another major theory of generative linguistics, provides exceptionally efficient apparatus for explaining the semantic affinity between more related sentences, e.g.

> This key opens that door.
>
> That door opens with this key.
>
> You can open that door using this key.
>
> That door can be opened with this key.

Researches of linguistic typology reveal that human languages fall into different types according to which grammatical, phonological, or lexical features they show preferences for. If some models are better at describing certain features, it must follow that some models will describe certain languages better than they do others. It is possible that **Transformational Grammar** (转换语法), a product of American linguistics, describes English better than it does other languages. It seems, as James (1980, pp. 63–64) suggests, that Applicative Generative Grammar, a model devised by the Russian linguist Shaumjan (1965), is eminently better suited to describing Russian, a language with a complex **morphology** (形态学, 词法), than it is to describe English.

Chao Yuen Ren (赵元任, 1892–1982), the famous Chinese American linguist and amateur composer, points out:

> The so-called linguistic theory is nothing but scientific conclusions derived from a comprehensive contrastive study of the languages of different nations in the world. (as cited in Wang, 1983, p. 40)

Most modern linguistic theories thus far formulated, as we know, are based upon the study of western languages. To form a really powerful, universally valid language theory or "Universal Grammar," as **Transformational Grammar** (转换语法) has purported to do, researchers of language are in constant need of testifying and modifying their theories against the findings derived from contrastive analyses made across different languages (including oriental languages).

1.2.2 The Practical Need for Contrastive Linguistics

The second reason for which **contrastive linguistics** (对比语言学) is desirable is that the study of contrastive data might suggest solutions to various practical linguistic problems, especially those which cannot be solved without the analysis of evidence from more than one language (Zabrocki, 1980, p. 53). Interlingual translation, for example, is a field with abundant problems of that kind.

We may consider an age-old issue of contention regarding poetic translation, that is, how to translate poetry in the form of poetry?

It is well known that poetry (verse) differs from plain prose and resembles music in that a poem displays an easily recognizable rhythm, which is achieved through the repetition of a certain pattern (called "**metric pattern**") in different parts of the poem. Different languages have different ways (i.e. metric patterns) to achieve the desired rhythm in a poem. (***Metric*** here means being written in the form of poetry, with regular strong and weak beats, i.e. rhythmic units known as "**metric units**" [节律单位].)

When translating a poem, should the translator rigidly copy its **metric units** (节律单位) and go to all lengths to reproduce them literally in the **target language** (目标语), or should they use instead the metric devices that are typical of the target language and that are **comparable**, but most probably not **corresponding**, to those in the **source language** (源语)? To find a reasonable solution to this issue, a **contrastive analysis** (对比分析) of the **verse meter** (诗律) (the regular and rhythmic arrangement of syllables according to particular patterns) of the languages involved is absolutely necessary.

Major metric units or devices in human languages include **quantity** (音量), **stress** (重音), number of syllables, rhyme, and **tones** (声调). American anthropological linguist Edward Sapir (1884–1939) (1921) contrasts the **verse meters** (诗律) of several major languages of the world and finds that **Greek** (希腊语) and **Latin** (拉丁语) verse uses a metrical system characterized by **quantity-timed rhythm** (长短音节奏型) because in those two languages syllables of short and long durations typically alternate with each other in a word, e.g.

Congito, ego sum. (R. Descartes)
"I think, therefore I am."

English words are noted for alternating stressed (heavy) and unstressed (light) syllables. Rhyme, which entered English verse rather late, is something decorative and far less important than the **stress** (重音). So English (as well as German) verse relies on an accentual, or **stress-timed rhythm** (轻重音节奏型), e.g.

`Deeply `I `sigh for the `fallen `flowers in `vain;
`Vaguely `I `seem to `know the `wallows `coming a`gain.

Syllables in French words are almost equally stressed and of approximately equal length; therefore, the **syllable-timed rhythm** (音节数节奏型), which is based upon the number of syllables in a rhythmic unit, is used in French poetic lines. Rhyme is also important in French metric pattern, as it can help to separate strings of loud and clear syllables, e.g.

Que ferai- /je des fleurs /tombeé?

De retour /sont-elles /mes vieilles /connaissances?

Chinese resembles French in that syllables of its words have few variations in either length or **stress** (重音). It is then quite natural that classical Chinese verse meter is likewise based upon the number of syllables of a rhythmic unit, upon rhyme and, most of all, upon its unique contrast in classes of even and changing **tones** (声调) (or **oblique and level tones** [平仄]). For example,

无可奈何花落去 ，　　似曾相识燕归来。

平仄仄平平仄仄　　仄平平仄仄平平

(晏殊"浣溪沙")

Since each language usually has its own unique or distinctive way(s) of producing rhythmic effects in rhymed speech, it is apparent that poetical translators will never do well blindly imitating or copying the metric form of the source poem. They should rather try to reproduce the **overall rhythmic or musical effect** of the original poem by bringing into full play the native metric resources of the **target language** (目标语).

Arthur Waley (1889–1966) was a prestigious English orientalist who translated from both Chinese and Japanese. Waley studied at King's College, University of Cambridge and once worked in the Oriental Division of the British Museum. He was the author of more than forty works and forty-six translations (including 《中国诗歌》 and 《道德经》), and was praised by Lü Shuxiang (吕叔湘) (1904–1998) as having made the most remarkable achievements in introducing Chinese and Japanese literature to the west in modern times, and by Fan Cunzhong (范存忠) (1903–1987) as having achieved the most notable results in the experiment of translating Chinese poems into English. His translations of Chinese poems, according to Fan, display a "spring-like rhythm" (Lin, 1997, p. 699). Waley admitted that when translating Chinese poetry he subconsciously followed the principle of **stress** (重音) contrast as is characteristic of English verse, seeing to it that the English translation for every Chinese character contains at least one stress (Waley, 1983, p. 38). The translations of the following two poems may be illustrative of this principle.

The first poem comes from *Shijing* (《诗经》, *The Book of Songs* or *The Book of Odes*), an anthology of verse dating from the 11th to 6th century BC, which became one of the Five Chinese Classics in the 3rd century BC:

摽有梅	Song

摽有梅	Plop fall the plums; but there are still seven.
其实七兮	Let those gentlemen that would court me
求我庶士	Come while it is lucky!
迨其吉兮	
	Plop fall the plums; but there are still three.
摽有梅	Let any gentleman that would court me
其实三兮	Come before it is too late!
求我庶士	
迨其今兮	Plop fall the plums; in shallow baskets we lay them.
	Any gentleman that would court me
摽有梅	Had better speak while there is time.
倾筐墍之	(Arthur Waley, Trans.)
求我庶士	
迨其谓之	

The second poem is one composed by the famous Tang poet Li Bai (李白)
(701–762):

月下独酌	**Drinking Alone by Moonlight**
李白	
花间一壶酒	A cup of wine, under the flowering trees;
独酌无相亲	I drink alone, for no friend is near.
举杯邀明月	Raising my cup I beckon the bright moon,
对影成三人	For he, with my shadow, will make three men.
月既不解饮	The moon, alas, is no drinker of wine;
影徒随我身	Listless, my shadow creeps about at my side.
暂伴月将影	Yet with the moon as friend and the shadow as slave
行乐须及春	I must make merry before the Spring is spent.
我歌月徘徊	To the songs I sing the moon flickers her beams;
我舞影零乱	In the dance I weave my shadow tangles and breaks.
醒时同交欢	While we were sober, three shared the fun;
醉后各分散	Now we are drunk, each goes his way.
永结无情游	May we long share our odd, inanimate feast,
相期邈云汉	And meet at last on the Cloudy River of the sky.
	(Arthur Waley, Trans.)

In translating English poems into Chinese, it is actually impossible to copy the stress-timed rhythm of the source lines simply because there is no marked **stress** (重音) and non-stress contrast in the Chinese language.

What can translators do to reproduce the rhythmic effects of the original poem then?

Some pioneering Chinese poets of *baihua shi* (白话诗, or vernacular free verse) and early translators of Anglo-American poetry, e.g. Wen Yiduo (闻一多, 1899–1946), made attempts to use the **syllable-group** (音节组) or "**pause**" (顿) as a basic **metric unit** (节律单位) in their work in the belief that it is a metric device which is rooted in Modern Chinese and is comparable to the **foot** (音步) in English verse. Their experimental efforts had good reasons but varying results. Some fared quite well, as is indicated in the following translation of American poet Philip Freneau (1752–1832)'s lyric "The Wild Honey Suckle":

野蜜花

The Wild Honey Suckle

Fair flower / that does / so come/ly grow,　　洁白的 / 花朵，

开得 / 多俊俏。

Hid in / this si/lent dull / retreat,　　躲在 / 绿荫中，

何等 / 静悄悄。

Untouched / thy hon/ied blos/som blow,　　蜜样花儿 / 喘着气，

有谁 / 知晓？

Unseen / thy lit/tle branch/es greet,　　纤细枝儿 / 在招手

有谁 / 看到？

No rov/ing foot / shall crush / thee here,　　那漫游的 / 脚步啊，

可别把你 / 踩碎。

No bus/y hand / provoke / a tear.　　那忙碌的 / 手指啊，

可别惹你 / 流泪。

(Wu 1987)

Others, however, were not so successful. An example might be Liang Zongdai (梁宗岱) (1903–1983)'s translation of Shakespeare's Sonnet 7:

Lo! / in the orient / when / the gracious / light　　看，/ 当 / 普照万物的 / 太阳 / 从东方
Lifts up / his burning / head, / each / under eye　　抬起了 / 火红的 / 头，/ 下界的 / 眼睛
Doth / homage / to his / new-appearing / sight,　　都对他 / 初升的 / 景象 / 表示 / 敬仰，
Serving /with looks / his / sacred / majesty;　　用目光 / 来恭候 / 他 / 神圣的 / 驾临。

What makes all the difference? The answer is simply that the translator of Freneau's lyric deliberately uses the Chinese **syllable-group** (音节组) for reproducing the pleasing sense of rhythm of the original poem, but does not seek a one-to-one correspondence between the syllable-group and the **foot** (音步), while the translator of Shakespeare's sonnet seems to have identified the Chinese syllable-group with the English foot and, on that cognition, substituted the former for the latter on a one-to-one basis.

It is understandable that Chinese poetical translators would take the **syllable-group** (音节组) as a metric unit comparable to the English foot, because it is something native to the Chinese language. The contrast in the number of syllable-groups is widely used in traditional Chinese poems (e.g. the *ci* poetry that originated in the Tang dynasty and flourished in the Song dynasty) and folk vocal arts to produce a rhythmic effect, just as the contrast in stressed and unstressed syllables (**foot** [音步]) is conventionally used in English rhymed texts for its musical impact. That said, the Chinese syllable-group and the English foot are only *comparable*, instead of *equivalent*, metric units in these two rather different languages. The problem with Liang's translation is that the translator mechanically (and wrongly) equates the Chinese syllable-group with the English foot, hence producing rather awkward lines throughout the translation. The translator is justified to resort to the Chinese **syllable-group** (音节组) in a bid to recreate the musical effects as conveyed by the **iambic pentameter** (抑扬格五音步) of the original poem, but should not seek a mechanical correspondence (neither in terms of number nor in terms of **distribution** [分布]) between these two metric devices.

As elaborated above, for the solution of both theoretical and practical problems involving language, findings obtained from **contrastive analysis** (对比分析) may simply be indispensable. It is perhaps in this sense that von Goethe (1749–1832) once remarked that a person who knows but one language does not know any language at all.

1.3 The History and Development of Contrastive Linguistics

Contrastive linguistics (对比语言学) originated in the United States during the Second World War. At that time, a lot of immigrants rushed into the country from different parts of the world to stay away from the war. They had to master English in order to make a new start in a foreign land. Later, when the United States stepped into the war after the Japanese surprise attack on Pearl Harbor, a large group of American soldiers were required to learn within the shortest possible time some ABCs of the languages of the belligerent states. That urgent need to learn foreign languages gave rise to the problem of how to teach a foreign language in a most effective and economical way. The solution found to the problem was **contrastive analysis** (对比分析). Fries (1945, p. 9) writes: "The most efficient [teaching] materials are those based on a scientific description of the language to be learned, carefully compared with a parallel description of the native language of the learner."

The psychological theory underlying this approach to language teaching was that of **stimulus-response** (刺激-反应) and associative learning of behaviorism (an influential school of psychology that dominated psychological theory in the U.S. between World War I and World War II and that seeks to explain animal and human behavior entirely in terms of observable and measurable responses to environmental stimuli).

The **stimulus-response theory** (刺激-反应理论) (or **S-R theory**) describes learning as the formation of associations between stimuli and responses. A **stimulus** (刺激) is something which produces a change or reaction in an individual or organism. A **response** (反应) is the behavior which is produced as a reaction to a stimulus. To illustrate graphically what a stimulus and a reaction are, Leonard Bloomfield (1887–1949), one of the founders of American structural linguistics, gives a parable of Jack and Jill taking a walk. Jill feels hungry (which, in this case, is the *stimulus*) and makes a *response* to that *stimulus* by asking Jack to pick her an apple. Her request in turn becomes a *stimulus* to Jack, who *responds* to it by picking an apple for Jill (Bloomfield, 1933, p. 24).

Related to the concepts of stimulus and response are the notions of reinforcement, extinction, stimulus generalization, and discrimination. **Reinforcement** (强化) is a stimulus which follows the occurrence of a response and affects the probability of that response occurring or not occurring again. Reinforcement which increases the likelihood of a response is known as **positive reinforcement** (正强化). Reinforcement which decreases the likelihood of a response is called **negative reinforcement** (负强化). If no reinforcement is associated with a response the response may eventually disappear. This is known as **extinction** (反应消退). If a response is produced to similar stimuli with which it was not originally associated, it is known as "**stimulus generalization** (刺激泛化)." Learning to distinguish between different kinds of stimuli is known as "**stimulus discrimination** (刺激区分)."

Learning involves the association of two entities, e.g. learning to drive means learning to associate the visual sensation of a red light with the need to decelerate or stop the vehicle. The study of this process constitutes Associationism in psychology, a study dating back at least to Aristotle. **Associationism** (联想说), or **associative learning** (联想性学习), refers to learning which happens when a connection or association is made, usually between two things. For example, when someone hears the word *table* they may think of the word *food*, because the word *food* is often used with or near the word *table*. This is a case of **association by congruity** (适合性联想). When someone hears the word *delicate*, they may think of the word *fragile*, because it has a similar meaning. This is a case of **association by similarity** (相似联想). When someone hears the word *happy*, they may think of the word *sad*, because it has the opposite meaning. What occurs here is the so-called **association by contrast** (对比联想).

The two "entities" associated in a learning task are a **stimulus (S)** (刺激) and a **response (R)** (反应). In language behavior, **S** is a communicative need while **R** is the utterance itself.

We may need to add here an explanation of the concept "utterance" because we shall use the term frequently throughout this book. In linguistics, **utterance** is a concept related to **discourse analysis** (话语分析). It refers to what is said by any one person before or after another person begins to speak, and may consist of

(1) just a word, such as B's reply in the following dialog:

A: Do you agree to what I said?
B: Yeah.

(2) a sentence or an elliptical clause, such as A's question and B's answer in:

A: Where's the supermarket?
B: Over there round the corner.

(3) more than one sentence, such as A's complaint in:

A: *Look, I'm really fed up. I've told you several times to wash your hands before a meal. Why don't you do as you're told?*
B: But Mum, listen …

To return to our discussion of Associationism in language learning, according to the aforementioned behavioristic claims about learning, to learn a foreign language means that the learner gradually forms in his or her mind an association between the communicative needs (which usually have already been learnt in one's mother tongue) and what is to be learnt: the foreign language utterances to express those needs.

At the same time when **behaviorist psychology** (行为主义心理学) was in its heyday, American **structural linguistics** (结构语言学) came to full bloom with its whole set of methods and procedures for conducting hierarchical **componential analysis** (构成成分分析) of the structures of language (e.g. He {*likes to* [*play* (*tennis*)]}. "他 {喜欢 [打 (网球)]}"). Language teaching was thus provided with what Fries called the basis of a scientific description of the language being taught.

The need for quick and effective second language teaching, the popularity of the behaviorist theory of learning, and the flourish of structural description of language— these three factors combined to bring about the birth of contrastive linguistics and its speedy development in the United States in the 1940s and 1950s. In 1941 Benjamin Lee Whorf (1897–1941) used the term "**contrastive linguistics**" (对比语言学) for the first time in his paper "Language and Logic" (Pan, 1997, p. 3).

It is not difficult to perceive that from the very beginning of its history, **American contrastive linguistics** was connected with foreign language teaching.

The pattern practice drills (e.g. 他喜欢打网球 / 篮球 / 乒乓球, etc.) kind of language teaching methodology, which derived insights and justification from structural linguistic description, became a vogue. Nothing seemed to be of greater potential value to language teachers and learners than a comparative and contrastive description of the learner's mother tongue and the **target language** (目标语). It was believed that if the structures of the mother tongue could be juxtaposed against those of the target language, course designers, teachers and learners would be in a better position to plan their teaching and learning, to foresee difficulties involved in language learning, and consequently to manage resources and direct teaching and learning effort in a better way. It was against that background that the 1960s saw a host of language teaching courses made available along with a range of contrastive projects published (typically between English and other world languages).

Beginning from the late 1960s, however, **contrastive analysis** (对比分析) came under severe criticism in the United States. It no longer claimed as much pedagogic attention as it used to. The decline of pedagogic interest in contrastive analysis was caused mainly by two circumstances.

(1) First of all, the theoretical basis of contrastive description appeared to be shaken by newly emerged approaches to psychology and linguistics. Specifically, **behaviorist psychology** (行为主义心理学) and **structural linguistics** (结构语言学) met with powerful challenges respectively from **cognitive psychology** (认知心理学) and **Transformational Grammar** (转换语法) in the 1960s.

Cognitive psychology (认知心理学) is a branch of psychology which deals with the study of the nature and learning of systems of knowledge, particularly those processes involved in thought, perception, comprehension, memory, and learning. It came to be related to linguistics, especially Noam Chomsky's **(Generative) Transformational Grammar** (生成转换语法), which links language structure to the nature of human cognitive processes. Cognitive psychology emphasizes the importance of the factors of understanding, conjecture, and thinking in the learning process. According to cognitive psychology, learning does not mean the formation of some **S-R** (刺激-反应) mechanism or a set of habits, but is a creative process of hypothesis testing.

In language learning **hypothesis testing** (假设检验) refers to the testing of ideas or "hypotheses" about a language to see if they are right or wrong. The most obvious way of doing this is to use relevant hypotheses to produce new utterances and see whether they work. One can also compare one's own utterances with those of other people speaking the same language, or imagine what other people would say in a particular situation and then see whether they actually say it.

For example, a young boy picking up his first language hears the adults around him making such utterances as *The cock crowed*, *The cat meowed*, etc. He wonders if he can say *Mom laughed*. So one day he tentatively says to his mother *Mom laughed*. His mother responds by saying *Oh, yes, my darling, Mom laughed*. The child then hypothesizes that one could add the sound /**d**/to the end of a word to express the pastness of an action. Some day, when he says *Dad goed*, however, his father corrects him, telling him that he can only say *Dad went*. Thus the boy gets to know that there are exceptions to the rule about the expression of pastness he has hypothesized: for some words there are special forms to express the pastness of action. It is in this way that the boy comes to acquire the knowledge of the past forms of English verbs.

When behaviorism was challenged by cognitivism, **structural linguistics** (结构 语言学) came under criticism from **Transformational Grammarians** (转换语法 研究者) for not postulating an *innate* mental mechanism or structure underlying any organized behavior, linguistic behavior included.

In philosophy, psychology, and linguistics there has historically been the confrontation between two theoretical positions, i.e. **innatism** (天赋论) (or **rationalism** [唯理论]) and **empiricism** (经验论). **Innatism** claims that human knowledge develops from structures, processes, and ideas which are in the mind at birth (that is, are *innate*), rather than from the environment; while **empiricism** (经验论) holds that all human knowledge comes from experience. The **innatist hypothesis** (天赋 假设) (also known as **innatist position** [天赋观], **nativist position** [天赋观], or **rationalist position** [唯理观]) about language argues that innate structures, processes, and ideas are responsible for the formation of the basic structures of language and for how these can ever be learned. This hypothesis or position has been used to explain how children are able to learn language.

The number of hypotheses about a new language that need to be tested, according to cognitive psychologists who hold the innatist hypothesis, is not infinite: some hypotheses are simply never formed, because every normal human being has innate knowledge of the so-called "**language universals**" (语言普遍项) at birth.

If the substance of these two studies (**behaviorist psychology** (行为主义心理 学) and **structural linguistics** (结构语言学) was called into question, the basis upon which to attempt contrastive description should certainly appear unstable.

(2) Secondly, a more complex, real-life condition also added to the decline of interest in the pedagogical power of **contrastive analysis** (对比分析). Language teachers discovered that the contrastive descriptions to which they had been exposed were only able to predict part of the learning problems encountered by their learners, and that those points of potential difficulty that were identified seemed to cause various and variable problems among different learners, and between the perception and the production of language. Language learning, in short, was less predictable from contrastive linguistic description than teachers had been led to believe.

Error analysts (错误分析研究者) distinguish two types of errors, that is, interlingual ones and intralingual ones. **Contrastive analysis (CA)** (对比分析) may predict the former but not the latter.

An **interlingual error** (语际错误) is one which results from language transfer, i.e. caused by the learner's native language, e.g. the incorrect French sentence *Elle regarde les* ("She sees them"), produced according to the **word order** of English, instead of the correct French sentence *Elle les regarde* (literally, "She them sees"), and the erroneous Chinese translation of *registered letter* ([in British English] a letter posted with special precautions for safety and for compensation in case of loss [保价信]) as "*挂号信," based on the similarity between the superficial **lexico-semantic structure** of the English original and that of the Chinese phrase挂 号信 (literally, "registered letter"). (In British English 挂号信 is actually *recorded letter* [a letter whose dispatch and receipt is recorded].)

An **intralingual error** (语内错误) is one which results from faulty or partial learning of the **target language** (目标语), rather than from language transfer (see Sect. 2.1.1). Intralingual errors may be caused by the influence of one target language item upon another. For example a learner may produce *He is comes*, based on a blend of the English structures *He is coming*, and *He comes*.

In this atmosphere of a certain unfulfilment it is not surprising that **contrastive analysis** (对比分析) lost some of its pedagogic impact. Researchers now tend to be skeptical of any plausible, or even possible, direct application of the results of contrastive analysis to the planning of curricula or the design of teaching materials. They stress rather its implicational value, its role as a source for experimental studies into the predictability of learner difficulty, its major theoretical contribution to studies into **interlanguage** (中间语) (the type of language produced by **L2 learners** (二语学习者) who are in the process of learning a language), its need to be combined with **Error Analysis** (错误分析) as a practical classroom research tool for teachers anxious to adjust their teaching to the state of knowledge of their learners (Based on James, 1980, pp. iii–iv).

The challenges **cognitive psychology** (认知心理学) and **Transformational Grammar** (转换语法) posed to **contrastive analysis** (对比分析) make a highly theoretical problem in this discipline. At the present stage of our study, it would suffice to know that claims made about language learning by behaviorist and cognitive psychologies and by structural and generative schools of linguistics are not absolutely irreconcilable with each other. They have different degrees of explaining power for different types of problems in foreign language learning.

What does merit our special attention at this point is that we should not associate **contrastive analysis** (对比分析) or **contrastive linguistics** (对比语言学) solely in terms of **L2 teaching** (二语教学). It is a narrow view that the value of contrastive analysis lies only in what it can contribute to practical language teaching. In fact there has always been more to contrastive analysis than making claims about learner difficulty. As we would find in the remaining chapters of this book, contrastive analysis has much to offer to the theory and practice of translation, to **L2 writing**, to the understanding and description of particular languages, to language typology, as well as to the study of **language universals** (语言普遍项).

The past few decades saw new developments of **contrastive linguistics** (对比语言学) in many countries in the world, not only in Europe and the United States, but also in such countries as Japan, South Korea, Singapore, Malaysia, Israel, Egypt, Iran, Jordan, etc. Since 1975 a number of international conferences and symposiums on contrastive linguistics have been held in the United States, Romania, Poland, Germany, and Finland. Many contrastive libraries and monographs have been published. In Poland, Fisiak's team has been working zealously in a project of Polish-English contrastive study. The journal *Papers and Research in Contrastive Linguistics,* which was created in Poland in 1973, has continually been published (Yu, 1994, p. ii). Another two journals, *Contrastive Linguistics* and *Contrastes* began to be published in Bulgaria and France respectively. Some renowned international journals, e.g. *Applied Linguistics* and *International Review of Applied Linguistics,* regularly carry papers on **contrastive linguistics** (对比语言学).

Contrastive linguistics (对比语言学) has long been engaging the attention of Chinese scholars. As early as in 1933, Yuan-Ren Chao (赵元任) carried out a contrastive study of English and Chinese **intonation** (语调). In recent years, many universities began to offer courses in contrastive linguistics and quite a number of research works have been published, notably Wu (吴洁敏, 1982), Xu (许余龙, 1992), Wang (王福祥, 1992), Yu (喻云根, 1994), Pan (潘文国, 1997), and Shao (邵志洪, 1997).

So, although **contrastive analysis** (对比分析) or **contrastive linguistics** (对比语言学) has been fraught with problems in the last few decades, it remains, paradoxically, highly vigorous. This is not really so difficult to understand, as for language workers, learners as well as teachers of foreign languages, it is a plausible and obvious thing to do. It is sound practice in search of a sound theory.

Questions for Discussion and Research

1. Read the following Chinese original and its English translation and try to answer some questions:

- Do you like the translation? Why or why not?
- What linguistic and/or extralinguistic knowledge is needed to translate this specific passage?
- Can you identify any differences between the Chinese and English languages from your comparative reading(s) of the two texts (respectively called the "source text" and the "target text")? How do these differences affect the way the translators communicate the meaning and style of the original in English?

尹雪艳着实迷人。但谁也没能道出她真正迷人的地方。尹雪艳从来不爱擦脂抹粉，有时最多在嘴唇上点着些似有似无的蜜丝佛陀；尹雪艳也不爱穿红戴绿，天气炎热，一个夏天，她都浑身银白，净扮得了不得。不错，尹雪艳是有一身雪白的肌肤，细挑的身材，容长的脸蛋儿配着一副俏丽甜净的眉眼子，但是这些都不是尹雪艳出奇的地方。见过尹雪艳的人都这么说，也不知是何道理，无论尹雪艳一举手、一投足，总有一份世人不及的风情。别人伸个腰、蹙一下眉，难看，但是尹雪艳做起来，却又别有一番妩媚了。尹雪艳也不多言、不多语，紧要的地方插上几句苏州腔的上海话，又中听、又熨贴。有些荷包不足的舞客，攀不上叫尹雪艳的台子，但是他们却去百乐门坐坐，观观尹雪艳的风采，听她讲几句吴侬软语，心里也是舒服的。尹雪艳在池子里，微仰着头，轻摆着腰，一迳是那么不慌不忙地起舞着；即使跳着快狐步，尹雪艳也从来没有失过分寸，仍旧显得那么从容，那么轻盈，像一毬随风飘荡的柳絮，脚下没有扎根似的。尹雪艳有她自己的旋律。尹雪艳有她自己的拍子。绝不因外界的迁异，影响到她的均衡。（白先勇.《永远的尹雪艳》）

Yin Hsueh-yen was genuinely bewitching, though no one could say precisely where her charm lay. She rarely bothered to put on makeup; at most she might touch her lips with a little Max factor now and then; so faint as to be barely noticeable. Nor did she care to wear vivid colours. All through the summer, when the weather was burning hot, she dressed entirely in silvery white, looking cool and fresh beyond words. Indeed, she had lovely snow-white skin and a slender figure, with sweet, exquisite eyes set in an oval face, but it was not these features that made her so extraordinary. Everyone who had ever set eyes on Yin Hsueh-yen said that, for some mysterious reason, every gesture of her hand and every movement of her foot held an alluring charm unmatched in al the world. While a yawn or a frown would have been unbecoming to others, in her it carried another kind of attraction. She spoke little: at crucial moments she might throw in a few words, ever so pleasant and soothing to the ear, in her Soochow-accented Shanghainese. Some patrons who could not afford to have her at their tables came nevertheless to the Paramount just to enjoy her radiant presence and listen to her soft Soochow speech, which seemed to make it all worthwhile. On the dance floor, her head slightly raised, her hips gently swaying, she always danced unhurriedly; even when it was a quick fox-trot, she never let go of herself displaying the ease and the suppleness of a windblown catkin drifting along, free of roots. Yin Hsueh-yen had her own rhythm; she moved to her own beat. No outside disturbance could affect her natural poise. (白先勇、叶佩霞 译)

2. What kind of study is **contrastive linguistics**? What is the status and objects of this study?
3. A **diachronic comparison** of Old English, Middle English and Modern English reveals that the grammar of the English language has become increasingly **analytic**. What changes do you think we may find out about the structure of the Chinese language if we trace its development?
4. What class of languages is Chinese slotted into in the **linguistic typology** of world languages? On what basis is the classification made?

References

Bloomfield, Leonard. (1933). *Language*. New York, NY: Henry Holt.

Fries, C. C. (1945). *Teaching and learning English as a foreign language*. Ann Arbor, MI: University of Michigan Press.

James, Carl. (1980). *Contrastive analysis*. Harlow, United Kingdom: Longman Group UK Limited.

Lin, Huangtian [林煌天 主编]. (1997).《中国翻译词典》. 武汉: 湖北教育出版社.

Pan, Wenguo [潘文国 著]. (1997).《汉英语对比纲要》. 北京: 北京语言文化大学出版社.

Sapir, Edward. (1921). *Language: An introduction to the study of speech*. New York, NY: Harcourt, Brace and Company.

Shao, Zhihong [邵志洪]. (1997).《英汉语研究与对比》. 上海: 华东理工大学出版社.

Waley, Arthur. (1983). 翻译小议 (刘英敏 译).《翻译通讯》, 1983 年第 8 期.

Wang, Fuxiang (Ed.) [王福祥 编]. (1992).《对比语言学论文集》. 北京: 外语教学与研究出版社.

Wang, Li [王力]. (1983)..《王力论学新著》. 南宁: 广西人民出版社.

Wu, Jiaxiang [吴新祥]. (1987 年 7 月). 等值论与诗歌翻译. 全国首届翻译理论研讨会论文, 中国青岛.

Wu, Jiemin [吴洁敏 编著]. (1982).《英汉语法手册》. 北京: 知识出版社.

Xu, Yulong [许余龙]. (1992).《对比语言学概论》. 上海: 上海外语教育出版社.

Yu, Yungen [喻云根]. (1994).《英汉对比语言学》. 北京: 北京工业大学出版社.

Zabrocki, Tadeusz. (1980). Theoretical contrastive studies. In J. Fisiak (Ed.), *Theoretical issues in contrastive linguistics* (pp. 43–56). Amsterdam, the Netherlands: John Benjamins B.V.

Chapter 2
The Principles and Methods of Contrastive Analysis

Any kind of comparative study demands a statement of the principles it depends upon and the methods that are employed. In this chapter, we will start by explaining the basic assumptions and hypotheses underlying **contrastive linguistics** (对比语言学) and distinguish the theoretical and applied levels of contrastive analysis. We will then elaborate the notion of the "third element" or common ground between the compared linguistic elements and outline the procedures for carrying out contrastive analysis.

2.1 Basic Assumptions and Hypotheses Underlying Contrastive Analysis (CA)

Classic **contrastive linguistics** (对比语言学) is based on the following three assumptions:

(1) the main difficulties in learning or using a new language are caused by **interference from the first language** (一语干扰作用);
(2) these difficulties can be predicted by **contrastive analysis** (对比分析) **(CA)**, which helps second language (**L2**) learners or users to perceive or recognize the differences between their first language (**L1**) and the new language they are learning or using; and
(3) teaching materials can benefit from contrastive analysis, which provides insight as to how the effects of **L1 interference** (一语干扰作用) can be reduced.

In this section, we are going to examine some fundamental **CA** problems associated with these assumptions.

P. Ke, *Contrastive Linguistics*, Peking University Linguistics Research 1, https://doi.org/10.1007/978-981-13-1385-1_2

2.1.1 The Psychological Basis of Contrastive Analysis: Transfer

In the study of learning, the notion of "**interference** (干扰作用)" is related to **transfer** (迁移), which is a basic concept in psychology.

Contrastive analysis (对比分析) draws on the theoretical resources of psychology as well as linguistics. This is inevitably so, since linguistics is concerned with the formal properties of language and not directly with learning, which is in essence a psychological matter. Since contrastive analysis is concerned with **L2 learning** (二语学习) (especially at an early stage of its history), it needs a psychological component. This required psychological component turned out to be the transfer theory.

Transfer (迁移) is the psychological hypothesis that the learning of **task A** will affect the subsequent learning of **task B**. For instance, if we know how to cycle, we may find it easier to ride a scooter or motor cycle. A student who scores well in mathematics may be expected to do well in other subjects of study which require good reasoning ability, too. We may also notice that a person who is good at playing Chinese military chess is quick in learning international chess, Japanese *go*, or other board games of strategic skill. If we substitute for "**task A**" and "**task B**" with **L1** (one's first or native language) and **L2** (one's second or foreign language) (二语) respectively in this definition, we would readily recognize the relevance of transfer theory to CA: it is that very psychological thing in **CA**. As a matter of fact, it has been recognized as the psychological foundation of **contrastive analysis** (对比分析).

In language learning **transfer** (迁移) refers to the effect of one language on the learning of another, as Robert Lado (1915–1995) points out: "individuals tend to transfer the **forms and meanings** and the **distribution of forms and meanings** (present author's italics) of their native language and culture to the foreign language and culture" (1957, p. 2).

Two types of language **transfer** (迁移) may occur, i.e. positive transfer and negative transfer. **Positive transfer** (正迁移) is also known as **facilitation** (易化作用). It is transfer which helps or facilitates language learning in another later situation, and may occur when both the native language and the **target language** (目标语) have the same form. **Negative transfer** (负迁移), also known as **interference** (干扰作用), is one that interferes with language learning in another later situation. Specifically, it refers to the use of a native-language pattern or rule which leads to an error or inappropriate form in the target language. For example, a Chinese student learning English may have no problem producing the correct English expressions *white bread* and *green tea* because these two phrases have the same lexico-semantic structures as their Chinese counterparts: 白面包 ("white bread") and 绿茶 ("green tea"). In this case, what the student has learnt in Chinese is positively carried over to his or her learning of the use of equivalent English phrases. We say that a positive transfer occurs here. Things are somewhat different, however, when the student intends to produce the English expressions for 黑面包

("black bread") and 红茶 ("red tea"). They might produce the erroneous forms of *black bread* and *red tea* because the correct English equivalents of these two phrases, *brown bread* and *black tea*, have lexico-semantic structures different from their Chinese counterparts. What the student has learnt in Chinese might be negatively carried over to, or interfere with, their production of the correct English forms. Here we have an instance of negative transfer.

2.1.2 The Strong and Weak Versions of Contrastive Analysis Hypothesis

Contrastive analysis (对比分析) has been discussed with regard to its role as a predictive device. Wardhaugh (1970, pp. 123–130) suggests that the so-called "**Contrastive Analysis Hypothesis** (对比分析假说)" exists in two versions, a strong one and a weak one. While the two versions are equally based on the assumption of **L1 interference** (一语干扰作用), they differ in that the strong version claims **predictive power** while the weak version, less ambitiously, claims merely to have **diagnostic power**, that is, the power to diagnose errors that have been committed.

Wardhaugh favors the weak version of **CA** hypothesis. According to him, using the weak version of **contrastive analysis** (对比分析) means that "reference is made to the two linguistic systems only in order to explain actually observed **interference** (干扰作用) phenomena" (Wardhaugh, 1970, p. 127).

Wardhaugh's argument, however, begs the question because it amounts actually to that the analyst is capable of deciding, without first conducting a **contrastive analysis** (对比分析), what kind of errors are attributable to **L1 interference** (一语干扰作用). Possessing such vital knowledge, he subsequently makes reference "to the two systems" or, in other words, conducts a contrastive analysis, in order to "explain" these errors. Surely such explanation is unnecessary, since the source of these errors must already have been known for them to be caused by **L1** in the first place (James, 1980, p. 185)! It is not difficult to see that Wardhaugh's argument is logically unsound.

Since the weak version of **CA** hypothesis is not so tenable, we hold the view that contrastive analysis is always predictive, and that the job of diagnosis belongs to the field of **Error Analysis** (错误分析) (EA).

2.1.3 The Predictive Power of Contrastive Analysis

It is the ambition of any science to transcend observation and predict the unobserved. It is appropriate for us to elucidate at this point what exactly **contrastive analysis** (对比分析) can predict and with what amount of accuracy it can make the prediction. There are two possible bases for prediction: either one can predict by generalizing from observed instances, or, more ambitiously, one can predict one phenomenon on the basis of observation of some other phenomenon. The **error analyst** (错误分析研究者) chooses the first path: having observed errors like **I must to go, *I should to learn* he generalizes to predict the likely occurrence of **I can to speak English*. The **contrastivist** (对比分析研究者) prefers the second path: on the basis of an analysis of two related linguistic systems he predicts learners' behavior. In other words, error analysts employ the **inductive method** (归纳法) in their prediction while contrastivists resort to **deductive method** (演绎法) in their prediction. (Based on James, 1980, pp. 181–182)

We should make a distinction at this point concerning the "prediction of error." In fact this phrase is ambiguous: it can mean either prediction *that* there will be error or prediction of the form of that error. Obviously, to claim that contrastive analyses have predictive capacity of the second kind would, given the present "state of the art," be quite presumptuous. So, rather than risk making wrong predictions about the form of errors, **contrastivists** (对比分析研究者) have more cautiously made predictions of an *either/or* type: learners with a certain **L1** learning this **L2** will produce either x or y types of errors; for example, French speakers tend to use *either /s/ or /z/* in French for **L2** English /θ/ and *either /t/ or /d/* in French for **L2** English /ð/.

There are, of course, limitations on the numbers of learner errors that contrastive analyses can predict, limitations stemming from the fact that not all errors are the result of **L1 interference** (一语干扰作用); that is, not all errors are interlingual ones. (Based on James, 1980, p. 146)

Several attempts have been made to determine the proportion of **interlingual** (that is, **L1-induced**) **errors** (语际错误) among all errors. Chau (1975) found 51% to be interlingual and 29% intralingual, strikingly confirming Richards (1971) who suggested 53% interlingual and 31% intralingual. Mukattash (1977, p. 5) found 23% of the syntactic errors in English of his Jordanian students to be cases of **L1** (Arabic) **interference** (一语干扰作用). Grauberg (1971, p. 261) found that for his advanced **L1** English learners of German "**interference** (干扰作用) from English … can be observed in 71 errors out of 193," that is, in 36% of all the cases. H. V. George estimated that about a third of errors are traceable to the **L1** (George, 1972).

By and large, then, between about a third and half of learner errors are apparently caused by the **L1-L2 mismatch**. **CA** can be expected to predict these errors (James, 1980, p. 146).

We may hence conclude that **contrastive analysis** (对比分析) can predict what aspects of **L2** might cause problems for the learners. Specifically, it can predict errors due to **L1 interference** (一语干扰作用) (i.e. **interlingual errors** [语际错误]), which account for about one third or more of total learner errors. But CA cannot predict the other half or more of learner errors, which are caused by insufficient command of **L2** (i.e. **intralingual errors** [语内错误]).

2.2   Theoretical Contrastive Analysis and Applied Contrastive Analysis

Just like what happens in many other fields, linguistic study is made at both the theoretical and applied levels. In **contrastive linguistics** (对比语言学), we distinguish two levels of analysis, i.e. **theoretical** or **"pure" contrastive analysis** and **applied contrastive analysis**.

Theoretical contrastive analysis (理论对比分析) or **pure contrastive analysis** (纯对比分析) tries to find suitable models and theoretical frameworks for comparison and to establish such key notions as congruence (等同), similarity (相似), and equivalence (等值) between the forms of different languages. It is concerned with the **universal categories** (普遍范畴) or **universal features** (普遍特征) (X) that are common to all languages or at least to the pair of languages being compared. It takes as its task the examination of how those universal categories or features (X) are realized and employed in specific languages, say A and B. In **contrastive phonology** (对比音系学), for example, the universal category X may be a group of phonological features. It is then the task of **theoretical contrastivists** (理论对比分析研究者) to compare how language A and language B draw on this group of phonological features to form their respective phonological systems Xa and Xb and in what way the two systems differ from each other.

Applied contrastive analysis (应用对比分析) has as its objective the application of the findings of theoretical contrastive analysis to the contrasting of two or more languages for certain practical purposes, notably **L2** teaching and learning, translation, **bilingual lexicography** (双语词典学), etc.

Applied contrastive analysis (应用对比分析) differs from **theoretical contrastive analysis** (理论对比分析) in that it is concerned with the problem of how a **universal category** (普遍范畴) X, realized in language A as Xa, is rendered in language B (Xb), instead of with the way in which some general linguistic characteristics are realized in two or more languages. In other words, what **applied contrastivists** (应用对比分析研究者) seek is the corresponding elements of Xa in B, i.e. Xb (Xu, 1992, pp. 14–16):

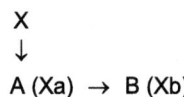

If such corresponding elements do not exist in B, Xb is said to have taken the **zero form** (often represented by "Ø"). In the following sentences, e.g. the indefinite article in English does not take a corresponding element (Xb) in Chinese:

We interpreted his silence as *a* refusal.
我们把他的沉默看成是Ø拒绝的表示。

It can be seen that **applied CA** is **unidirectional** whereas **theoretical CA** is **bidirectional** or **multidirectional**.

Since in the one-way traffic of applied contrasts only Xa and Xb are set in comparison, there exists the danger that the **contrastivist** (对比分析研究者) may overlook the X (the **universal category** [普遍范畴] or **universal feature** [普遍特征]) underlying them. Again, let's take the article as an example. When comparing the **surface syntax** (表层句法) of English and Chinese, we may notice that the English language contains articles such as *an* and *the* while the Chinese language has none. Some contrastivists (Oller and Redding, 1971) report that students whose native language contains articles show a much better command of the use of English articles than those whose native language does not. According to that report, Chinese students may encounter difficulties when learning English articles.

On a more abstract (and hence more universal) level, however, we may observe that articles in English are used primarily to distinguish between **definite reference** (特指) and **indefinite reference** (非特指). This definite/indefinite reference contrast is the very **universal feature** (普遍特征) X that underlies the comparison. The observation derived from the unidirectional contrast that English articles are represented in **Chinese syntax** (汉语句法) as zero form might mislead the learner into thinking that Chinese does not have ways to distinguish definite reference from indefinite reference. As a matter of fact, the differentiation made between definite reference and indefinite reference is something universal (X) in human languages. The contrast between definite reference and indefinite reference does exist in Chinese and are at least partially represented by such syntactic devices as **word order** (Xu, 1992, p. 17). For instance, definite noun phrases usually appear before the verb while indefinite noun phrases are usually placed after the verb, as in:

苹果我吃了。

I ate *the apple*.

我吃了苹果。

I ate *an apple*.

> ... The entry I was left with was an entry only one week old. "I want Maurice. I want ordinary corrupt human love."
> *It's* all I can give you, I thought. I don't know about any other kind of love, ...
>
> (Greene 1975, p. 125)
>
> ... 最后剩下的一则日记写了只有一个星期: "我要莫里斯。我要平平常常的、堕落的、凡人的爱。"
> 我想: "我所能给你的一切就是这个。我不知道还有什么别的样子的爱。"
>
> (柯平, Trans. 《恋情的终结》)

We may look at another example, which is interestingly indicative of how the negligence of this **universal feature** (普遍特征) of definite/indefinite reference and its specific way of representation may cause awkward mistranslations. In this specific case, the negligence has for ages (indeed, even up to the very present day) inadvertently affected the Chinese translation of the first line of Hamlet's famous soliloquy:

To be, or not to be, **that is the Question**:
(Whether 'tis nobler in the mind to suffer
The slings and arrows of outrageous fortune,
Or to take arms against a sea of troubles,
And by opposing end them? ...)

(Shakespeare. Hamlet, III, I, 56–60)

死后还是存在, 还是不存在——这是问题; (梁实秋, Trans.)

生存还是不生存: 就是这个问题: (曹禺, Trans.)

生存还是毁灭, 这是一个值得考虑的问题; (朱生豪, Trans.)

活下去还是不活: 这是问题。(卞之琳, Trans.)

是存在还是消亡, 问题的所在; (孙大雨, Trans.)

干, 还是不干, 这就是问题。(陈嘉, Trans.)

存在, 还是毁灭, 就这问题了。(林同济, Trans.)

All the translators whose translation is printed here have devoted their attention almost exclusively to the interpretation of the first half of the sentence, specifically the verb *be*, to the negligence of the appropriate way to render the meaning of definite reference as conveyed by the article *the* in the second half of the sentence. They could not have possibly failed to recognize the definite reference of the noun "question" since it is preceded by the definite article *the*, but none of them seemed to have put to himself the question of how to render this notion of definite reference into Chinese. As a result, their translations of the sentence are not only awkward, but also incorrect in that they give the false impression that Hamlet is not trying to pinpoint the answer to the question which must have been going on in his mind in some elusive way for a long time (i.e. as the next two lines indicate, **which option is "nobler in mind": to suffer the insult of outrageous fortune, or to fight and end all that troubles him, most probably at the cost of his own life?**), but seems to be finding on that particular moment that he is suddenly confronted with the question of life or death.

Prof. Chen Guohua (陈国华) (Chen, 1997, p. 15) made a contrastive study of the conventional ways by which definite reference and indefinite reference are made in English and Chinese, and proposed the following translation (slightly revised by the present author), which correctly represents the definite reference of the original and which, in the present author's opinion, is the sole correct and coherent one of all the translations ever published of this famous line by Shakespeare:

是生, 还是死, 问题就在这里:
(哪一种做法精神上更高贵,
是忍受狂暴命运射来的矢石,
还是拿起刀枪与苦海拼搏,
以抗争将一切了结?...)

As we can easily perceive in Prof. Chen's translation, the first line leads naturally to the succeeding lines because it correctly transfers, by way of taking proper care of the notion of definite reference as conveyed by the article *the*, the original logical tie between them. The translation of the whole soliloquy thereby appears coherent (logical and consistent) in the context of the story.

This example illustrates that **theoretical contrastive analysis** (理论对比分析) is important in that it deals with problems that are closer to the essence of things under investigation. In this specific case, a theoretical contrastive analysis of the different ways English and Chinese employ to make definite reference and indefinite reference will help the translator to render a special question in Shakespeare's work into Chinese in an appropriate way. In a more general sense, however, the contrastive analysis made may give Chinese students who learn English or English students who learn Chinese some generalized (and therefore extensively significant) conception of the relationship between the function of English articles and that of Chinese **word order**.

In this book, we shall tackle both the theoretical and applied aspects of **contrastive linguistics** (对比语言学). We shall try to give a balanced account of the two and see to it that the theoretical analysis discussed have at least a potential bearing on the practical problems we may encounter in language use and study.

2.3 Criteria for Comparison

Before going into a discussion of this topic, we had better go back to first principles and ask ourselves a simple question: how do we ever set about comparing anything?

Normally, the first thing we do is to make sure that we are comparing like with like: this means that the two (or more) entities to be compared, while differing in some respect, must share certain attributes. This requirement is especially strong when we are contrasting, that is, looking for differences, since it is only against a background of sameness that differences are significant (James, 1980, p. 169). We may, e.g. compare English verbs with Chinese nouns or Chinese adjectives with English adverbs, but these comparisons obviously do not make much sense since the objects being compared are totally different things. To make sense of our comparisons, we must compare, say, English verbs with Chinese verbs, Chinese adjectives with English adjectives, and the like. We shall call this background of sameness the "**constant**" (常量) and the differences the "**variables**" (变量). In the theory of **contrastive linguistics** (对比语言学) the constant has traditionally been known as the *tertium comparationis* (Latin = the third element in comparison, i.e. the factor which links or is the common ground between two elements in comparison) (比较参照物) or **TC** for short.

In the previous section we distinguish two types of contrastive analysis: theoretical contrastive analysis and applied contrastive linguistics. **Theoretical contrastive analysis** (理论对比分析) does not investigate how a given category present in language A is represented in language B. Instead it looks for the realization of a **universal category** (普遍范畴) X in both A and B. **Applied contrastive analysis** (应用对比分析), on the other hand, is concerned with the problem of how a universal category X, realized in language A as X(a), is rendered in language B as X(b). In both cases, there exists this universal category or **universal feature** (普遍特征) X, which is the **TC** for **contrastive analysis** (对比分析). It is our concern in this section to characterize **TC** in broad terms.

In the next chapter, we shall come to find that for phonetic and phonological **CA**, the **International Phonetic Alphabet (IPA)** (国际音标), a system of symbols for representing the pronunciation of words in any language according to the principles of the **International Phonetic Association** or, at a more fundamental level, a limited number of distinctive phonological features, might be strong candidates for **TC**. In the fourth chapter, we shall see that for lexical **CA** the probably universal set of **semantic components** (语义成分) would be very useful for **TC**. In this section we shall discuss the **TC** for grammatical **CA**.

Over the years three candidates have been proposed for the **TC** by which grammatical **CA** can be carried out. They are: the **surface structure** (表层结构), the **deep structure** (深层结构), and **translation equivalence** (翻译等值).

2.3.1 The Surface Structure (SS)

In **generative linguistics** (生成语言学) the surface structure and the **deep structure** (深层结构) are a pair of important notions regarding the structure of a sentence. The **surface structure** (表层结构) is the syntactic structure of the sentence which a person speaks, hears, reads or writes. In other words, it is the actually observed structure of a sentence, e.g. the passive structure in the following sentence:

The newspaper was not delivered today.

The **deep structure** (深层结构) is much more abstract and is considered to be there in the speaker's, writer's, hearer's, or reader's mind. The deep structure for the above sentence would be something like:

(NEGATIVE) someone (PAST TENSE) deliver the newspaper today (PASSIVE).

The items in brackets are not lexical items but grammatical concepts which shape the final form of the sentence.

In the scheme of **grammar** (语法) formulated by **Transformational Grammarians** (转换语法研究者), rules which describe the **deep structure** (深层结构) are in the first part of the grammar (**Base Component**). Rules which transform these structures (**transformational rules**) are in the second part of the grammar (**Transformational Component**). (We shall deal with these notions in a more elaborate way in Chap. 5 where we address grammatical **CA**.)

Most of the contrastive analyses ever conducted have taken **surface structure** (表层结构) categories as the **TC**. This does not mean that they yield superior **TCs**. There are advantages as well as disadvantages for doing so.

First, there is no denying that it is **surface structures** (表层结构) that **L2 learners** (二语学习者) are confronted with, and that they have to master in order to communicate. As Jakobovits (1970, p. 73) observes: "… similarities and differences of surface features may be more relevant for the operation of transfer effects in second language learning than deep structure relations." In other words, learners would naturally equate surface structures. So the surface structure seems to be a convenient **TC** for grammatical **CA**.

There are, however, disadvantages for basing **CA** on the **surface structure** (表层结构).

(1) First, as Stockwell et al. (1975, p. 3) point out, surface grammar "… tells us little or nothing about the way in which sentences are formed. It is **grammar** (语法) conceived largely from the hearer's point of view."

(2) The main objection to using the **surface structure** (表层结构) as the **TC** is that it leads to interlingual equations that are superficial and insignificant. As Widdowson (1974) points out, we are hereby led to identify as sames the categories that have very different *values* in the economy of the respective **grammar** (语法), as well as different conditions for *use* in real-life settings. In the following illustrations, for instance, the surface-structure **TC** implies the equation of the verb forms in 1) and 2) whereas in situations of *use* (i.e. pragmatically) it is just as frequently 3), not 2), that is equivalent to 1), although formally 3) is closer to the English sentence 4) in that they both take the present perfect tense:

    1) The postman opened the door.
    2) Le facteur ouvrit la porte.
    3) Le facteur a ouvert la porte.
    4) The postman has opened the door.

This is because French **passé simple** has very limited use. What is comparable to English past tense is French **passé composé**. This example suggests that what is correspondent formally does not always correspond pragmatically. **Formal correspondence** is just not a reliable basis for cross-language comparison. For this reason **contrastivists** (对比分析研究者) (James, 1969; Wagner, 1970) proposed that a more satisfactory **TC** would be the **deep structure** (深层结构) (based on James, 1980, pp. 170–171), which we shall discuss in the following.

2.3.2   The Deep Structure (DS)

The **deep structure** (深层结构) is one of the most fundamental and innovative conceptions in **generative linguistics** (生成语言学). In Noam Chomsky's theory, it acts as the basis of semantic realizations in **utterances** (for definition, see Sect. 1.3 "The History and Development of Contrastive Linguistics") and is closely related to **Competence** (语言能力) (see Sect. 1.1.2 "Micro-contrastive Linguistics and Macro-Contrastive Linguistics" for definition), which Chomsky argues to be the real aim of linguistic investigation.

A question which may arise at this stage is: why is a level of syntactic description deeper than the overtly observed structure necessary or, in other words, why do we need the notion of the **deep structure** (深层结构)?

The notion of the deep structure is desired mainly for two reasons.

(1)   One reason is that a postulated **deep structure** (深层结构) will help to simplify the statement of semantic rules.

It is obvious that in order to understand a sentence correctly, one needs to be able to tell its subject from its object. (Just consider what a great difference in meaning there exists between the much quoted phrases of "Dog bites the man" and "Man bites the dog". [Alfred Harmsworth, a British newspaper magnate: "When a dog bites a man, that is not news, because it happens so often. But if a man bites a dog, that is news."]) We know that **grammar** (语法) has as one of its chief functions to aid in the understanding of sentences. So it should provide means for identifying the subjects and objects associated with particular verbs in the sentence.

It is equally obvious that, since what is concerned here is understanding or meaning, the subjects and objects referred to are not concepts in superficial structures but those in logical or underlying structures.

It is possible for superficially dissimilar sentences of a language to be para-phrases of one another, that is, they convey the same ideational content. In the following two pairs of sentences, for instance, a) and b) have different superficial structures, but native speakers of English feel that they have identical **logical subjects** (逻辑主语):

1a)   To find the fossils of a dinosaur is exciting.
 b)   It is exciting to find the fossils of a dinosaur.

2a)   There's a hole in my bucket.
 b)   My bucket has a hole in it.

On the other hand, the following two sentences have the same superficial structure, but the **logical subjects** (逻辑主语) of their predicates are perceived to be different:

3a) John is easy to please.
  b) John is eager to please.

Traditional grammar (语法) did adopt a logical approach to **syntax** (句法). But by defining, for example, the subject as "the performer of an action," it could not account for the difference in meaning between countless pairs of sentences like the above one. This shows that there is no simple way to identify the **logical subject** (逻辑主语) on the level of superficial structure of a sentence.

It is for this reason that Noam Chomsky ingeniously developed the notion of a deeper level of syntactic description—the **deep structure** (深层结构), on which the relations between subjects and verbs can easily be determined.

With Chomsky, the **logical subject** (逻辑主语) of a verb is defined as the **noun phrase** (NP) immediately before it in the deep structure. Some syntactic rules are formulated to turn deep structures into **surface structures** (表层结构). In this way, the semantic interpretation of the sentence becomes both explicit and simple. Sentences can be judged to be synonymous or intralingual paraphrases of each other *when and only when* they have the same deep structure. For example, 1a) and 1b) may be taken as synonymous because they have the same deep structure [1a)]. A transformation named "**EXTRAPOSITION**" will move the subject to the end of the sentence, putting at its original position a "dummy" subject *it*, and thus produces Sentence 1b). By the same course of analysis, 3a) and 3b) are taken to be sentences with different meanings since they have different deep structures. The **logical subject** (逻辑主语) of 3a) is the underlying "SOMEBODY" while that of 3b) is "John."

(2) Another reason that we need the notion of **deep structure** (深层结构) is that it helps to simplify the statement of syntactic rules, too.

(a) First of all, the introduction of the notion of **deep structure** (深层结构) makes it easy to make statements of the relationships among apparently different sentences in an explicit way. Let us examine the following group of sentences, which are so diverse in their **surface structures** (表层结构) that they appear to be different sentences:

4a) For Mary to sing the song was hard.
  b) The song was hard for Mary to sing.
  c) Mary was hard to sing the song.
  d) It was hard for Mary to sing the song.

By appealing to deep structure analysis, however, we may clarify their relationships in a clear and uniform way: 4a) is regarded as the kernel of the four sentences (that is, its structure is perceived to underlie the other three sentences). By applying **OBJECT RAISING** transformation we derive 4b); by applying **SUBJECT RAISING** transformation we derive 4c); and by applying **EXTRAPOSITION** transformation we derive 4d). The four sentences are therefore said to be related and indeed synonymous to each other because they have a common **deep structure** (深层结构).

(b) On the other hand, apparently similar or identical structures may have under them different **deep structures** (深层结构). It is due to this fact that ambiguities rise in language. The notion of deep structure displays strong power in explaining syntactic ambiguity. For instance, in the following humor (linguistically, humors often rely on ambiguities for their comic effects), two deep structures happen to share one common **surface structure** (表层结构).

> A big-game hunter was showing a charming young lady the skin of a lion that he had shot. "One night," he explained, "I heard the roar of a lion: I jumped out of bed, raised my gun, took careful aim and shot it in my pajamas."
>
> "Good heavens," the young lady exclaimed, "How ever did it get into your pajamas?"

The **deep structure** (深层结构) meaning intended by the hunter ("I, who was in pajamas, shot the lion.") happens to take the same superficial form as another deep structure, that is, "I shot the lion, which was in my pajamas." The young lady missed (or deliberately ignored) the meaning carried by the first deep structure of the sentence (i.e. the meaning intended by the boastful hunter) and interpreted what the guy said according to the second deep structure, hence the humorous effect.

In the above we made pure linguistic justifications for the conception of the **deep structure** (深层结构). We may now turn to consider the relevance of the notion of deep structure to **contrastive analysis** (对比分析).

Apparently, the notion of deep structure has several advantages for contrastive purposes:

(1) The purported universality of the **deep structure** (深层结构) makes it a convenient **TC** for **contrastive analysis** (对比分析). It is at least possible to argue that **interlingual paraphrases** (语际释义), that is, pairs of sentences from two different languages having the same ideational content, are likewise derived from a common deep structure. Note that the idea of intralingual paraphrase implies that the deep structure is language-specific, while that of interlingual paraphrase implies that it is language-independent, just as Chomsky (1967, p. 80) points out: "It seems to be true that the underlying deep structures vary slightly, at most, from language to language, ... It is pleasant to discover that they do not vary much from language to language." If this is true, the deep structure ought to serve as a viable **TC**.

(2) The second advantage of the concept of **deep structure** (深层结构) for **CA** is that it can be used as a yardstick by which the degrees of difference or equivalence between languages can be measured. If a shared deep structure is converted into a language-specific **surface structure** (表层结构) by the sequential application of transformations, then the points in their transformational derivations at which equated deep structure representations of two languages begin to diverge, can be taken as a measure of their differences: "the differences between languages must come at various levels of intermediate structure" (Di Pietro, 1971, p. 26). The "earlier" they diverge, the greater the difference; the "later," the less. In this way it is possible to describe degrees of

equivalence or disparity between languages in terms of correspondences between the *rules* of their respective **grammar** (语法): we gain the double advantages of quantification and explicitness. (Based on James, 1980, pp. 171–172)

On the other hand, however, the proposal of adopting the **deep structure** (深层结构) as the **TC** for contrastive grammatical analysis has one serious drawback, that is, it fails to take into account the fact that sentences—of the *same* or of *different* languages—with a common deep structure are not necessarily communicatively or pragmatically equivalent. In other words, even though we can demonstrate the common origin of two such sentences as:

Le facteur a ouvert la porte.

The door was opened by the postman.

we shall merely mislead the learner if we try to equate them in terms of their communicative potential. The contexts where the first is used in French are not the same as contexts where the second is used in English. They may have the same propositional content, but they are certainly not pragmatically equivalent (James, 1980, p. 174). Specifically, the French sentence may be a response to the question "What did the postman do?" while the English sentence may be a reply to the question "What happened to the door?" (Widdowson, 1974).

So there comes the need for us to move on to consider the third candidate for **TC** in **contrastive analysis—translation equivalence** (翻译等值).

2.3.3   Translation Equivalence

It is to our knowledge that grammatical elements convey **grammatical meaning** (语法意义), which is part of the total meanings of a message. This means that differences in grammatical structure affect the total meaning of an utterance or sentence. So the equivalence of a pair of sentences in two languages in meaning may work as the **TC** for grammatical **CA**.

We also know that translation theorists set great store by semantic equivalence between the source text and the target text. We see then that **translation theorists** (翻译理论研究者) and **contrastivists** (对比分析研究者) ally themselves here in the pursuit of a common objective: the definition of translation equivalence (Wilss, 1977).

To the layman, **translation equivalence** (翻译等值) is synonymous with sameness of meaning. According to this view, the contrastivist should equate pairs of sentences of **L1** and **L2** which "mean the same." Here he runs into a big problem, however: how to determine whether a **L1** and a **L2** sentence do mean the same? Even bilinguals who know the two languages very well will disagree about this. *Le Rouge et le Noir*, e.g. has been understood by Prof. Xu Yuanzhong as something like "魂归离恨天" to the cry of many other famous translators of French literature. Therefore, **contrastivists** (对比分析研究者) and **translation theorists** (翻译理论研究者) must seek some *objective* definition of **translation equivalence** (翻译等值).

One way to define **translation equivalence** (翻译等值) is in terms of **deep structure identity** (深层结构相同), since the **deep structure** (深层结构) of a sentence, according to Chomsky (1965, p. 16), is a representation "… which incorporates all information relevant to the single interpretation of a particular sentence." This amounts to a claim that the deep structure equals meaning, which implies that identity of the deep structure equals sameness of meaning (James, 1980, p. 175).

However, this view has been effectively challenged and repudiated in both linguistic and Translation Studies communities in recent years. We may employ a logical method known as *reductio ad absurdum* ("reduction to absurdity": proving the falsity of a premise by showing that its logical consequence is absurd or contradictory) (归谬法, 反证论法) to prove that **translation equivalence** (翻译等值) is not equal to **deep structure identity** (深层结构相同). For data we may consider the responses to negative-polarity questions in English and Chinese. In answering a negative-polarity question, Chinese and English speakers use *yes* and *no* in somewhat different ways. The Chinese speaker uses *yes* or *no* on the basis of whether he agrees with the questioner making the specific hypothetical statement about something while the English speaker uses *yes* or *no* depending his judgment of the truth or falsity of the thing itself. So the English negative-polarity question *Didn't you go to school today?* will be answered by *Yes* if the child did go, by *No* if he did not. In Chinese, the same question (你没有去上学吗?) is answered with *No* (不是的) if the child did go, and with *Yes* (是的) if he did not. It follows that "… the English *yes* and the Chinese *no,* and the English *no* and the Chinese *yes* are **translation equivalents** (翻译等值成分)." Surely this cannot be true. We cannot say that these responses of opposite polarity have identical deep structure, if indeed they can be said to have any structure at all!

There is, however, a far simpler reason than that we explained above why **deep structure identity** (深层结构相同) does not guarantee **translation equivalence** (翻译等值). This is that meaning, and equivalence of meaning, are of several types, and the **deep structure** (深层结构) is predicated or based on but one of these, to the exclusion of the others. The deep structure is concerned with the **propositional meaning** (命题意义) or "**ideational meaning**" (概念意义) (Halliday, 1970) that single isolated sentences convey. There are, however, at least two further kinds of meaning a sentence may carry, i.e. "**interpersonal meaning**" (人际意义) and "**textual meaning**" (语篇意义) as Halliday calls them (James, 1980, p. 178).

We may also define meaning more precisely in sociosemiotic terms (for an introduction to sociosemiotic theory of meaning, see Ke, 1996, pp. 75–81) and distinguish three broader categories of meaning, i.e. **referential meaning** (指称意义) (**RM**, the relationship between verbal signs and entities/processes in the world which they refer to or describe), **pragmatic meaning** (语用意义) (**PM**, the relationship between verbal signs and their users, including identificational, expressive, associative, social or interpersonal, and imperative or vocative meanings), and

intralingual meaning (言内意义) (**IM**, the relationship between verbal signs themselves, including phonetic and phonological meanings, graphemic meaning, morphological/lexemic meaning, syntactic meaning, and discoursal/textual meaning).

With reference to the Fig. 2.1, which shows these three categories of meaning (and the individual meanings falling under them), we may analyze the notion of meaning in a more elaborate and explicit way.

In linguistic communication, as in any other sort of communication, there are at least five essential elements involved: the **Topic** (传通主题) (the message transmitted), the **Code** (语码) (the system of symbols with which the message is processed and sent out), the **Sender** (发讯人) (the encoder of the message), the **Receiver** (收讯人) (the decoder of the message), and the **Channel of Contact** (传通渠道) (the way or settings in which the message is conveyed from the Sender to the Receiver). Each of the three categories of sociosemiotic meaning is related primarily to one or more of these five elements.

The **ideational meaning** (概念意义) or **referential meaning** (指称意义) is related to the conceptual or cognitive aspect of the topic of communication.

The interpersonal meaning (人际意义) or pragmatic meaning (语用意义) of a sentence determines what kind of **speech act** (言语行为) it performs for its user: to praise, condemn, refuse, agree, and so on (Fig. 2.2).

The textual meaning (语篇意义) or **intralingual meaning** (言内意义) of a sentence determines what information it contributes to the message: how it helps maintain **cohesion** (接应, 接气) and **coherence** (连贯统一), what rhetorical effects are aimed at, etc.

All linguistic items have **intralingual meaning** (言内意义) since linguistic signs by definition function within the structure of interrelated units of a language. Almost all expressions also have **referential meaning** (指称意义). And quite frequently words, phrases, sentences, etc. are charged with **pragmatic meaning** (语用意义), because we use language to comment as well as to state, to do things as well as to communicate information.

The three categories of meaning, however, differ in their relative degree of prominence in different contexts. Generally speaking, in technical contexts (typically, science and academic writings), **referential meaning** (指称意义) is almost exclusively important. In general or "institutional" contexts (typically, news report, publicity material, official guides, handbooks, instruction manuals, etc.) (Newmark, 1988, p. 44), **pragmatic meaning** (语用意义) as well as **referential meaning** (指称意义) may be important. And in literary contexts, a high degree of foregrounded

Fig. 2.1 The universal category/feature *X* and its realizations in Language A (*Xa*) and Language B (*Xb*)

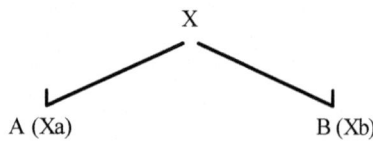

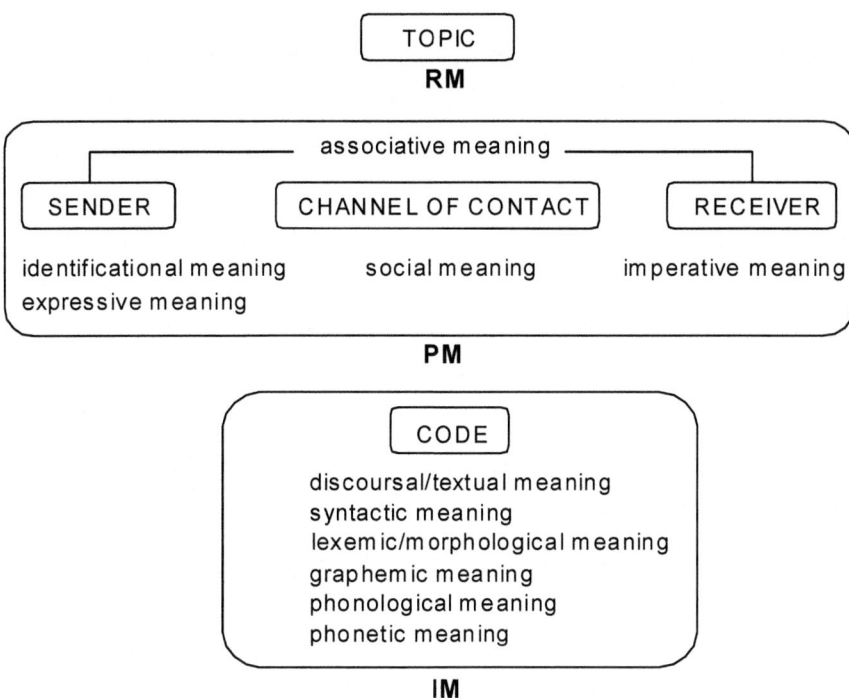

Fig. 2.2 A sociosemiotic model of meaning

pragmatic meaning (语用意义) and **intralingual meaning** (言内意义) may be registered.

For two sentences from different languages to be translationally equivalent they must convey the same referential (ideational) *and* pragmatic (interpersonal) *and* intralingual (textual) meanings. But **deep structure identity** (深层结构相同) means the sameness of only one of these three types of meaning, namely the ideational or **referential meaning** (指称意义). Therefore it is not an adequate guarantee for **translation equivalence** (翻译等值). For **contrastive analysis** (对比分析) we ought to equate **L1** and **L2** forms which, no matter how far they diverge superficially, are referentially (or in Newmark's terms, semantically), pragmatically, and, to a lesser degree, intralingually, equivalent. The term of qualification "to a lesser degree" is added here to **intralingual equivalence** (言内意义等值) because this dimension of equivalence is often rather difficult to attain. Just think of how hard it would be to render into **L2** a word play, such as a palindrome (that is, a word, phrase, etc. that reads the same backwards as it does forwards), e.g.

deed/level

"客上天然居, 居然天上客" (an antithetical couplet associated with the name of a shop in Beijing; Emperor Qianlong is said to have composed the first half of the couplet while Ji Xiaolan, his grand secretary, completed the second half.)

Referential and **pragmatic equivalence** is a different case. It is not only indispensable to the success of communication on almost all occasions, but also largely possible to be achieved in translation.

So we conclude that **translation equivalence** (翻译等值)—rigorously defined thus in sociosemiotic terms—is the best available **TC** for **grammatical contrastive analysis** (语法对比分析).

We have by now noticed that in this search for criteria against which languages should be compared grammatically, **contrastive linguistics** (对比语言学) and translation theory meet each other and sort of join hands.

2.4   Procedures of Contrastive Analysis

Any **contrastive analysis** (对比分析) involves two steps: first, there is the stage of description when each of the two languages is described on an appropriate level; then comes the stage of juxtaposition for comparison.

Structural linguists used to observe the rule that a language is described in a hierarchy of orders or levels, from the lowest phonetic and phonological levels to the highest textual and pragmatic levels. These levels of description, according to **structural linguistics** (结构语言学), should not be "mixed." In other words, it was a regulation within **structural linguistics** (结构语言学) that the description on, say, the level of **phonology** (音系学), should be carried out without reference to the other linguistic levels. To invoke, for instance, grammatical factors to facilitate the description of the phonology of a language or vice versa, was viewed as illegitimate and this "**mixing of levels** (层面混淆)" was ruled out of court. Nowadays mixing is allowed, and sometimes found to be necessary to account for some facts of language.

In the first stage of **contrastive analysis** (对比分析), the observance of levels can be adhered to, but it will frequently be necessary, at the comparison stage, to cross levels. Let's look at some examples of what may be called **interlingual level shifts** (语际层面推移) or **level crossings** (层面跨越)

5a) He wanted to escape.   Il voulait s' échapper.
  b) He tried to escape.   Il a voulu s' échapper.

6a) 厂里让她下岗了。   Her plant laid her off.
  b) 厂里让她下岗了?   Did her plant lay her off?

7a) I don't lend my books to anyone.   Je ne prête mes livres à personne.
  b) I don't lend my books to `anyone.   Je ne prête pas mes livres à n'importe qui.

In 5) what is a lexical distinction in English is expressed through a grammatical, or more precisely, a morphological contrast within French respectively: we have an **interlingual level shift from lexis** (词汇) **to grammar** (语法). In 6) we see that questions are distinguished from statements in Chinese by **intonation** (语调), and in English by the grammatical device of *DO*-**INSERTION**: a **phonology-to-grammar level shift**. In 7) the two English sentences are differentiated through intonation, a device operating on the phonological level, whereas French uses two distinct lexical items to convey the same difference: we have a **level shift from phonology** (音系学) **to lexis**. (Based on James, 1980, pp. 29–31)

2.5   Questions for Discussion and Research

1. What is **transfer**? Use examples from your own learning experience to illustrate the notions of **positive transfer** and **negative transfer.**
2. What are theoretical CA and applied CA respectively concerned with?
3. Make a comparative reading of the different Chinese translations of the first line of Hamlet's famous soliloquy in William Shakespeare's tragedy *Hamlet* and judge if they do justice to the original. You are also encouraged to translate this line by yourself and state the reason for translating it your way:

   To be, or not to be, that is the Question:

   (Whether'tis nobler in the mind to suffer

   The slings and arrows of outrageous fortune,

   Or to take arms against a sea of troubles,

   And by opposing end them?...)

   (Shakespeare. *Hamlet*, III, I, 56–60)

   死后还是存在, 还是不存在——这是问题; (梁实秋, Trans.)

   生存还是不生存: 就是这个问题: (曹禺, Trans.)

   生存还是毁灭, 这是一个值得考虑的问题; (朱生豪, Trans.)

   活下去还是不活: 这是问题。(卞之琳, Trans.)

   是存在还是消亡, 问题的所在; (孙大雨, Trans.)

   干,还是不干, 这就是问题。(陈嘉, Trans.)

   存在,还是毁灭, 就这问题了。(林同济, Trans.)

4. What is meant by "**interlingual level shifts**" or "**level crossings**"? Why may they be necessary in contrastive analysis?
5. What do we mean when we say that CA can **predict errors**? **Error analysis** distinguishes two types of errors: **interlingual errors** and **intralingual errors**. What type of errors can CA be reasonably expected to predict?
6. Compare the following sentences:

   If it's going to rain, I wish it would rain.
   If it's going to rain, I wish it would.

In the second sentence, *rain* is transformationally deleted because it is the same as the preceding *rain* ("deletion under identity"). Do the two sentences mean the same? See if the following implications are equally applicable to both sentences:

desire for the rain
impatience at the rain's inability to make up its mind

In the following two sentences, decide whether the implications of (a) acceptance or determination and (b) resignation are equally applicable to both:

If I have to drive it in, I'll drive it in.
If I have to drive it in, I will.

Does it appear that even with as simple a transformation as deletion we cannot be sure that there will not be some change in meaning (Bolinger, 1981, p. 106)?

References

Bolinger, D., & Sears, D. A. (1981). *Aspects of language* (3rd ed.). New York, NY: Harcourt Brace Jovanovich.

Chau, T. T. (1975). Error analysis, contrastive analysis, and students' perception: A study of difficulty in second-language learning. *IRAL, 13*(2), 119–143.

Chen, G. [陈国华]. (1997). 论重译莎剧. Manuscript submitted for publication.

Chomsky, N. (1965). *Aspects of the theory of syntax*. Cambridge, MA: MIT Press.

Chomsky, N. (1967). The general properties of language. In C. H. Millikan & F. L. Darley (Eds.), *Brain mechanisms underlying speech and language* (pp. 73–88). New York, NY: Grune & Stratton.

Di Pietro, J. R. (1971). *Language structures in contrast*. Rowley, MA: Newbury House.

George, H. V. (1972). *Common errors in language learning*. Rowley, MA: Newbury House.

Grauberg, W. (1971). An error analysis in German of first year university students. In G. E. Perren & J. L. M. Trim (Eds.), *Applications of linguistics*. Cambridge: Cambridge University Press.

Greene, Graham. (1962). The end of the affair. Harmondsworth, United Kingdom: Penguin Books.

Greene, Graham. (2001). 《恋情的终结》 (Ke, Trans.). 南京: 译林出版社. (Original work [The End of the Affair] published 1951).

Halliday, M. A. K. (1970). Language structure and language function. In J. Lyons (Ed.), *New horizons in linguistics*. Harmondsworth: Penguin Books.

Jakobovits, L. A. (1970). *Foreign language learning: A psycholinguistic analysis of the issues*. Rowley, MA: Newbury House.

James, C. (1969). Deeper contrastive study. *IRAL, 17*(2), 83–95.

James, C. (1980). *Contrastive analysis*. Harlow: Longman Group UK Limited.

Ke, P. (1996). A socio-semiotic approach to meaning in translation. *Babel, 42*(2), 74–83.

Mukattash, L. (1977). *Problematic areas in English syntax for Jordanian students*. Amman: University of Amman.

Newmark, P. (1988). *A textbook of translation*. London: Prentice Hall.

Oller, J. W., & Redding, E. Z. (1971). Article usage and other language skills. *Language Learning, 21*(11), 85–95.

Richards, J. C. (1971). Error analysis and second language strategies. *Language Sciences, 17,* 12–22.

Stockwell, R. P., et al. (1975). *The grammatical structures of English and Spanish*. Chicago, IL: University of Chicago Press.

Wagner, K. H. (1970). *The relevance of the notion "deep structure" to contrastive analysis*. University of Stuttgart PAKS Project Report No. 6.

Wardhaugh, R. (1970). The contrastive analysis hypothesis. *TESOL Quarterly, 4*(2).

Widdowson, H. G. (1974). The deep structure of discourse and the use of translation. In S. P. Corder & E. Roulet (Eds.), *Linguistic insights in applied linguistics* (pp. 129–142). Paris: Didier.

Wilss, W. (1977). *Ubersetzungswissenschaft: Probleme und Methoden*. Stuttgart: Klett.

Xu, Y. [许余龙]. (1992).《对比语言学概论》. 上海: 上海外语教育出版社.

Chapter 3
Phonetic and Phonological Contrastive Analyses

In this and the next few chapters, we shall deal with micro-contrastive linguistics (微观对比语言学), concentrating on the first four levels of linguistic description, i.e. **phonetics** (语音学), **phonology** (音系学), **lexis** (词汇), and **grammar** (语法).

3.1 Phonetics and Phonology

One question that may arise as we start this chapter would be: what is the most basic difference between **phonetics** (语音学) and **phonology** (音系学)? The answer is that the difference is one between type and token.

In linguistics, a **type** (类符) is a class of linguistic items, e.g. **phonemes** (音位), words, utterances (see Sect. 1.3 "The History and Development of Contrastive Linguistics" for the definition of "utterance"); a **token** (形符) is an example or a physical manifestation of a class. For example, *hello, hi, good morning* are three different tokens of the text or discourse type "Greeting" in **phatic communication** or **phatic communion** (寒暄). There are nine letter-tokens in the word *phonology* (i.e. there are nine physical manifestations of each of the different letters of the English alphabet that appear in the word *phonology*), but there are only *seven* letter-types (different letters) in the word *phonology*. Children may often be found to confuse a type and a token, as is shown in the following humor:

Teacher: Tommy, name five things that contain milk.
Tommy: Butter and cheese, ice-cream and two cows.

A distinction can be drawn between phonetics and **phonology** (音系学) in terms of this differentiation between type and token. **Phonetics** (语音学) studies human speech sounds in general, that is, the **type** of speech sounds; while **phonology**

© Peking University Press and Springer Nature Singapore Pte Ltd. 2019
P. Ke, *Contrastive Linguistics*, Peking University Linguistics Research 1,
https://doi.org/10.1007/978-981-13-1385-1_3

(音系学) studies the specific speech sounds as employed in different languages, i.e. the **tokens** of human speech sounds.

Phonetics (语音学) studies how people physically produce and perceive different sounds to create speech. **Phonetics** is not concerned in any way with the meaning connected to speech sounds, but **phonology** is. **Phonology** (音系学) studies how speech sounds are structured and combined to create meaning in words, phrases and sentences. In **generative linguistics** (生成语言学), phonology is considered a part of **grammar** (语法) and, just as there are grammar rules governing the **morphology** (形态学, 词法) of words and the **syntax** (句法) of sentences, there are phonological rules governing the structure of speech sounds in specific languages.

A division of the phonetic sciences (i.e. the scientific studies of human speech sounds and the sound systems of specific languages) into these two main branches immediately poses a problem for the **contrastivist** (对比分析研究者): is he to do **contrastive phonetics** (对比语音学) or **contrastive phonology** (对比音系学)?

The short answer is: Both. **Contrastive phonetics** (对比语音学) will involve the **contrastivist** (对比分析研究者) in making detailed descriptions of the sounds of a pair of languages and then somehow equating certain of these sounds interlingually for purposes of comparison. **Contrastive phonology** (对比音系学) will require him to investigate and then compare the specific functions comparable sounds (**phonemes** [音位]) in different languages perform in their own sound systems. In other words, contrastive phonetics compares the physiological and physical properties of speech sounds while contrastive phonology compares the functions of speech sounds.

But can **contrastive phonetics** (对比语音学) be made before or independent of **contrastive phonology** (对比音系学), that is, without reference to the differences speech sounds have in their functions? It can, by taking as the criterion for comparison the articulatory grid employed in the **International Phonetic Alphabet (IPA) Chart** (国际音标表): on this articulatory framework the **contrastivist** (对比分析研究者) can compare similar sounds of **L1** and **L2** and match them. The feasibility of this approach is guaranteed by the fact that the world's languages do tend to employ sounds produced by a limited number of combinations of articulatory features. This is not surprising in view of the fact that human vocal apparatus is physiologically uniform throughout the world. Perhaps the most interesting fact about the pronunciation of language in general is that there are enormous possibilities in the number and variety of sounds that the human vocal apparatus can produce, and yet only a small fraction of this potential variety is actually put to use in natural languages. (Based on James, 1980, pp. 71–73).

In the following we shall first study **contrastive phonetics** (对比语音学) and then **contrastive phonology** (对比音系学). Finally, we shall consider **contrastive analysis** (对比分析) on the suprasegmental level, which goes beyond the scope of individual sounds of vowels, consonants, and semi-vowels and extends over more than one sound in an utterance.

3.2 Contrastive Phonetics

When studying the sounds of human language, the phonetician is concerned with three facets of the reality of sound, i.e. the physiological, the physical, and the psychological. These three different realities of sound are respectively the objects of investigation of three different branches of **phonetics** (语音学): articulatory phonetics, acoustic phonetics, and auditory phonetics.

3.2.1 Articulatory Phonetics

Articulatory phonetics (发音语音学) deals with the way in which speech sounds are produced. In this section we shall first examine human organs involved in voice production (i.e. articulators) and the dynamics of voice production and then discuss the problem of the modulation of speech sounds.

3.2.1.1 Vocal Organs (Articulators) and the Dynamics of Voice Production

Vocal organs (发音器官) are also known as **speech organs** (发音器官) or **articulators** (发音器官). Human vocal organs and their close neighboring organs include (See Fig. 3.1):

- **chest muscles** (胸部肌肉): They alternately raise (expands) and lower (contracts) a person's rib cage (胸腔) and diaphragm (the large muscular membranous partition between one's lungs and stomach that helps one breathe [横隔膜]). Although they are not exactly a "vocal organ," we may list them here on the ground that they are actually the primary engine of a voice production process.
- **diaphragm** (横隔膜): This is the principal muscle of respiration. The combined movement of the rib cage (胸腔) and the diaphragm expands and contracts the lungs.
- **lungs** (肺): Each of the pair of organs situated within the rib cage, consisting of elastic sacs with branching passages into which air is drawn, so that oxygen can pass into the blood and carbon dioxide be removed. The lungs expands and contracts by the combined movement of the rib cage (胸腔) and the diaphragm (横隔膜), thereby inhaling and exhaling air. The air exhaled from the lungs and forced between the vocal cords is the source of voice.
- **larynx** (喉): The part of the respiratory tract between the pharynx (咽) and the trachea (气管), having walls of cartilage (软骨) and muscle, forming an air passage to the lungs and holding the vocal cords in humans and other mammals. In non-technical use the larynx is called the "**voice box**."
- **vocal cords** (声带): Folds of membranous tissue which project inwards from the sides of the larynx to form a slit across the glottis (声门) in the throat. Vocal cords may vibrate in response to the passage between them of air exhaled from

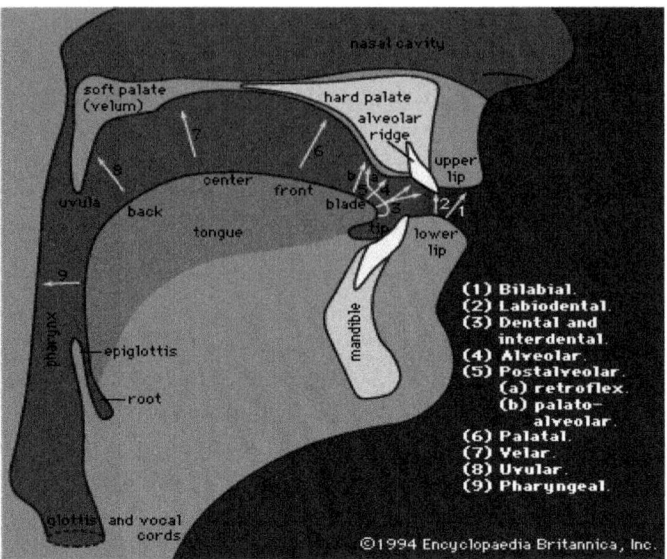

Fig. 3.1 Location of vocal organs and possible places of articulation. Retrieved from **phonetics** (2010). Encyclopædia Britannica. *Encyclopaedia Britannica Ultimate Reference Suite.* Chicago: Encyclopædia Britannica

the lungs to produce voiced onsonants, e.g. /*b*/, /*d*/ *and* /*g*/. The frequency of these vibrations determines the pitch of the voice. The vocal cords are shorter and thinner in women and children, accounting in part for their higher-pitched voices.

- **glottis** (声门): The space between the vocal cords. It affects voice modulation through expansion or contraction. For ordinary breathing the vocal cords are relaxed and widely separated. For voiced sounds, including all vowels and some consonants, such as the initial sounds of *b*in, *z*ip and *th*is, the vocal cords are pressed lightly together, the air forced between them produces vibration and thus voice. Involved in producing **glottals** (声门音) (sounds produced by the sudden opening or shutting of the glottis before or after an emission of breath or voice, as the *h* sound in the English word *hat*).
- pharynx (咽): (After the Greek word for "throat") The membrane-lined cavity at the back of the nose and mouth, where the passages to the nose and to the mouth connect with the throat. It is the passageway for both food and air. Involved in producing **pharyngeals** (咽音, 喉音) (a speech sound produced by articulating the root of the tongue with the pharynx, a feature of certain consonants in Arabic and some other languages, e.g. in Somali, *xood*, "cane").
- **epiglottis** (会厌): A flap of cartilage at the root of the tongue, which is depressed during swallowing to cover the opening of the windpipe.
- **esophagus** *or* **oesophagus** (食道): The muscular, membranous tube for the passage of food from the pharynx to the stomach. Also called **"gullet"**.
- **uvula** (小舌): (*Also called*: **palatine uvula**) A fleshy extension at the back of the soft palate which hangs above the throat. Its chief function so far as most speakers of English are concerned seems to be to get red and inflamed when one gets a "sore throat," but in other languages and in some dialects of English

it is used in the production of speech sounds. Involved in producing **uvulas** (小舌音) (a speech sound articulated with the back of the tongue and the uvula, as *r* in French and *q* in Arabic.

- **soft palate (velum)** (软腭): The fleshy, flexible part towards the back of the roof of the mouth. Acts as a valve for the production or suppression of **nasality** (鼻音性). When a nasal sound (such as the initial sound in "mouse") is to be produced, the soft palate moves forwards so that the stream of air, whose exit through the mouth is blocked elsewhere (in the case of "mouse" by closed lips), is forced up and out through the nose. Otherwise the velum is moved back and up to block the nasal exit, and the air is forced out entirely through the mouth. Of course, in reality there are many gradations between nasal and oral sounds, and a certain degree of nasality is present even when one does not intend it. Also involved in producing **velars** (软腭音) (a speech sound pronounced with the back of the tongue near the soft palate, as in *k* and *g* in English).
- **hard palate** (硬腭): The bony front part of the roof of the mouth. Involved in producing **palatals** (腭音) (a speech sound made by placing the blade of the tongue against or near the hard palate, e.g. *y* in *yes*).
- **tongue** (舌头): The most flexible and most frequently used vocal organ for modulating speech sounds. Involved in the production of many vowels and consonants.
- **alveolar ridge** (齿槽): The ridgelike border of the upper and lower jaws containing the sockets of the teeth, involved in producing **alveolars** (齿龈音 , 齿槽音) a consonant pronounced with the tip of the tongue on or near this ridge, e.g. *n, s, d, t*).
- **teeth** (牙齿): Involved in producing **labiodentals** (唇齿音).
- **lips** (嘴唇): Involved in producing **bilabials** (双唇音) and **labiodentals** (唇齿音).
- **mandible** (颌, 颚, 颚骨]): The jaw or a jawbone, especially the lower jawbone in mammals and fishes.

The dynamics of voice production may be outlined in the following (where the double arrow sign [⇒] indicates the direction of the movement of primary articulation drive, and the single arrow sign [→] indicates the direction of the movement of an air stream exhaled from the lung and finally shaping into a speech sound):

- **chest muscles** ⇒ the **rib cage** and the **diaphragm** ⇒ **lungs** → the **larynx (vocal box)** (therein modulated by the position and state of the **vocal cords**, which expand and contract to control the space between them—**glottis**) → the **pharynx** (therein modulated by the position and state of the root of the tongue) →

  - ↗the **nasal cavity** (therein modulated by the position and state of the **soft palate [velum]**)
  - ↘the **oral cavity** (therein modulated by the position and state of such **active articulators** as the **uvula**, **lower teeth**, **lower lip**, and most importantly, the **tongue**)

3.2.1.2   The Modulation of Speech Sounds

By "modulation of speech sounds" we mean the exertion of a modifying or controlling influence on the original stream of air exhaled from lungs so that a specific sound is articulated. In articulatory studies of sound a distinction is made between the **manner of articulation** (发音方法) and the **place of articulation** (发音位置) (also called **point of articulation**), both of which are involved in modulating the air stream passing through the upper respiratory tractor and the oral cavities to produce a sound.

For example, **vowels** (元音) are made by shaping the air stream that passes through our oral cavity rather than by obstructing it, while **consonants** (辅音) are made either by blocking the air completely (as when pronouncing **stop** (塞音) [=plosive] consonants, e.g. [**p/b**], [**t/d**], [**k/g**], etc.) or constricting it so that it comes through noisily (as when pronouncing **fricative** (擦音) consonants, e.g. [**f/v**], [**θ/ð**], [**s/z**], etc.).

By and large, three essential conditions of the vocal organs determine what a speech sound formed is like:

(a) the position of the lips and the tongue
(b) how far open the mouth is
(c) whether or not the **vocal cords** (声带) are vibrating (Fig. 3.2).

For instance, in English [**p**]/[**b**] are **bilabial stops** (双唇塞音), i.e. stops formed by closing or nearly closing both lips with the back of the tongue touching or near the soft palate; [**f**]/[**v**] are "**labiodental fricatives** (唇齿擦音), i.e. fricatives articulated with the lower lip and upper teeth; and [**ŋ**] is a **velar nasal** (软腭鼻音), i.e. a nasal (consonant articulated by lowering the soft palate so that air resonates in the nasal cavities and passes out the nose) made with the back of the tongue touching or near the soft palate.

With reference to what is examined above, the first approach to **phonetic contrastive analysis** (语音对比分析) would be characterized as physiological. It is concerned with the comparison of **L1** and **L2** sounds with a shared articulatory basis (as visually represented on the **International Phonetic Alphabet [IPA] Chart** [国际音标表]).

Fig. 3.2 Three most essential aspects of the vocal organs that determine what a speech sound is like

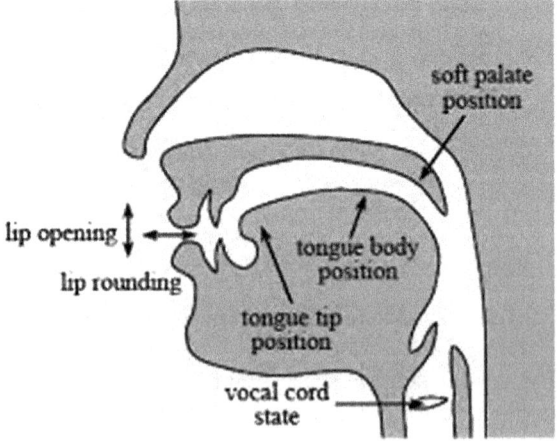

For example, the English **diphthong** (双元音) [eɪ] and the Chinese diphthong (ei) are similar in the **manner of articulation** (发音方法), but different in the **place of articulation** (发音位置). The vowel [e] in the English diphthong [eɪ] (as in *bake, cake,* and *take*) is a **spread front sound** (展唇前元音), i.e. a vowel sound formed by raising the tongue, excluding the blade and tip, towards the hard palate and with the opening between the lips extended laterally, while the (e) in the Chinese diphthong (ei) (as in *bei* "north" and *gei* "give") is a **spread mid sound** (展唇中元音), i.e. a vowel sound pronounced with the tongue in a position approximately intermediate between high and low, as the vowel in *but*, and with the opening between the lips extended laterally. To pronounce the English diphthong [eɪ] as one would do when articulating the Chinese diphthong (ei) is a mistake commonly found with Chinese beginners of English (Fig. 3.3).

3.2.2   Acoustic Phonetics

When a speech sound is produced it travels through the air and causes minor air disturbances or sound waves. **Acoustic phonetics** (声学语音学) is concerned with the trip speech sounds make to reach our ears. Specifically it deals with how speech sounds are transmitted through the air and are received by the ear before they are processed by our neurological system.

The physical properties of sound include the following.

Fig. 3.3 The position of the tongue and the degree of openness of the mouth when different vowels are articulated (as represented in IPA Chart, 2005)

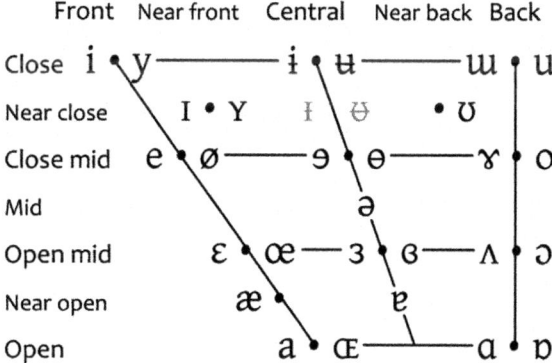

Vowels at right & left of bullets are rounded & unrounded.

3.2.2.1 Frequency

The **frequency** (音頻) at which a sound (in the case of speech sounds, the vocal cords) vibrates determines the **pitch** (音高) of a sound (i.e. our sense that a sound is "higher" or "lower").

The basic frequency at which a sound vibrates is known as the **fundamental frequency** (基频), generally abbreviated to F_0 and read as "F nought."

The range of frequencies that a young adult can hear is extremely wide—from about 20 to 20,000 Hz. It is not possible to hear vibrations lower ("**infrasonic** [次声的]") or higher ("**ultrasonic** [超声的]") than this. The most important speech frequencies lie between 100 and 4000 Hz. The fundamental frequency of the adult male voice, e.g. is around 120 Hz; the female voice, around 220 Hz.

3.2.2.2 Amplitude of Vibration

The **amplitude of vibration** (振幅), i.e. the extent to which an air particle moves to and fro around its rest point, contributes to the intensity of the sound. Together with other factors (such as frequency and duration), it determines the **loudness** (响度) of a sound.

3.2.2.3 Timbre

The **timbre** (or **sound quality**) (音色) of a voice or musical sound is its character or quality as distinct from its pitch and intensity. It is the overall impression that a listener obtains of a speaker's voice or of a musical source. Specifically, it refers to those characteristics of a particular voice that enable the listener to distinguish one voice from another, e.g. when a person is able to identify a telephone caller. In other words, **timbre** helps a listener to determine the identity of the source of a sound.

When a sound is produced by an object vibrating in a periodic way, not only a simple sine wave is generated, but other amounts of energy are also generated by the same vibration, all of which are correlated with the basic sine wave (or "sine curve") in a simple mathematical relationship: they are all multiples of the fundamental frequency. Thus an F_0 of 220 Hz will set up a "sympathetic" set of frequencies at 440, 880 Hz, and so on. These multiples are known as **overtones** (泛音) or **harmonics** (泛音; 和声). (In music, "**harmonic**" often denotes a note that sounds together with the main note being played and is higher and quieter than that note, e.g. a high quiet note played on the violin by touching the string very lightly [和声].) Depending on the nature of the vibrating object (e.g. the material it is made of, or its thickness), different sets of **harmonics** are established, and these are heard as differences in **timbre** (Fig. 3.4).

Fig. 3.4 The fundamental and the first six overtones of a vibrating string

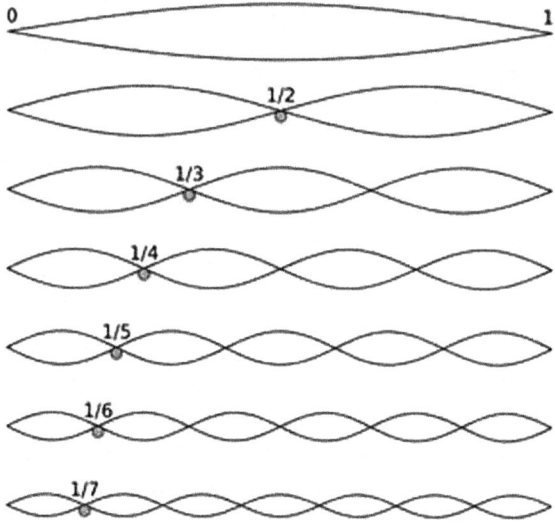

When speech sounds are produced, the moving articles of air from the lungs may form **periodic** (regular) **patterns** or **aperiodic** (irregular) **patterns**. In the former case, what is heard would be **musical sounds** (乐音) while in the latter case, **noises** (噪音). **Vowels** (元音) are musical sounds, **voiceless consonants** (清辅音) are noises, and **voiced consonants** (浊辅音) are musical sounds which are tinged with some noises (Crystal, 1987, pp. 133–134).

It is easy to see that the second approach to **phonetic contrastive analysis** (语音对比分析) would be physical rather than physiological, and would be associated with the acoustic properties of speech sounds (Fig. 3.5).

If we compare the initial consonants **[p]** in the French word *pâle* and the English word *pal*, e.g. we can establish that the English **plosive** (爆破音) (=stop) in this initial position is accompanied by a puff of breath or "**aspiration** (送气)," but the French plosive is not. While the difference can be traced to an articulatory source it is more easily demonstrated and described in physical, acoustic terms. There are even instruments, such as the **sound spectrograph** (声谱仪), which can record the occurrence of such aspiration. Similarly, there are acoustic differences, which can

Fig. 3.5 Musical sound and noise

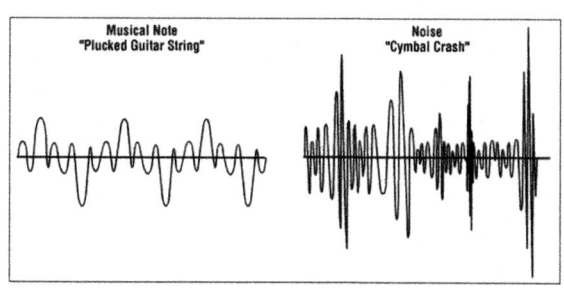

be demonstrated instrumentally, between the "similar" vowels in English *spleen* [sp*l*i:n] and German *Spiel* [ʃpɪ*l*] "game." An **acoustic** approach to **phonetic contrastive analysis** (语音对比分析) consists therefore in comparing **L1** and **L2** sounds that have much in common physically and noting the differences accompanying this similarity.

3.2.3 *Auditory Phonetics*

Auditory phonetics (听觉语音学) is the study of how speech sounds are perceived by the listener. To take a simple unilingual example: it can be shown that the /p/ in *pit* differs from the /p/ in *spit*: in the former /p/ is **aspirated** (送气的), but in the latter it is not. Nevertheless, the English ear does not send to the English brain any instruction to register this phonetic difference: auditorily, and mentally, [**p^h**] and [**p**] are perceived as the same **phoneme** (音位) /p/.

Notice that we are now speaking of two **allophones** (音位变体).

Incidentally, *allo-* is a **combining form** (构词成分) signifying "variation," e.g. an **allomorph** (语素变体) is one of a set of forms that a morpheme may take in different contexts: the *-s* of *cats*, the *-en* of *oxen*, and the *zero suffix* (零后缀) of *sheep* are **allomorphs** of the English **plural** morpheme.

By "**allophones**" (音位变体) we mean the group of different forms of a **phoneme** (音位) (the smallest unit of sound in a language which can distinguish two words, e.g. the phonemes /t/ and /d/ differentiate the word *ten* from the word *den*).

The morpheme **-eme**, by the way, refers to the smallest differentiating element in some system, e.g. in narratology, an element or part of a joke is called a "jokeme" (Berger, 1997, p. 164).

The **International Phonetic Alphabet (IPA)** (国际音标), a most commonly adopted type of visual representation of speech sounds using a **phonetic alphabet** (音标), actually includes two systems of transcribing or notating the speech sounds of languages across the world, i.e.

- broad transcription (宽式音标) (**phonemic transcription** [音位音标])
- narrow transcription (严式音标) (**phonetic transcription** [语音音标])

The **broad transcription** (宽式音标) (positioned between slashes) is also known as "**phonemic notation**" (音位音标). It disregards all allophonic differences and transcribes only the more noticeable phonetic features of an utterance. It is not really a phonetic transcription, but a representation of the phonemic structure (**phonology** [音系学]) of a language. The strength of the **broad transcription** is that it allows more widely applicable statements to be made about the pronunciation of a diverse language community and thus more suitable for providing pronunciation data in foreign language dictionaries. The weakness of a **broad transcription** is that it can not reflect the dialectal variations of a language's phonetic system.

The **narrow transcription** (严式音标) (positioned within brackets) is also known as "**phonetic** or **allophonic notation**" (语音音标) (语音变体音标). It encodes more information about the phonetic variations of specific **allophones** (音位变体) in the utterance and can be described as a transcription of the **phonetics** (语音系统) of a language. The merit of the **narrow transcription** (严式音标) is that it describes the phonetic system of a language accurately and helps students to learn exactly the right sound. The disadvantage of a **narrow transcription** is that it is rarely representative of all speakers of a language. In some British accents, for instance, the **/r/** in *very* is pronounced as a **tap** (轻拍音) (i.e. a speech sound which is produced by striking the tongue quickly and lightly against the part of the mouth behind the upper front teeth). A further disadvantage in less technical contexts is that **narrow transcription** involves a larger number of unfamiliar symbols.

In the aforementioned example, we used both **phonemic** and **phonetic notations** in IPA to transcribe the **/p/** sound in *pit* and *spit* respectively: we stated that in the former **/p/** is **aspirated** (送气的), but in the latter it is not; nevertheless, the English ear simply ignores this phonetic difference and perceives **[pʰ]** and **[p]** as the same **phoneme** (音位) **/p/**. (In the **narrow transcription**, diacritics [marks such as an accent, placed over, under or through a letter in some languages, to show that the letter should be pronounced in a different way from the same letter without a mark or marked differently, e.g. *pʰ*] are used to mark allophones.) The example implicates that we should use a **narrow transcription** (严式音标) when it is necessary to clarify the difference between two allophones (音位变体), but when there is no necessity to distinguish between two allophones, a **broad transcription** would be sufficient and preferred.

In this sub-section, we have been talking about **tokens** of the same **type**, which have equal functions in the phonetic system of a given language. We are no longer concerned with physical or physiological reality, but with *psychological* reality. Our domain is now what James (1980, p. 73) calls "**functional phonetics** (功能语音学)" or **phonology** (音系学). Although the principle here has been illustrated with intralingual examples, it applies equally well interlingually and is the foundation for phonological **CA**, which we are going to discuss in the following section.

3.3 Contrastive Phonology

3.3.1 Phonological Contrastive Analysis

Human beings can make a wide range of sounds but, interestingly, only a small number of them are actually used in **human** speech. **Phonology** (音系学) identifies the set of speech sounds for each language, investigates how these sounds are arranged to form meaningful units (i.e. words, phrases and sentences) and what function each sound performs in the sound system of that language. Specifically, the phonological system of a language includes:

(a) a set of sounds the language selects to use and their features
(b) rules which specify how sounds interact with each other.

Contrastive phonology (对比音系学) identifies comparable speech sounds for two or more languages and investigates what functions these sounds perform in the sound system of each language (i.e. the functional statuses of comparable speech sounds in different languages).

3.3.1.1 The Functional Statuses of Comparable Speech Sounds in Different Languages

Let us consider the case of **laterals** (边音) (i.e. consonant sounds produced by placing a part of the tongue against the palate so that air flows around it on both sides) in English and in Russian. Each of these two languages has two lateral sounds. The "clear" [l] (as in *look*) and the "dark" [ɫ] (as in *stool*) of English are both **alveolar laterals** (齿龈边音)—laterals formed with the tip of the tongue touching or near the inner ridge of the gums of the upper front teeth, as when *t*, *d*, and *s* are produced. But [l] is produced with simultaneous higher raising of the front of the tongue than of the back, while [ɫ] has the opposite configuration. [l] occurs before vowels and [ɫ] elsewhere (before consonants and finally).

Russian has two laterals also: [ɫ] and [lʲ], the former **velarized** (软腭音化), the latter **palatalized** (硬腭音化). [ɫ] is a lateral fricative, usually voiced, with mid-tongue depressed, resulting in a "dull," "hollow" sound of low tonality, something like [ɫ] in English *bull*. There is ample justification for equating the Russian and English laterals on both articulatory and acoustic grounds.

But what is the functional status of each? For the English speaker [l] and [ɫ] are **allophones** (音位变体) of the same **phoneme** (音位) in that each sends the same "message" to the brain, namely that in either case the /l/ phoneme is being used. This can be tested by intentionally switching the clear and dark variants within a word: to the English speaker, [ɫɪp] is still *lip* and [fɪl] is still *fill*, and when he hears an Irishman say [fɪl maɪ glæs] for Received Pronunciation (RP) [fɪɫ maɪ glæs] the message is clear. For the Russian [ɫ] and [lʲ] have different status by signaling differences in meaning: [daɫ] means "he gave" while [dalʲ] means "the distance." The important point to be made in this context is that objectively similar sounds of two languages can have different functional statuses; in **L1** the differences may be disregarded and the two speech sounds viewed as "the same," while in **L2** the same objective difference is upheld as constituting a functional difference. This possibility is the cornerstone of **contrastive phonetics** (对比语音学) and **contrastive phonology** (对比音系学). (Based on James, 1980, pp. 73–74).

3.3.1.2 Pronunciation Problems Caused by Phonemic Asymmetries and by Allophonic Differences

The pair of notions of **phoneme** (音位) and **allophone** (音位变体) proposed by **structural phonologists** (结构音系学家) is significant in that it helps to identify two categories of pronunciation problems which **L2 learners** (二语学习者) face: problems resulting from **phonemic asymmetries** (音位非对应) (non-correspondences) between the two languages, and those resulting from **allophonic differences** (音位变体差异). The assumption is that the first category will be the source of more fundamental distortions, often leading to unintelligibility while the second category merely leads to "foreign accent" without much impairment of communication. This assumption is normally upheld by observation of learners' speech (James, 1980, p. 81).

For example, the sound [b] in the English word *bin* is an unaspirated (不送气的) voiced consonant. A Pekingese may pronounce the word as "宾" [**pɪn**]; a native of Shanghai, on the other hand, is likely to pronounce it—in Shanghai dialect—as "贫" [**bʰn**]. Both of them would be making a pronunciation error when they do so, of course. But are their errors of the same type? If not, what kind of error did they make respectively? And which error is a more grave one?

The Pekingese uses a **voiceless** Chinese **phoneme** (音位) **(b)** (represented by **/p/** on the **IPA chart**) in place of the **voiced** English phoneme **/b/**, which contrasts with the **voiceless** phoneme **/p/**. The native of Shanghai uses a dialect sound which resembles the English phoneme **/b/** in being **voiced** but differs from it in being **aspirated**.

Obviously, both errors resulted from a **negative transfer** (负迁移) or **interference** (干扰作用) of the Chinese sound system. But they are different in nature and degree of gravity.

In English the **voiced/voiceless contrast** (清浊对比) is a **phonemic** one, which affects the intelligibility of the speech while the **aspirated/unaspirated contrast** (送气/不送气对比) is just an **allophonic** one, which makes the speech sound "foreign" but without impairing its intelligibility.

The Pekingese, using a **voiceless** Chinese **phoneme** (音位) **/p/** for a **voiced** English phoneme **/b/**, makes a **phonemic error** (音位错误), while the native of Shanghai, using a dialect sound which resembles the English phoneme **/b/** in being **voiced** but differs from it in being **aspirated**, only makes an **allophonic one** (音位变体错误).

A **phonemic error** is more grave than an **allophonic one**, because it results in unintelligibility. Therefore, the error made by the Pekingese is much more grave than the one made by the native of Shanghai.

3.3.1.3   The Functional Loads of Comparable Phonological Contrasts in Different Languages

Another important notion proposed by structural phonologists is that of functional load. **Functional load** (功能负载量) refers to the relative importance of linguistic contrasts in a language.

Not all the distinctions or contrasts within the structure of a language are of the same importance. For example the majority of the consonants in English form a **voiced/voiceless contrast** (清浊对比):

/p/-/b/
/t/-/d/
/k/-/g/
/f/-/v/
/s/-/z/
/ʃ/-/ʒ/
/ts/-/dz/
/tr/-/dr/

Since the contrast between voiced/voiceless consonants serve to distinguish many words in English (*pig-big, tare-dare, class-glass, ferry-very,* etc.), that contrast is said to have a high **functional load** in English.

Other contrasts in English, such as that between /θ/ and /ð/ (in words like *wreath* and *wreathe*), are not used to distinguish many words and are thus said to have a low **functional load**.

The distinction between the **aspiratedness** and **unaspiratedness** (送气/不送气对比) of consonants helps to distinguish a large number of words in Chinese:

(pa)-(ba) 琶-芭
(ti)-(di) 替-递
(kong)-(gong) 空-弓
(qi)-(ji) 旗-集
(chi)-(zhi) 池-织
(tongshi)-(dongshi) 同事-董事
(tuzi)-(duzi) 兔子-肚子
(ketou)-(gedou) 磕头-格斗

Therefore the **aspirated/unaspirated contrast** (送气 / 不送气对比) of consonants is said to have a high **functional load** in Chinese.

3.3.2 Two Phonological Models

For phonological analysis we have a two-way choice between **taxonomic phonology** (结构音系学) or **structural phonology** (结构音系学) and **generative phonology** (生成音系学). In the following we are going to consider these two models and their relative strengths and weaknesses.

3.3.2.1 The Taxonomic or Structural Phonology

The **taxonomic** or **structural phonology** (结构音系学), as we have seen, is characterized by an effort at classifying items into classes and then sub-classes. In taxonomic phonology, the distinctive speech sounds of a language are first classified as vowels and consonants; the consonants are then classified as stops, fricatives, nasals, etc.; the stops may be further classified as **voiced** and **voiceless** and so on.

So far as phonological **CA** is concerned, this approach has been found to work pretty well on the whole.

The failing of taxonomic phonology in **contrastive analysis** (对比分析) is its inability to differentiate **productive difficulty** (产出性困难) from **receptive difficulty** (接受性困难): it is assumed that what is difficult to perceive by the learner will in fact be difficult for him to produce. Such is not the case. There are a great number of examples of an asymmetry between the learner's receptive and productive control of phonological segments. The English speaker may hear the /k/:/x/ contrast between German *locker* (/lɔkə/, "loose") and *Loch* (/lɔx/, "hole") but is unable to produce the sound /x/.

3.3.2.2 Generative Phonology

Generative phonology (生成音系学) stems from America (Chomsky and Halle, 1968) but is rooted in European phonological theory of the 1940s. Like **generative syntax** (生成句法), **generative phonology** (生成音系学) assumes that surface-structure phonology is derived from the deep-structure phonology by means of transformations. The phonological rules mediate between the **systematic phonemic level** (系统音位学层面) (at which all distinctive feature information is specified) and the **systematic phonetic level** (系统语音学层面) (at which all phonetic information is specified).

This is the major weakness of the model for purposes of **contrastive analysis** (对比分析): the phonological **deep structure** (深层结构) is assumed to contain forms which are deleted from the surface representation. *King*, for example, is given the deep structure [*kiŋg*] from which the [g] is deleted. This notion of phonological deep structure not only lacks psychological reality, but seems to contradict it, with its postulation of these quasi-mystical underlying forms. Given the choice between taxonomic and generative phonology, while accepting that the latter is probably more powerful for "pure" linguistic purposes, we should opt for the former and weaker, for the reason that it is more practical and concrete.

There is however one element of generative phonology, the element it inherited from **Prague School** (布拉格学派) (a linguistic tradition which began with the founding of the "Prague Linguistic Circle" in 1926 and which developed many ideas that have influenced modern linguistic thought) phonology, which has proved useful in phonological **CA**: the concept of **distinctive features** (区别性特征). Distinctive feature phonology as proposed by **Roman Jacobson** (1896–1982) was a development of **Nikolai Trubetzkoy** (1890–1938)'s distinctive opposition approach. It operates on the assumption that the **phoneme** (音位) is not the most convenient unit for phonological analysis, since it can be analyzed into a set of phonological "components" or features, which are more fundamental than the phoneme itself (James, 1980, pp. 81–82). The features are generally shown in the form of a **binary opposition** (二项对立), that is, the feature is either present [+] or absent [−]. Thus the English phoneme /t/ is a composite of the features [+**voiceless** (清 [音])], [+**apical** (舌尖音)], [+**stop** (塞音)], which distinguish it from /d/, from the **labials** (唇音) /p/, /b/, from the **palatals** (腭音) /tʃ/, /dʒ/, /ʃ/, from the **velars** (软腭音) /k/, /g/, and so on.

The approach adopted by generative phonology has two obvious advantages.

(1) The first is the gain in economy: whereas a language may use from 30 to 40 **phonemes** (音位), it is possible to exhaustively characterize such a language using no more than a dozen **distinctive features**. Chomsky and Morris Halle (1968) mainly adopts the following distinctive features:

syllabic (音节性)	consonantal (辅音性)
vocalic (元音性)	high (高位音)
low (低位音)	back (后位音)
anterior (前部音)	coronal (舌尖音)
obstruent (阻塞音)	continuant (延续音)
nasal (鼻音)	lateral (边音)
strident (糙音)	sonorant (响音)
voiced (浊音)	delayed release (迟除阻音)
aspirated (送气音)	segment (音段音)

(Xu 1992, p. 101)

Further economy is gained by the binarity of **distinctive feature** specifications: the presence (+) and absence (−) of one and the same feature can be used as a classificatory index, sparing the analyst the need for multiplication of categories.

(2) The second advantage, which is of particular interest to the **contrastivist** (对比
分析研究者), is the *universality* of **distinctive features**: **phonemes** (音位), in
contradistinction to distinctive features, are certainly not universal, as we have
seen, but distinctive features are. The universal set of features can thus serve as
a ***tertium comparationis*** (比较参照物) for phonological **CA** (James, 1980,
pp. 82–83). In using the universal set of features as a TC, we would be in a
better position to make fair comparisons between the sound systems of different
languages.

3.4 Suprasegmental Contrastive Analysis

In spoken utterance, two broad classes of sound units or speech features are usually
identified and distinguished:

(1) **segments** (音段 ; 音段特征): serially ordered individual sounds which are
identifiable and separable from each other, such as vowels, semi-vowels, and
consonants.
(2) **suprasegmentals** (超音段 ; 超音段特征) (also called **prosodies** [韵律结构] or
prosodic features [韵律结构特征]): aspects or features of phonetic structure
above the level of individual sounds, such as **tempo** (节律) , **stress** (重音),
pitch (音调), and **juncture** (音渡).

Suprasegmental features accompany or are added over individual consonants
and vowels. They are not limited to single sounds but often extend over syllables,
words, or phrases. **Tempo** (节律) (also known as **speech rate** (言语速率)
expressed in words per minute or syllables per second), e.g. is conditioned by pause
rate (slower speech involves more pausing), or by variations in articulation rate (the
speed with which the syllables themselves are produced, regardless of pauses in
between the words), or by both, and affects a series of utterances or a stretch of
discourse. In Spanish, the **stress accent** (重音) is often used to distinguish between
otherwise identical words: *término* means "term," *termíno* means "I terminate,"
and *terminó* means "he terminated." In Mandarin Chinese, **tone** (声调) is a distinctive suprasegmental (超音段; 超音段特征) (see Sect. 3.4.1 for detail). English
"*beer dripped*" and "*beard ripped*" are distinguished by word **junctures** (词间音
渡). (Based on Suprasegmental, 2010)

The distinction made between segments and **suprasegmentals** (超音段; 超音段
特征) is especially favored by American structural linguists.

In the following we are going to make a **contrastive analysis** (对比分析) of
Chinese and English with regard to two suprasegmental properties—**pitch** (音调)
and **juncture** (音渡).

3.4.1 The Contrastive Analysis of Pitch

Pitch (音调) refers to the relative height of speech sounds as perceived by a listener. In **suprasegmental phonology** (超音段音系学), there are two significant elements of pitch: **tone** (声调) and **intonation** (语调).

3.4.1.1 Tone

Tone (声调) refers to the height of **pitch** (音调) and a unit of change of pitch which is associated with the pronunciation of syllables or words and which affects the meaning of the word. In **tone languages** (声调语言), such as Chinese, Vietnamese, and Thai, a difference in **pitch** (音调) is a distinctive feature used to distinguish lexical items; in other words, the meaning of a word depends on the tone used when pronouncing it.

Tonal contrasts in Chinese, e.g. make **phonemic distinctions**. When an American student stepped into a Chinese restaurant and said:

我要吃轿 (饺) 子。

and when a British lad talked about:

我的老伴 (老板) 儿 ……

They all made pronunciation errors resulting from **phonemic asymmetries** (音位非对应) between English and Chinese. So their errors would cause unintelligibility on the part of the Chinese listeners, at least at the beginning of the communication.

3.4.1.2 Intonation

Intonation (语调) (or **pitch movement** [音调变动]) refers specifically to the change of **pitch** (音调) to convey grammatical or attitudinal information rather than vocabulary differences. In this sense, it is opposed to tone (声调). In English, for example, four or five different intonations have been identified by linguists as suprasegmental devices to modulate or affect the meaning and function of utterances in discourse:

- Intonation 1   fall in pitch
- Intonation 2   rise in pitch
- Intonation 3   a slight rise in pitch
- Intonation 4   fall in pitch followed by a rise
- Intonation 5   rise in pitch followed by a fall.

In a **tone language** (声调语言) such as Chinese, changes in pitch are used mainly to distinguish different words with the same pronunciation, e.g. *jiā* (家, "home"), *jiá* (夹, "to clip"), *jiǎ* (假, "false"), *ji* (嫁, "to marry").

In an **intonation language** (语调语言) such as English, changes in pitch are used mainly to:

(1) perform **grammatical functions** (语法功能) (for instance, to show whether an utterance is a statement or a question, For example,

Ready?↗,

or what part of a sentence is being questioned, e.g. as a response to the statement

The Smiths has hired a new maid.

one may ask:

Who↗

if one wants to know who has hired a new maid, or

Who↘

if one wonders who has newly been hired by the Smiths;

(2) give additional information to that given by the words of an utterance, For example,

I GOT↘ the prize. [it was doubtful whether I would]

or

(3) indicate the speaker's attitude to the matter discussed or to the listener, For example,

But I TOLD↘ you.

In terms of intonation, English is a **stress-timed language**, which means the length of time between any two neighboring stressed syllables is roughly the same, no matter how many unstressed syllables occur in between. For the convenience of discussion, it is necessary to introduce a new term—**foot** (音步), which typically starts with a stressed syllable and ends before the next stressed syllable. For example, in the following utterance,

|THANK you for|GIVing me such a| WONderful | **TIME** |

there are four feet. It is to be noted that while the second foot is made up of as many as five syllables, the last foot contains only one syllable. Nonetheless, the time the speaker spends on each of the four feet should be roughly the same.

In comparison with English, in which **intonation** (语调) performs so varied functions, Chinese has much fewer fluctuations in its intonation. Contrary to English, Chinese is a **syllable-stressed language** where the timing of all syllables tends to be the same, regardless of their stress. The fact that in Chinese changes of **pitch** (音调) are largely associated with the pronunciation of just syllables or words makes it relatively easier for Chinese speech sounds to be electronically synthesized on the computer (Microsoft, e.g. set about developing Chinese voice synthesizing softwares before it took up the development of English ones).

3.4.2 The Contrastive Analysis of Juncture

In **phonology** (音系学), **juncture** (音渡) refers to:

(1) a pause or other phonological feature or modification of a phonological feature, such as the lengthening of a preceding phoneme or the strengthening of a following one, marking a transition or break between sounds, especially marking the phonological boundary of a word, clause, or sentence
(2) the point in a word or group of words at which such a pause or other junctural marker occurs.

In English **junctures** (音渡) can be observed in such words as ***night-rate*** and ***re-seed*** and are absent in such words as *nitrate* and *recede*. (Based on Juncture, 1987)

Going above the word level, we have a special kind of syntactic structure (known as "**alternative structure** [二选结构]"), which includes alternative **junctures** (音渡) and allows for more than one **deep structure** (深层结构) being assigned to one single **surface structure** (表层结构), hence resulting in structural (grammatical) ambiguity (the state of having more than one possible meaning).

By "**alternative structure** (二选结构)" we mean constructions of modification which present two or more possible interpretations but presuppose that only one is true, e.g.

pregnant women and babies ["(pregnant women) and babies" or "pregnant (women and babies)?]

It is usually difficult for **machine translation (MT)** (机器翻译) systems to treat alternative structures automatically, especially those encountered in Chinese texts, where characters and words are not typographically set off from each other by a space, thereby causing additional difficulties for the translation engine to parse sentences into contextually meaningful structures, e.g. the Chinese sentence *Bai tian e zai hu li you yong* (白天鹅在湖里游泳。) "[literally] white sky/day goose in lake swim" may be segmented in the following ways, resulting in two totally different interpretations of the sentence:

白天|鹅|在|湖里|游泳。 **"By day geeze** swim in the lake."

白|天鹅|在|湖里|游泳。 **"White swans** are swimming in the lake."

The following is a real-life case of structural ambiguity caused by alternative structure:

下午鸭鸭同小姨玩汽车。小姨把他的玩具公共汽车称作"拖拉机"。鸭鸭以为小姨说的是"拖垃圾",便很严肃地纠正她说:"小姨,它是布吉 [《汤玛士小火车》里的公共汽车],它不拖垃圾!" (Author's diary, July 10, 2010)

To translate such potentially ambiguous sentences from Chinese into other languages, **machine translation (MT)** (机器翻译) systems must be programmed first to segment words and phrases in a context-sensitive way. In other words, ambiguous lexical chunks and sentence constructions must be segmented at right junctures and hence disambiguated, with unacceptable and unsuitable word combinations excluded from being processed in the next step of source text analysis. (Based on Ke, 2009)

3.5 Questions for Discussion and Research

1. **Articulators** (vocal organs or speech organs) are organs involved in the production of speech sounds. What are **active articulators** and what are **passive articulators**? Name four of each of them.
2. How can we determine whether a single speech sound is a **phoneme** or not?
3. The sound **[b]** in the English word *bin, e.g.* is an unaspirated voiced vowel. Influenced by local dialects, people in different areas of China may pronounce the word somewhat differently. A Pekingese may pronounce the word as "宾" **(bin)/[pɪn]** while a native of Shanghai is likely to pronounce it as "贫" **(pin)/ [bʰɪn]**. Both of them would make pronunciation errors when they do so, of course. But are their errors of the same type? If not, what kind of error do they make respectively? Which kind is a more grave one? And why?
4. Use examples to illustrate how **suprasegmental features** can affect the meaning or function of an utterance.
5. Can **contrastive phonetics** be made independently of **contrastive phonology**; if so, on what basis?
6. What are the three branches of **phonetics**?
7. Give examples of **phonemic contrast** and **allophonic contrast**.
8. Comment on the strengths and weaknesses of the **taxonomic** and **generative** approaches to phonological CA.
9. Changes in **pitch** are realized as **tone** or **intonation** in different languages. What functions do tone and intonation perform in English and Chinese respectively?

References

Berger, A. A. (1997). *Narratives in popular culture, media and everyday life*. Thousand Oaks, CA: SAGE Publications Inc.

Chomsky, N., & Halle, M. (1968). *The sound pattern of English*. New York, NY: Harper & Row.

Crystal, D. (Ed.). (1987). *The Cambridge encyclopedia of language*. Cambridge, United Kingdom: Cambridge University Press.

James, C. (1980). *Contrastive analysis*. Harlow, United Kingdom: Longman Group UK Limited.

Juncture. (1987). In S. Flexner (Ed.), *Random House Webster's unabridged dictionary* (2nd Ed.). New York, NY: Random House Inc.

Ke, P. (2009). Machine translation. In M. Baker & G. Saldanha (Eds.), *The Routledge encyclopedia of translation studies* (2nd ed., pp. 162–169). London, United Kingdom & New York, NY: Routledge.

Suprasegmental. (2010). Encyclopædia Britannica. In *Encyclopaedia Britannica ultimate reference suite* [DVD-ROM]. Chicago, IL: Author.

Xu, Y. [许余龙]. (1992). 《对比语言学概论》, 上海: 上海外语教育出版社.

Chapter 4
Lexical Contrastive Analysis

Lexicology is the study of the **lexical items** or **vocabulary items** (词项) of a language.

A **lexical item** is also called a "**lexeme** (词位)". It is the smallest meaningful unit that is an item in the **vocabulary** (词汇) of a language. It may be simply a word (**word-lexeme** [单词词位]), but it can also be a phrase (**phrasal lexeme** [短语词位]).

A **lexeme** (词位) is an abstract unit. It can occur in many different forms in actual spoken or written sentences, and is regarded as the same **lexeme** (词位) even when it is **inflected** (that is, being added with an **affix** [词缀] or changed in some other way according to the rules of the **grammar** [语法] of a language). For instance, in English, all inflected forms of a word such as *speak, speaks, spoke, spoken, speaking* belong to one and the same **lexeme** (词位) *speak*. Similarly, such expressions as *speak highly of, speak ones' mind, so to speak, tall talk, talk big, all talk and no cider* would each be considered a single **lexeme** (词位) (phrasal lexeme). In a dictionary, each **lexeme** (词位) merits a separate entry or sub-entry.

All the lexemes in a language considered as a collection is known as the language's **lexicon** (词库) or vocabulary.

Broadly speaking, **lexicology** consists of two divisions:

(1) **Lexical morphology** (词汇形态学), which studies the form and changes in the form of the **lexemes** (词位) of a language primarily from the point of view of **word formation** (构词) (derivation and compounding).
(2) **Lexical semantics** (词汇语义学), which studies (**a**) the meanings and changes in the meanings of **lexemes** (词位) through time and (**b**) the relations between the **lexemes** (词位) of a language.

Lexical **CA** may be conducted with reference to these two divisions.

© Peking University Press and Springer Nature Singapore Pte Ltd. 2019
P. Ke, *Contrastive Linguistics*, Peking University Linguistics Research 1,
https://doi.org/10.1007/978-981-13-1385-1_4

4.1   Contrastive Lexical Morphology

Morphology (形态学, 词法) is the study of the **structural forms** of a word, both from the point of view of inflections and of word-formation. It is traditionally located between **phonology** (音系学) (linguistic study at the level of sounds) and **syntax** (句法学) (linguistic study at the level of sentences).

So far as a word is concerned, three kinds of linguistic forms may be distinguished, i.e. the **phonetic form**, the **graphemic form**, and the **structural form**. The phonetic form of a lexical item is the object of study of **phonetics** (语音学). The graphemic form of a lexical item is the object of study of **graphemics** (文字学) (the study of a language's writing system). The third kind of form, the **structural form**, is the object of study of **lexical morphology** (词汇形态学).

4.1.1   *Lexical/Derivational Morphology and Inflectional Morphology*

Lexical morphology (词汇形态学) is also known as "**derivational morphology** (派生形态学)". It is actually one of the two parts of **morphology** (形态学, 词法), the other part being **inflectional morphology** (屈折形态学).

Inflectional morphology (屈折形态学) studies the way in which words vary (or "**inflect** [(使) 发生屈折变化]") in order to express grammatical contrasts in sentences, such as singular/plural, perfect/imperfect, or past/present. Traditionally, this study was referred to as "**accidence**". *Tree* and *trees*, for example, are two forms of the "same" word; the choice between them, **singular** versus **plural**, is a matter of **grammar** (语法), i.e. something regarding the expression of **grammatical meanings** (语法意义), and is therefore part of grammar. Since **inflectional morphology** (屈折形态学) falls within the scope of grammar, it will not be our concern in the present chapter.

What we shall discuss in this section is **lexical morphology** (词汇形态学), which studies the principles governing the construction of new words, without reference to the specific grammatical role a word might play in a sentence. For example, in the formation of *lovely* from *love*, or *unlock* from *lock*, we see the formation of different words, with their own grammatical properties.

4.1.2   *Morpheme*

A **Morpheme** (语素) is the smallest meaningful unit in the meaning system of a language, that is, it is the smallest meaningful element into which words can be analyzed. If we take something away from or change something in a morpheme, we shall definitely alter or destroy its meaning. For example, if we remove the letter *f* from the English word *form*, which is a morpheme, what is left—*orm*—will not make any sense. If we remove the letter *m* from the word *form*, we shall get *for*, which is nevertheless a different morpheme and has another meaning. If we replace the letter *k* in *peak* (the pointed summit of a mountain) with some other letter(s), say, *t* or *ce*, we shall likewise get different morphemes which refer to other things (*peat*: a brown soil-like material characteristic of boggy, acid ground, consisting of partly decomposed vegetable matter and widely cut and dried for use in gardening and as fuel [泥炭,泥煤]; *peace*: freedom from disturbance).

Morphemes can be classified into "free" and "bound" forms, i.e. "free" morphemes and "bound" morphemes.

4.1.2.1 Free Morpheme

A **free morphemes** (自由语素) (or **free form** [自由语素]) can occur as a separate word, e.g. *class, very, good, yes.*

4.1.2.2 Bound Morpheme

A **bound morpheme** (粘附语素) (or **bound form** [粘附语素]), e.g. *un-, dis-, -ly, -tion*, cannot occur on its own. It must be used along with other morphemes and it functions in a word either as an **affix** (词缀) or as a **combining form** (构词成分).

Affix

An **affix** (词缀) is a **bound morpheme** (粘附语素) which is added to a word and changes its meaning or function. The function of an affix can be inflectional (**inflectional affix** [屈折词缀]), e.g. *lexes* (the plural form of *lexis*), or derivative (**derivative affix** [派生词缀]), e.g. *lexical* (the adjectival form of *lexis*), *dislike* (the derivative antonym of *like*).

An **infix** (词缀) is an affix which is inserted *within* a **stem** (词干) (see in the following paragraph for the definition of *stem*). In many languages, **infixation** (附加中缀法) is a normal morphological process. For example, in Tagalog (他加禄语), an Indonesian language spoken in the Philippine Islands, the form *um* is infixed within the form *sulat* "to write" to produce *sumulat*, which means "wrote."

In Chinese, some words and phrases with the verb-object or verb-complement structures may be infixed, e.g. 洗澡 "bathe" may be infixed by the form 一 次 "one time" to become 洗一次澡 "take a bath." And the form 不 "not" may be inserted within the word 推动 "to push forward" to produce 推不动 "be unable to push (something) forward" or "(something) be unable to be pushed forward." In colloquial Chinese, some words or phrases may even be inserted with some nonce elements to express a strong affective meaning, e.g. *daomei* (倒霉) "ill-fated": *dao-babeizi-mei* (倒八辈子霉) "ill-bloody-fated." The nearest examples of infixation in

English are such emphatic or cursing forms as *abso-**blooming**-lutely awful, handi-**bloody**-cap, im-**fucking**-possible, propa-**fucking**-ganda.*

Combining Form

A **combining form** (构词成分) is a **bound morpheme** (粘附语素) that can form a new word by combining with another combining form, a word, or sometimes an affix. The combining form *geo-*, for example, can form the word *geology* with the combining form -(*o*)*logy*.

The main classes of **affixes** (词缀) are the **prefixes** (前缀) (e.g. *un*kind) and **suffixes** (后缀) (e.g. love*ly*), but **infixes** (中缀) are also possible.

4.1.2.3 Stem (Base Morpheme) and Root

Two concepts related to affix are "**stem**" (词干) and "**root** (词根)."

The **stem** (词干) (or "**base form** [派生词基础式] /**base morpheme** [派生词基础语素]") is that part of a word to which an **inflectional affix** (屈折词缀) is or can be added. For example, *push* in the word **pushed** or *desk* in the word **desks**.

The stem of a word may be:

(1) a simple stem consisting of only one morpheme, e.g. *build*. In this case, the **stem** (词干) is known as the "**root**" (词根);
(2) a root plus a **derivational affix** (派生词缀), e.g. *build + -er = builder*;
(3) two or more roots, e.g. *build + up = build-up*.

The way to form new words by adding **derivative affixes** (派生词缀) to a base form is called **derivation** (派生). We have seen many examples of this in the above. The way to form new words by adding two base forms together is known as **compounding** (复合), e.g. *black + bird = blackbird*. English **compounds** (复合词) are usually distinguished from phrases by reduced stress on one of the base forms and by changes in meaning (compare '*black*' *bird*, and '*black*' *bird*).

The relationships between different morphemes as discussed above may be summarized in the following diagram (Fig. 4.1):

4.1.3 A Comparison of the Makeup of English and Chinese Word Stock

A comparison of the constitution of English and Chinese word stocks may lend some insights into the structural property of the lexical systems of these two languages.

	free morpheme / form (can occur as separate words), e.g. *pen, to, good, yes*					root (one-morpheme stem), e.g. *build*
Morpheme		affix	(in terms of functions)	inflectional affix, e.g. *-s, -ed* (added to a stem — inflection, e.g. *builds*)	+	stem / base form / base morpheme (stem + stem = compounding, e.g. *webpage*)	1 root + 1 derivative affix, e.g. *builder*
				derivative affix, e.g. *-less, dis-* (added to a stem — derivation, e.g. *webless*)		2 or more roots, e.g. *worksite*
	bound morpheme / form (must be used with another morpheme, as an affix or combining form)		(in terms of positions)	prefix: *un-, dis-*			
				infix: *sulat* "write", *sumulat* "wrote"; *-bloody-, -不-, -八辈子-*			
				suffix: *-ly, -tion*			
		combining form (can form a new word by combining with another combining form, a word or sometimes an affix), e.g. *geo-, bio-*					

Fig. 4.1 Different morphemes

We know that the more a language depends on the changes of a word's form to show a change in its meaning or **grammatical function** (语法功能), the more **synthetic** (具综合语特征) or **inflectional** (具屈折语特征) it is; conversely, the less a language depends on the changes of a word's form to show a change in its meaning or grammatical function, the more **analytic** (具分析语特征) or **isolating** (具孤立语特征) it is.

A word's form may be changed in two ways: by **inflection** (屈折变化) or by **derivation** (派生). In Chinese there are almost no **inflectional affixes** (屈折词缀) and there are very few **derivative affixes** (派生词缀) (among them are perhaps such forms as -化 "-ize" (现代化, 本地化, etc.), -迷 (-粉丝) "fan" (足球迷, 张曼玉 的狂热粉丝, etc.), -友 "enthusiast" (摄 [影发烧] 友, 驴友, etc.), -屋 "-house" (饼 屋, 咖啡屋, etc.), -族 "-nik" (披头族, 月光族, 尼特族, 点赞族, etc.). Therefore, Chinese words register very few changes in their form, which imparts a strikingly analytic feature to the lexical system of the Chinese language.

The **vocabulary** (词汇) of **Modern Chinese** (现代汉语) consists of two kinds of words, i.e. *danchun ci* or **mono-morphemic words** (单纯词) (like 天, 地) and *hecheng* **ci** or **multi-morphemic words** (合成词) (like 葡萄, 浪漫).

According to some statistics (Xu, 1992, pp. 128–129), about 20% of the items in the **lexicon** (词库) (the collection of lexemes in a language) of Modern Chinese are **mono-morphemic words** (单纯词), which include **mono-syllabic** ones (单音节 词) (apart from some rare exceptions such as 甭 "need not," 孬 "not good," and 仨 "three persons/objects," mono-syllabic words in Chinese are largely mono-morphemic), **bi-syllabic** ones (e.g. 葡萄 "grape," 坎坷 "uneven; full of frustrations," etc.), **tri-syllabic** ones (e.g. 维尼纶 "polyvinyl alcohol fiber" and 喀 斯特 "Karst"), **quadri-syllabic** ones (e.g. 卡 拉OK "Karaoke") and those with more than four syllables (e.g. 英特纳雄耐尔 *"Internationale"*).

Although relatively small in number, **mono-morphemic words** (单纯词) in Chinese are used much more frequently than **multi-morphemic words** (合成词), which refer to such words as 课本 "coursebook," 课堂 "classroom," etc. and which account for 80% of the total **vocabulary** (词汇) of Modern Chinese. The frequency of occurrence of **mono-morphemic words** (单纯词) accounts for approximately 70% of total lexical usages. Of the **multi-morphemic words** (合成词), the majority must be **compounds** (复合词) instead of **derivatives** (派生词) since, as indicated above, there are almost no **inflectional affixes** (屈折词缀) and very few **derivative affixes** (派生词缀) in Chinese.

In Modern English, however, the number of **derivatives** (派生词) and that of **compounds** (复合词) are in the ratio of about **1:1** (at least so far as the new words that emerged after the Second World War are concerned). As was made clear in the previous section, a **derivative** (派生词) is formed of one **stem** (词干) and one or more **affixes** (词缀). And an **affix** (词缀), for that matter, is a **bound morpheme** (粘附语素) which is added to a word (hence changing its form!) to modify its meaning or function.

Since **derivatives** (派生词) mean changes in word forms, the above ratio of derivatives to compounds in Modern English (**1:1**) and the facts that **70%** of the lexical items used in Modern Chinese are **mono-morphemic words** and that there are *almost no* **inflectional affixes** and *very few* derivative affixes (therefore very few **derivatives**) in Chinese **multi-morphemic words** indicate that the lexical structure of English is much more **synthetic** (具综合语特征) (i.e. depending on changes in word forms to show a change in the meaning or grammatical function of a word) than that of Chinese.

4.2 Contrastive Lexical Semantics

Modern linguists study meaning primarily by making a detailed analysis of the way words and sentences are used in specific contexts and thereby distinguish two types of semantic meaning: **lexical meaning** (词汇意义) and **sentence meaning** (句子意义).

Lexical meaning (词汇意义) is the meaning of words and is dealt with by **lexical semantics** (词汇语义学).

Sentence meaning (句子意义) is the meaning of sentences. The meaning of a sentence can evolve or be conditioned on different levels of linguistic structure. As may be perceived from our discussion of meaning from the sociosemiotic perspective in Sect. 2.3 ("Criteria for Comparison"), sentence meaning, while evidently being related to the **Topic of communication** (传通主题) (hence overlapping **referential meaning** [指称意义] and to the **Participants** in an event of communication (hence overlapping **pragmatic meaning** [语用意义]), may also be realized on such levels of linguistic description as **phonetics** (语音学) and **phonology** (音系学) (e.g. **prosodic meaning** [韵律意义], which is realized through **suprasegmentals** (超音段;超音段特征) or **prosodies** [韵律结构], that is, variations in **speech rhythm** [言语节律], **stress** [重音], **pitch** [音调], **intonation** (语调), and **juncture** [音渡]).

This suggests that sentence meaning is a dynamic notion, which is involved not only in the syntactic part of the description of a language (as we shall find in Chap. 5), but also on other levels of linguistic description, e.g. phonetics and phonology (as we have seen in Chap. 3), and in such areas of study as **pragmatics** (语用学) and the so-called "**truth-conditional semantics**" (真值条件语义学), which investigates **sentence meaning** (句子意义) using ideas derived from philosophy and logic (Crystal, 1987, p. 107) and defines the meaning of a given proposition as being the same as, or reducible to, its truth conditions (the condition under which a proposition is true) (so, for example, "Nanjing was the capital of ten ruling dynasties in ancient China" is true if and only if Nanjing was the capital of ten ruling dynasties in ancient China).

Diagrammed, sentence meaning has the following dimensions:

```
                    ┌ Pragmatic dimension—studied by pragmatics
 Sentence meaning—┤ Syntactic dimension—studied by syntax
                    │ Referential dimension—studied by truth-conditional semantics
                    └ Phonological dimension—studied by phonetics and phonology
```

In this section we shall focus on a contrastive study of **lexical meaning** (词汇意义).

Lexico-semantic contrasts are oftern conducted in three focal areas, that is, **motivation of words** (词汇理据), **sense relationships** (系统意义关系) (related to **collocation** [搭配], **lexical fields** [词汇场], and **lexical gaps** [词汇空缺]), and **semantic features** (语义特征). In the following we are going to consider **CA** in these three areas one by one.

4.2.1   The Motivation (Internal Form) of Words

In everyday usage, **motivation** means "(being provided with) a strong reason for doing something," e.g. *The stronger the motivation, the more quickly a person will learn a subject.* But the word is used in a special technical sense in the discussion we are now undertaking (i.e. **lexical semantics** [词汇语义学]).

By **motivation** (理据), we mean certain relationships that may be perceived to exist between the form of a word and its meaning or between its **primary meaning** (原初意义) and its **associative meaning(s)** (联想意义).

The motivation of a lexical item is also known as its **internal form** (词语内部形式). Stephen Ullmann (1914–1976), the Hungarian-born British linguist and one of the founders of modern **semantics** (语义学), classifies words into **opaque** ones and **transparent** ones, claiming that every language contains conventional, opaque words whose form and meaning are not related to each other in any way. On the other hand, however, each language will also contain words that are at least in some measure motivated and hence transparent (Ullmann, 1962).

Generally speaking, individual words may feature four kinds of motivation:

4.2.1.1 Phonetic Motivation

Phonetic motivation (语音理据) is the relationship between the phonetic form of a word and its **referential meaning** (指称意义) (the relationship between linguistic signs and the entities in the world which they refer to or describe).

What we call **onomatopoeic words** (拟声词), i.e. words that sound like the noise or natural sounds they describe, are phonetically motivated words, e.g.

> *buzz* (a low, continuous humming or murmuring sound, made by or similar to that made by an insect)
> *rustle* (a soft, muffled crackling sound like leaves or pieces of paper moving or rubbing against each other)
> *tinkle* (a light, clear, ringing metallic sound)
> *rat-a-tat-tat* (a series of short, sharp sounds, as that made by knocking on a door)

In many languages, a particular kind of bird that lays its eggs in other birds' nest is onomatopoeically named after its characteristic two-note call. In Chinese its name is *bugu*; in English, *cuckoo*; in French *coucou*; in Spanish, *cuclillo*; in German, *Kuckuk*; in Russian, *kukushka*; and in Hungarian, *kakuk*.

4.2.1.2 Graphemic Motivation

Graphemic motivation (书写理据) is the relationship between the written form of a word and its **referential meaning** (指称意义). Typical examples of graphemically motivated words may be found in ideographic languages such as Chinese. Most Chinese characters that contain the radical 雨 "rain," for example, carry the meaning related to meteorological phenomena involving precipitation, vapor, etc. So we have such characters as 雪 "snow," 雾 "fog/mist," 霁 "(of rain or snow) to stop," 露 "dew," 霞 "morning/evening glow," etc.

4.2.1.3 Morphological Motivation

Morphological motivation (语素理据) refers to the relationship between the morphological make-up of a word and its **referential meaning** (指称意义). In Sect. 4.1.2, we noted that a **combining form** (构词成分) adds new referential meaning to another combining form or a word and that a **derivative affix** (派生词缀) adds new referential meaning to a **stem** (词干) (**base form** [派生词基础式]).

On that account both **derivatives** (派生词) and **compounds** (复合词) are morphologically motivated words, e.g. *musician, driver, classmate, takeaway.*

Folk etymology (俗词源), that is, a popular way of modifying the form of a word or phrase to make it seem to be derived from a more familiar word, may be regarded as an attempt at "(forcefully) finding" **morphological motivation** (语素理据) for unfamiliar words. For example, *asparagus* is an unfamiliar term in English, with its semantic structure opaque, so some people pronounce it as something like "sparrow grass." The new interpretation does not necessarily make any sense, but somehow it seems more plausible than what it replaces. This is especially clear in the folk etymologies invented by children. One child was convinced that *bakin' powder* was "bacon powder," another that *ice cream cone* was "ice cream comb" (Bolinger, 1981, p. 248). In humorous writings, folk etymology is sometimes intentionally utilized, For example,

> **Midwife**: The second wife of a man who marries three times.

4.2.1.4 Semantic Motivation

Semantic motivation (语义理据) is the relationship between the **primary meaning** (原初意义) of a word and its **associative meanings** (联想意义) (**extended meaning** [引申意义], **figurative meaning** (比喻意义, 喻义), etc.). For instance, we may understand what one means when s/he calls another person "a wolf in sheep's clothing" if we know that famous fable by ancient Greek storyteller Aesop.

4.2.1.5 A Contrastive Analysis of the Morphological Motivation of English, German, and Chinese Words

In the following we shall make a **contrastive analysis** (对比分析) of the **morphological motivation** (语素理据) of English, German, and Chinese words.

Ferdinand de Saussure (1857–1913), the famous Swiss historical linguist and a founder of modern linguistics, argues (1916) that German displays a greater amount of **morphological motivation** (语素理据) than English while Chinese is the least morphologically motivated language. Chinese, according to de Saussure, is a typically "lexical language" in contradistinction to **Proto-Indo-European** (原始印欧语) and **Sanskrit** (梵文), which are typically "grammatical languages."

The first half of de Saussure's judgment is right but the second half (that Chinese is the least morphologically motivated language) is largely wrong because de Saussure was making a synchronic comparison of several modern languages and yet the basis on which he drew his conclusions about the Chinese language was apparently **classical Chinese** (古汉语).

Morphological motivation (语素理据) (the relationship between the morphological make-up of a word and its referential meaning) is by definition related to the morphological construction or make-up of a word. Hence **derivatives** (派生词) and **compounds** (复合词), which contain more than one morpheme, may be morphologically motivated while mono-morphemic words, which are made up of only one morpheme, are usually not morphologically motivated (although they may be phonetically or graphemically motivated, as was illustrated above).

In classical Chinese, most words were indeed mono-syllabic and mono-morphemic, hence normally not morphologically motivated. Things are quite different with Modern Chinese, however. As explicated in the previous section, in **Modern Chinese** (现代汉语) multi-morphemic words (most of which are disyllabic) account for 80% of the total lexical items and among these the majority must be compounds, since there are almost no **inflectional affixes** (屈折词缀) and very few **derivative affixes** (派生词缀) in the Chinese language. Therefore Modern Chinese must have a much greater chance of being morphologically motivated than classical Chinese.

If we examine Table 4.1 in which German, English, and Chinese nouns are juxtaposed for a comparison of their **morphological motivation** (语素理据), we shall see that Chinese nouns are almost as much morphologically motivated as German ones in that they depend on **compounding** (复合) for **word-building** (构词).

Learners of English-Chinese translation may wonder why when needs arise to borrow elements from other languages English usually adopts a foreign item directly while Chinese tends to translate it; for example, the Italian term *maf(f)ia* (a

Table 4.1 A contrast of the morphological motivation of German, English, and Chinese nouns

German	English	Chinese
Ehelosigheit ("marriage" + negative suffix + noun suffix)	Celibacy	独身 ("single living")
Erdteil ("earth part")	Continent [<L continuous land]	大陆 ("great land")
Fingerhut ("finger hat")	Thimble [<OE]	顶针 ("needle-pusher")
Handschuh ("hand shoe")	Glove [<OE]	手套 ("hand sheath")
Nilpferd ("Nile horse")	Hippopotamus [<Gk horse + river]	河马 ("river horse")
Scheidung ("separate" + fem. noun ending)	Divorce	离婚 ("leaving marriage")
Schlittschuh ("sledge shoe")	Skate [<OF stilt]	溜冰鞋 ("skating shoe")
Schnittlauch ("split leek")	Chive [<L onion]	细香葱 ("thin fragrant leek")
Wasserleitung ("water leader")	Aqueduct [<L water + lead]	引水管 ("water-leading pipe")
Ursache ("origin matter")	Cause	原因 ("original reason")

secret terrorist group in Sicily; originally opposed tyranny but evolved into a criminal organization in the middle of the 19th century) was introduced into the English language in its original form (i.e. maf[f]ia) but put into *heishou dang* or "black-hand party" (黑手党) when introduced into Chinese.

The cause of this marked difference in preferred strategies for introducing foreign items can most probably be found in the character of English and Chinese word stocks.

Modern English borrows words freely from languages of the most diverse origins, e.g.

> **Blitz** (a sudden military attack, especially from the air < German)
> **matador** (a person who fights and kills the bull in a bullfight < Spanish)
> **sputnik** (any of a series of Soviet satellites sent into Earth orbit, especially the first, launched October 4, 1957 <Russian)
> **rabbi** (a person trained in Jewish law, ritual, and tradition and ordained for leadership of a Jewish congregation, especially one serving as chief religious official of a synagogue <Hebrew)
> **galosh** (a waterproof overshoe that protects shoes from water or snow <Gaelic)
> **tomahawk** (a light axe used as a tool or weapon by American Indians <Algonquian Indian)
> **sampan**, **cheongsam**, and **chopsuey** (<Chinese)

And when it did so, it usually, as indicated by the items above, just transliterated the borrowed items instead of trying to naturalize their **morphemes** (语素). This must be at least in part due to the fact that historically the English language borrowed words extensively from every major language of the world, including such "classical" languages as Latin and Greek, and such "national" languages as Danish, Icelandic, Norwegian, Swedish, and French, and from numerous minor languages; and, as a result, the **vocabulary** (词汇) of the English language became increasingly heterogeneous and less morphologically motivated, with the average user not bothering so much about how the morphological form of a word is related to its meaning.

The case with Chinese is quite different. Chinese, at least **Modern Chinese** (现代汉语), is in fact a markedly morphologically motivated language. As its speakers, we seem to have long been accustomed to the practice of figuring out the meaning of a word by looking into the characters or **morphemes** (语素) it is made up of. Thus when the Chinese language does borrow from other languages, it normally resorts to "**loan translation**" (借译), i.e. literally translating each individual morpheme in a source word or each individual word in a source phrase or sentence into a correspondent morpheme or word in the target language so that the morphemes of the items borrowed may be naturalized or partially naturalized.

In the first few decades of the 20th century, when western and Russian cultures were introduced into China in a big way, there was a time when Chinese translators merely transliterated the new terms they brought to their readers. For example, *democracy* appeared in Chinese as "德谟克拉西," *telephone* as "德律风," *inspiration* as "烟士批里纯", and *president* as "伯里玺天德." These transliterated borrowings have proved unpopular with Chinese readers. Nowadays they have all been superseded by more motivated translations: 民主 ("people domination"), 电话 ("electric speech"), 灵感 ("spirit feeling"), and 总统 ("general administrator").

Sometimes, though, Chinese speakers and translators tend to go too far in their eagerness to find motivation for a borrowed word. This is especially true with the translation of trademarks. The familiar *Coco-Cola* (rendered into Chinese as "可口可乐" ["tasty and pleasant"]), *Pepsi(-cola)* (rendered into Chinese as "百事可乐" ["everything is enjoyable"]), *Vermouth* (rendered into Chinese as "味美思"), *Omo* (rendered into Chinese as "奥妙"), *Safeguard* (rendered into Chinese as "舒肤佳"), *Acstar* (rendered into Chinese as "发嘉丽"), and *Sprite* (meaning "a small or elusive supernatural being; an elf or a pixy [小妖精]" but rendered into Chinese as "雪碧") need not be discussed. Two recent introductions were "柏丽" ("Cypress Beautiful") for Sweden floor board *Pergot* and "固特异" ("especially tough and extraordinary") for American name brand auto tire *Goodyear*.

4.2.2 Sense Relationships

In **semantics** (语义学) (the study of linguistic meaning), we distinguish two important notions: reference and sense. **Reference** (所指意义) is the relationship between words and the objects (entities), events, and qualities they stand for.

In its narrower sense, *reference* is used only for the relationship between linguistic expressions and specific phenomena, such as the phrase *Tommy's dog* and "Tommy's dog," and not classes and types, such as the word *dog* which means the type of the animal.

In its wider sense, *reference* is used for the relationship between linguistic expressions and classes and types, such as the word *ocean* and any ocean (referent) in the real world or in a fictional or possible world.

Reference as used in both its narrower and wider senses is identical with what semanticists traditionally called "**denotation**" (外延意义) (the object or concept to which a term refers, or the set of objects of which a predicate is true). It is also identical with what we call "**referential meaning**" (指称意义) (the relationship between linguistic signs and the entities in the world which they refer to or describe) (See Sect. 2.3.3 and Ke, 1996, pp. 75–81).

Sense (系统意义) is the place a word or phrase (**lexeme** [词位]) holds in the system of relationships with other words in the **vocabulary** (词汇) of a language. For example, the English words *bachelor* and *married* have the **sense relationship** (系统意义关系) of *bachelor = never married*. In English we have *longhand* (ordinary handwriting, in which the words are written out in full, as distinguished from *shorthand* or from *typing*, e.g. *The director scratched out the speech in longhand*) because there exists the word *shorthand* (a quick way of writing using special signs or abbreviations, used especially to record what a person is saying).

The primary focus of modern **semantics** (语义学) is on the **sense** (系统意义) of words and phrases rather than on their **reference** (所指意义).

There are several kinds of **sense relationship** (系统意义关系) between **lexemes** (词位). Some result from the way words or phrases occur in sequences. These are known as **syntagmatic** or sequential **semantic relations** (横组合语义关系). ("**Syntagm**" is a linguistic unit consisting of a set of linguistic forms [**phonemes** (音位), words, or phrases] that are in a sequential relationship to one another.) For example, if we hear the sentence *He is a very kind _____*, we would "know" that the omitted word will be one of a very small set (e.g. *man, person,* etc.). In this sentence the words *kind* and *man/person,* etc. maintain a sort of **syntagmatic semantic relationship**.

Other **sense relationships** (系统意义关系) between **lexemes** (词位) result from the way in which words or phrases can substitute for each other. These are known as **paradigmatic** or substitutional **semantic relations** (纵聚合语义关系). ("**Paradigm**" is a set or list of linguistic items that form mutually exclusive choices in particular syntactic roles. English **determiners** (限定词), e.g. form a paradigm: we can say *a book* or *his book* but not **a his book*.) For instance, in the sentence *He is a _____ man*, we may put in the blank many different qualifiers, e.g. *kind/evil*. The substitution of *evil* for *kind* results in a change of meaning that we recognize as an "opposite." In this sentence the words *kind, evil,* etc. form a paradigmatic semantic relationship.

4.2.2.1   Syntagmatic Semantic Relationship: Collocation

Collocation (搭配) is related to the co-occurrence of words and phrases. The object of the study of collocation is the **co-occurrence relationships** (共现关系) between lexical items. "You shall know a word by the company it keeps," said the British linguist J. R. Firth (1890–1960) (1957), referring to the **syntagmatic** (横组合的) tendency of **lexemes** (词位) to work together ("collocate") in predictable ways. *Blond,* e.g. collocates with *hair, flock* with *sheep,* and *neigh* ([of a horse] making a long high-pitched cry) or *whinny* ([of a horse] making gentle neighing sound) with *horse.* In Chinese, one 打篮球 "plays basketball," but 踢足球 "plays football."

Quite often a word in different **collocations** (搭配) may mean differently, as is shown by the following humor:

Teacher: I need a responsible child to fetch me something.
Tommy: I'll go. Every time something happens at home, my dad says I'm responsible!

Collocations (搭配) differ greatly between languages, and provide a major difficulty in commanding foreign languages. In English, one "faces" problems and "interprets" dreams; but in modern Hebrew, people have to "stand in front of" problems and "solve" dreams. In Japanese the verb for "drink" collocates with water and soup, but also with tablets and cigarettes (Crystal, 1987, p. 105). In Chinese a poor writer or literary translator may be described as 糟蹋 or 糟践

("spoiling/ruining") literature, but never "murdering" literature, as one would say in English. Likewise, a dazzling reading lamp "hurts" eyes in Chinese but "kills" eyes in English.

To write or translate idiomatically, **L2** learners and users should pay particular attention to the **collocation** (搭配) of words. That often means consulting a good dictionary with sufficient information on the collocation of **L2** words whenever they are *not absolutely sure of* (not just when they are *unsure of*) the way one word goes with another to communicate a particular meaning, e.g.

> He *did hard labor* for three years. 他劳改过三年。
> He *did hard work* for three years. 他辛辛苦苦工作了三年。
>
> She is *not a little* afraid of snakes. 她怕蛇怕得厉害。
> She is *not a bit* afraid of snakes. 她一点也不怕蛇。
>
> I have *seen him through.* 我帮他渡过了难关。
> I have *seen through him.* 我看透了他。
>
> He is a *medicine man.* 他是个巫师。
> He is a *medical man.* 他是个医生。

Chinese beginners of English tend to make such ungrammatical sentences as

> **Because* I am ill, *so* I won't go to school.

because they are not aware of the **collocational limitations** (搭配限制) on the words *because* and *so*. For the same reason, international students who have not acquired complete knowledge of the norms governing the collocation of Chinese transitive verbs with their objects may make the following ungrammatical Chinese sentences:

> *我在1990年结婚了她。
> *昨晚,我在街上捡 (见) 到我太太,我们一起去参观我奶奶。
> *今天早餐,我吃我太太和面条 (我和我太太吃面条)。

The more fixed a **collocation** (搭配) is, the more we think of it as an "**idiom**" (成语), i.e. a pattern to be learned as a whole, and not as the "sum of its parts." Thus we find French *broyer du noir* (literally, "grind" + "black"), meaning "have the blues" or "be browned off" a nice instance of the arbitrary use of color terms. Idioms are hard nuts to crack in translation, especially when its meaning as a whole and the meanings of its constituent words are employed at once to create a punning effect, as is shown in the following humors:

> When my brother, a notorious spender, came home for a visit, he told my father that he was going to get married and settle down. Said Dad, "Why don't you stay single and settle up?"
>
> "I put quite a few suggestions for improving the business into the suggestion box. Did you receive them?"
>
> "Yes. Did you see the office boy with wastebasket?"

"I did, sir."

"Well, he's carrying out your suggestions."

A solid contrastive study of the **idioms** (成语) of English and Chinese would certainly contribute much to the practice of translation between these two major languages in the world (See Chen, 1982).

4.2.2.2   Paradigmatic Semantic Relationships

David Crystal (1987, p. 105) distinguishes several familiar types of **paradigmatic semantic relations** (纵聚合语义关系):

Synonymy

Synonymy (同义) denotes the relationship of "sameness" of meaning, e.g.

mix
blend
merge
mingle
fuse

Words rarely (if ever) have *exactly* the same meaning. There usually exist stylistic, regional, expressive, or other subtle differences between their meanings, e.g. *hide* and *conceal* are regarded as a pair of synonyms, but *conceal* is more formal than *hide*. *Jolly* is explained as meaning "very" in English dictionaries but, as Newmark (1988, p. 114) notes, *jolly* in *jolly good* is a slight middle-class intensifier, which can only be over-translated in French (*drôlement*) and under-translated in German (*ganz, vielleicht*)—both languages missing the connotation of social class. In the following episode, an American student of Chinese obviously failed to note the fact that synonyms are not really interchangeable words:

A Chinese teacher ran into her American student on an avenue on the campus in the evening and asked him if he was taking a walk. The American student smiled and said, "对!我正在这里徘徊." His Chinese teacher, stifling a chuckle, asked him if he knew what "徘徊" means in Chinese. "Sure!" said the American student, "徘徊就是在一个地方来回来去地走着."

Context must also be taken into account when there are several synonymous words to choose from. Two **lexemes** (词位) might be synonymous in one sentence but different in another: *range* and *selection* are synonyms in

What a nice ____ of furnishings

The hotel offers a wide ____ of facilities.

but not in

Its mountain ____s, winding rivers, lush farmland and native bush sparkle beneath cloud-filled skies.

Antonymy

Antonymy (反义) is the relationship of "oppositeness of meaning." Antonyms are in fact very different from synonyms. There may be no true synonyms, but there are several kinds of real antonyms, including:

(1) **gradable antonyms** (可分级反义词), such as *big/small, good/bad*, which permit the expression of degrees, e.g. *very big, quite small*, etc. (between extremes there often existing gradations or degrees of change, e.g. between light and pitch black there are: *dim, dark, darkened*, etc.);
(2) **nongradable antonyms** (不可分级反义词) (also called **complementary terms** (互补项), which do not permit degrees of contrast, such as *single/married, male/female;* it is not possible to talk of *very male, quite married*, etc., except in jest; and
(3) **converse terms** (互逆项), which present two-way contrasts that are interdependent on each other, such as *buy/sell* or *parent/child*; one member presupposes the other.

Hyponymy

Hyponymy (上下义) refers to the notion of "inclusion," whereby we can say that "an X is a kind of Y." For example, *rose* is a **hyponym** (下义词) of *flower, car* of *vehicle*. Therefore we may say "A rose is a kind of flower" and "A car is a kind of vehicle." Several **lexemes** (词位) can be "**cohyponyms**" (同级下义词) of the same **superordinate** (上义词) (general term), e.g. *rose, pansy, tulip*, etc. are the cohyponyms of *flower*.

In English, Chinese, and many other languages, the word *animal* is a strange **lexeme** (词位), because it can be used at three levels in a hierarchy of inclusion (See Fig. 4.2):

(1) in a classification of living things, it contrasts with *plant* and *microorganism* (or *microbe*, including bacterium, fungus, and virus), to include birds, fishes, and insects (in other words, it is the **cohyponyms** (同级下义词) of *plant* and *microorganism*);
(2) it contrasts with *bird, fish,* and *insect* to include humans and beasts, that is, it is the **cohyponyms** (同级下义词) of *bird, fish,* and *insect;*
(3) it contrasts with *human*, i.e. it is the cohyponym of *human*.

Thus when we say "Human beings are a kind of animal," we use the word "animal" to refer to the group of living things that contrast with "microorganism" and "plant" ("Human beings are not plants or microorganism."). When we say "The horse is an animal," we use the word "animal" to refer to any animal that is not a

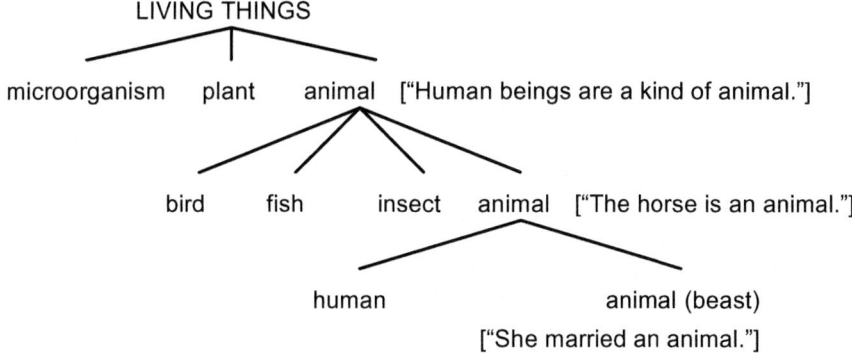

Fig. 4.2 Three levels of hyponymic relationship the word *animal* enters into

bird, fish, or insect. When we say "She married an animal," however, we use the word to refer to any four-footed creature, especially a mammal, which does not belong to human beings. In this case what we actually mean to say with the metaphor is that the woman married a brutal, debased, or beastly man who behaved just like any non-human animal. As we can see, the word "animal" in these three usages belong respectively to three different levels of inclusion or **hyponymy** (上下 义). Children may sometimes ignore or confuse between the three levels of senses in which the word is used, as we can see in the following humor.

> Tommy was only two years old, but his father was very proud of him. Once his father was talking to a visitor, telling the man how clever his son was.
> "The boy is only two years old," he said, "and he knows all animals. He's going to be a great naturalist. Here, let me show you."
> He took a book of natural history from the bookshelf, placed Tommy on his knee, opened the book and showed him a picture of a giraffe.
> "What's that, Tommy?"
> "Horsey," said Tommy.
> Next a tiger was shown, and Tommy said, "Pussy."
> Then Tommy's father showed Tommy a picture of a lion, and Tommy said, "Doggy."
> And when a picture of a chimpanzee was shown, Tommy said, "Daddy!"

Translators need to be sensitive to terms that are used in different levels of inclusion in different contexts. For example, *court of law* is "法院" in Chinese; but when it is used in parallel with *court of equity* (衡平法法院) in the U.K., the U.S., or other common law countries, it should be rendered as "普通法法院." Likewise, *contractor* is "承包商" when used independently; but "总包商" when used along with *subcontractor* (分包商). "农牧业税" should be *farming and husbandry taxes* instead of *agricultural and husbandry taxes* because *agriculture* includes *husbandry*.

Incompatibility

By **incompatibility** is meant the relationship of mutual exclusiveness between sets of words that are members of the same **superordinate category** (上义范畴). For example, *red, green*, etc. are incompatible **lexemes** (词位) within the category *color*: it would not be possible to say "I am thinking of a single color, and it is green and red." On the other hand, *red* is not incompatible with such words as *round* or *dirty* (something can be at once "red and round," e.g. a balloon). Terms for fruit, flowers, weekdays, and musical instruments illustrate other incompatible sets. Once again, we must be prepared for some unexpected usages as in English, where *black, white*, and *gray* are not always included within the category of *color* (as with *black-and-white* films and *black-and-white* TV).

4.2.2.3 Lexical Fields and Lexical Gaps

Closely linked to **hyponymy** (上下义) is the notion of **lexical field** (词汇场). The concept of lexical field was introduced into linguistics by German scholars, chiefly J. Trier (1934), for the purpose of delimiting the **lexicon** (词库) into cohesive subsystems.

Lexical field (词汇场) is also known as "**word field** (词汇场)" or "**semantic field** (语义场)". It refers to a group of related words or phrases (i.e. **lexemes** [词位]) organized into a system within which each item interrelates with and sort of defines the other items.

The lexical field of COLOR in English, e.g. includes eleven basic items: *white, black, red, green, yellow, blue, brown, purple, pink, orange, and gray*. The items in the field define each other: we cannot really understand the meaning of a specific item, say, *orange*, without knowing its relationship with the other items in the same field, say, *red* and *yellow*. (When one mixes red and yellow, one will get orange.) In the Chinese lexical field of COLOR, we cannot really know what kind of a color 青 ("greenish blue" or "bluish green") is without knowing its position relative to 绿 "green" and 蓝 "blue" in the same field. A similar example is the lexical field of ACADEMIC CONFERENCE SESSIONS, which include *plenary session* (大会), *concurrent session* (分组会议), and *workshop* (专题讨论).

We may view the **vocabulary** (词汇) of a language as a system of subsystems: these very subsystems are the **lexical fields** (词汇场) in the **lexicon** (词库) of the language. The lexical field is similar to the thesaurus (e.g. *Roget's Thesaurus*), and contrasts with the conventional dictionary, which is organized alphabetically and in which the **semantic relations** (语义关系) between words and expressions are usually not indicated.

The absence of a word in a particular place in a **lexical field** (词汇场) of a language is called a **lexical gap** (词汇空缺).

To express a concept, especially a complicated one, we have two lexical devices.

(1) First, we may **lexicalize** (词汇化) it, i.e. give it a specific name, e.g. *a mare, enlarge a photo.*

(2) Secondly, we may describe it in a circuitous or roundabout way, i.e. by "circumlocution" (in the literal sense of the word), e.g. *a female horse, make a photo larger,* or *cause a photo to become larger.*

The first lexical device is known as **synthetic expression** (综合式表达) and the second one, **analytic expression** (分析式表达).

The synthetic way of expressing a concept is usually used where the referent is **lexicalized** (词汇化) (that is, there is a word for it in the language's **vocabulary** [词汇]). The analytic way of expressing a concept will be used whenever some notion has to be expressed and yet there is not a ready-made word for it in the **target language** (目标语)'s **Lexicon** (词库) or, to put it in another way, whenever a **lexical gap** (词汇空缺) exists somewhere in the relevant **lexical field** (词汇场) of the language.

With reference to other languages, every language has lexical gaps in its **semantic fields** (语义场). This very fact explains why bilinguals and translators alike find it easier to describe or talk about something in one language than in another. For example, the concepts expressed directly in German with single words *verdeutschen* and *Zweitspracherwerb* have to be expressed indirectly in English with phrases: "to translate into German" and "second language acquisition." The Chinese language has different names for different kinds of boiled or steamed stuffed wheaten food: 包子, 饺子, and 馄饨. But to English speakers, all these have but one name—dumpling (a small piece of dough, boiled or baked, often enclosing meat, fruit, etc.): the contrasts between them are simply not **lexicalized** (词汇化) in the English language.

Kinship is important in all societies. The comparative study of kinship has been one of the central concerns of social or cultural anthropology. One approach to comparative kinship study is the analysis of **kinship terminology** (亲属称谓术语). In the following we shall make a short contrastive study of the English and Chinese lexical fields of consanguineous kinship terminology (亲属称谓术语). For the purpose of clarity, let's first make a diagram of the contrasts between the kinship systems of the two languages (or "language-culture") (see Table 4.2).

When we look over Table 4.2, the first thing we would notice is that the Chinese consanguineous **kinship terminology** (亲属称谓术语) is much more complicated than its English counterpart. After an item-by-item comparison of these two systems, we would find that the Chinese kinship terms are based upon five parameters, that is, ***generation from ego*** (辈分), ***linearity*** (直系) (being in a direct line of descent or ancestry) ***vs. collaterality*** (旁系) (being descended from the same stock but by a different line; offshoot), ***gender*** (性别) (male vs. female), ***seniority versus juniority*** (长幼), and ***paternal*** (父系) ***vs. maternal*** (母系), while its English counterpart involves only three parameters: generation from ego, male vs. female, and linearity vs. collaterality. In the case of cousin, English adopts a simpler, symmetric term, negating even the male-female contrast. As a result, the Chinese **word field** (词汇场) of consanguineous kinship terminology is much more

Table 4.2 English and Chinese consanguineous kinship terminology

Collateral Distance [how closely the offshoot members of one's family are related to one]					Genealogi-cal Distance [how closely the members of one's family are related to one in a line of descent]
4th	**3rd**	**2nd**	**1st**	**0**	
				great-grandfather/ great-grandmother 曾祖父/母 外曾祖父/母 ↙ ↓	**+3**
			granduncle/ grandaunt 伯祖父/母 叔祖父/母 姑公/婆 姨公/婆 舅公/婆 ↙	grandfather/ grandmother 祖父/母 外祖父/母 ↙ ↓	**+2**
	one's parents 2nd cousin ↙	one's parent's 1st cousin 堂(表)伯/母 堂(表)叔/婶 堂(表)姑/父 表姨/父 表舅/母 ↙	uncle/aunt 伯父/母 叔父/婶母 姑母/父 姨母/父 舅舅/母 ↙	father/mother [linear relative one generation higher than oneself] 父/母 ↙ ↓	**+1**
3rd cousin	2nd cousin (the child of one's parent's 1st cousin) 远房堂兄/姐 远房堂弟/妹 远房表兄/姐 远房表弟/妹 ↓	(1st/full) cousin/cousin- german (the son or daughter of one's uncle or aunt) 堂兄/姐 堂弟/妹 表兄/姐 表弟/妹 ↓	brother/sister 兄/姐 弟/妹 ↓	Ego 本人 ↓	**0**

Table 4.2 (continued)

		2nd cousin once removed 从兄/姐 从弟/妹 从表兄/姐 从表弟/妹	1st cousin once removed (a child of one's 1st cousin) 堂房侄儿/女 堂房外甥/女 表侄儿/女 表外甥/女 ↓	nephew/niece 侄儿/女 外甥/女 ↓	son/ daughter 儿/女 ↓	-1
			1st cousin twice removed	grandnephew/ grandniece 侄孙/女 侄外甥/女	grandson/ granddaughter 孙儿/女 外孙/女 ↓	-2
					great- grandson/ great- granddaughter 曾孙儿/女 曾外孙/女	-3

The arrow means "giving birth to."

complex than that of the English one. This fact cause difficulties in the translation of some English kinship terms, as the following case indicates:

Three *cousins* of the French President were also to receive diamonds.
法国总统的三位远亲后来也接受了一些宝石。

Objectively, the "three cousins" mentioned here may be three males, three females, two males and one female, or two females and one male (four possibilities of combination); they may be of three different ages (three possibilities of combination); and they may be relatives on either the paternal or the maternal side (two possibilities of combination). So there are in all 24 (4 × 3 × 2) possible combinations of the three individuals in terms of gender, age, and paternal/maternal contrasts. If we take into account the possibility that one or more of them may be **second cousins** (the children of one's parent's first cousin, i.e. one's 远房堂兄弟姐妹 and 远房表兄弟姐妹), the possible combinations of the three would be increased to an incredibly large number. In French there is at least one feminine form of *cousin—cousine—*to distinguish the male cousin from the female one, hence less possible combinations in our case (although only by half—not quite significant a reduction so far as translation into Chinese is concerned). But the English language has only one general term—*cousin—*to serve as both the nominal term and the form of address for a vast number of different members of an extended family, including the children of one's uncles and aunts (**first cousins**) and the grandchildren of one's granduncles and grandaunts (**second cousins**). Facing so formidable a number of possibilities, the translator of the above sentence could do no more than equivocating about the referent of the term, rendering it as "远亲"

("distantly related relative"). "远亲," however, is a term of broad coverage, including such relatives as one's granduncle/grandaunt, grandnephew/grandniece, etc. and is therefore not an exact translation. But we doubt if anybody could come up with a better Chinese term for it.

4.2.3 Semantic Features

In the third chapter we showed how **phonemes** (音位) may be analyzed into phonological features. In a similar way, **lexemes** (词位) can be shown to be composed of semantic features.

Semantic features (语义特征) or **semantic components** (语义成分) are the smallest elements of meaning in a word. The meaning of words may be described as a combination of semantic features. We may, for example, consider the following sets of words in English:

man	woman	child
bull	cow	calf

We feel that these two groups of words represent a common pattern vertically, so that we could set up a proportion like:

man : woman : child = bull : cow : calf

Both "man" and "bull" are (+ male), "woman" and "cow" (+ female), and "child" and "calf" (+ immature). Horizontally, we see further contrasts: all words in the first set are (+ human), all words in the second set (+ bovine). The entire set of semantic features which distinguish these items from each other can then be summarized in Table 4.3:

The features we have isolated here are **semantic components** (语义成分). Each **lexeme** (词位) is a complex of such components or features: "calf," for example, is specifiable as (+ bovine, + immature), which corresponds to the dictionary definition of this item as "young cow" or "baby of a cow."

James (1980, pp. 93–95) notes a **contrastive analysis** (对比分析) of the lexical field of COOKING in English and German in terms of **semantic features** (语义特征). There are, according to James, two procedural options for the contrastive analysis of **lexical fields** (词汇场) from two languages:

(1) **From componential analysis** (构成成分分析) **to translational matching:** We may produce an independent specification of **L1** and **L2 lexemes** (词位) (and

Table 4.3 Semantic features distinguishing related items from each other

	+ *male*	+ *female*	+ *immature*
human	man	woman	child
bovine	bull	cow	calf

senses) for the same field. This may be done with a native speaker supplying the **L2** inventory, and each lexeme being analyzed componentially. Then follows a matching procedure: those **L1** and **L2** lexemes or senses receiving the same features are by definition **translation equivalents** (翻译等值成分).

(2) **From tentative translation to componential analysis** (构成成分分析): We may utilize **translation equivalence** (翻译等值). This approach starts with tentative translations and the subsequent componential analysis as a check on their "fit."

Let us illustrate the first approach by reference to the field of COOKING in English and German: the field for English has been analyzed by Lehrer (1969). She regards *cook* as having three senses:

(a) Its most general sense *cook1* means "to prepare a meal" and this belongs to the field of household tasks with *clean, wash, repairs*, etc.
(b) *Cook$_2$* is less general and contrasts only with *bake*, that is, it refers to the preparation of all foods other than those sold in bakeries.
(c) *Cook$_3$* is the most marked sense, and the one on which our **contrastive analysis** (对比分析) will focus: it involves the application of heat in some way to food.

The **lexical field** (词汇场) covered by *Cook$_3$* can be divided into six main categories headed by the **lexemes** (词位) *boil, simmer, fry, roast, toast /broil* (*Broil* is an American English usage meaning "to cook directly under a heating unit or directly over an open fire." It is matched in British English by *grill* and *toast*.), and *bake* (the specific sense). These six lexemes, then, are **hyponyms** (下义词) of *Cook$_3$*, which is the **superordinate** (上义词) of the field.

Let us take a subset of **lexemes** (词位) from the *cook* field in English and German. First we assign to them their **semantic features** (语义特征), and then we shall be in a position to do the **contrastive analysis** (对比分析).

C_1–C_5 refer to the five **semantic features** (语义特征) whereby these sets of **lexemes** (词位) can be specified and differentiated. By convention "**+**" signifies that the lexeme is marked by having the relevant component, "**−**" that it is marked by lacking it, and "**O**" that it does not apply distinctively one way or the other.

Note what equations and nonequations (contrasts) this analysis reveals:

• *cook$_3$= kochen$_1$*: both mean to prepare food in any of the ways specified by C_1–C_5.
• *boil = kochen$_2$*: i.e. in water, on flame, rapidly.
• *simmer = kochen$_3$*: i.e. in water, on flame, gently.

Braten is specified positively only by the absence of water in the cooking process, all the other features being non-distinctive (marked by O). Now *braten* can be with fat or without, i.e. dry; one can also *braten* in the oven or on the flame. In fact *Bratkartoffeln* ("*fried potatoes*") are cooked in a pan, on the flame, with fat, that is, they *are fried*; while *ein Rindbraten* is prepared in the oven, without fat: it is *roast beef*. In other words *braten* is a more general term, occupying the semantic space of both *fry* and *roast*. To differentiate the senses of *braten* we could establish two terms *braten$_1$* (=fry) and *braten$_2$* (=roast).

Such a division could be motivated from within German if we introduced more features. The most obvious candidates for these features would be **selectional features** (选择性特征) or **selectional restrictions** (选择性限制) (that is, restrictions on the types of noun phrase which can occur in a clause with particular verbal elements; for instance, in English the noun must agree with the verb in number— *The child likes Disneyland* /*The children like Disneyland*—and, on the semantic level, some nouns can only collocate with certain verbs—"*The children like Disneyland*" is all right, but "**The child pleases Disneyland*" is incorrect). We would say that *braten1* selects objects like *Schinken* "bacon," *Spiegeleier* "fried eggs" while *braten2* selects as objects such nouns as *Rind* "beef," *Schweine* "pork," and *Kalbs* "veal."

Toast selects the same features as *rösten*: *Röstbrot* ("roasted bread") is *toast* (n.). However, the relationship is not always so clear-cut: we have *Röstkartoffeln* "baked potatoes," *Röstpfanne* "frying pan," and *Röstofen* "kiln (a furnace or oven for burning, baking, or drying, especially one for calcining lime or firing pottery)."

C$_1$–C$_5$ fail to distinguish *roast* from *bake*. But we can distinguish this pair if we resort to further specification by **selectional features** (选择性特征) *Bake/backen* select objects composed of flour (*cake/Kuchen/Gebäck*) while *roast/braten* select animal substances, i.e. meats.

The studies of **lexical field** (词汇场) and **semantic features** (语义特征) carry important implications for some key problems in translation studies.

(1) First, the fact that a notion can be expressed using a set of semantic features makes it possible for second language users (including translators) to describe or refer to any unlexicalized entities in the **target language** (目标语); in other words, any **lexical gap** (词汇空缺) in a word field of the target language can in principle be filled in by an **analytic expression** (分析式表达方式) which incorporates the essential semantic features of a concept or notion the speaker intends to communicate. This is highly significant for the solution of the long-standing debate over the issue of **translatability** (可译性) or **untranslatability** (不可译性) among **translation theorists** (翻译理论研究者) (Wilhelm von Humboldt [1767–1835], Willard Van Orman Quine [1908–2000], Virginia Woolf [1882–1941], Jacques Derrida (1930–2004), etc. hold that translation is ultimately impossible).

For example, German has a set of simple **lexemes** (词位) for "brush" like *Bürste, Pinsel, Besen*, which are not **lexicalized** (词汇化) in English, but the English language manages to come up with the complex equivalents *hair/ clothes brush, painting brush*, and *sweeping brush*. It is this possibility of **interlingual paraphrase** (语际释义) which guarantees, at least so far as the translation of **referential meaning** (指称意义) is concerned, the feasibility of translation, even in cases where one of the languages has a "lexical gap."

(2) Secondly, just as Lyons (1968, p. 472) points out, **semantic features** (语义特征), like phonological features, may be universals:

It has frequently been suggested that the **vocabulary** (词汇) of all human languages can be analyzed, either totally or partially, in terms of a finite set of **semantic components** (语义成分) which are themselves independent of the particular semantic structure of any given language.

This postulation is of great practical as well as theoretical importance for the study of meaning in translation. To solve a complicated problem, we need to reduce it to its basic component parts (Consider how German mathematician and philosopher Leibniz [1646–1716]'s creation of the binary system of numbers [1 and 0], a system which uses combinations of a very limited number of basic elements [not unlike **semantic features** (语义特征)], affected the development of computer science!). A small, limited set of **semantic features** (语义特征) that are manageable by men (and computers as well) will definitely be conducive to the solution of the problem of meaning on the level of **lexis** (词汇), which in turn will help to solve practical problems related to interlingual translation.

4.3 Three Active Areas

There are a number of areas where lexical **CA** has been actively carried out, notably:

- anthropology
- translation
- bilingual lexicography.

4.3.1 Anthropology

Many of the problems to which contrastive lexicology ultimately has to address itself were the concern of scholars in anthropology throughout the 20th century.

In the 1920s and 1930s American linguists and anthropologists Edward Sapir (1884–1939) and his pupil Benjamin Lee Whorf (1897–1941), taking up the tradition of placing great value on the diversity of the world's languages and cultures as started with the romantic idealism of the late 18th century, concerned themselves with the problem of the relationship between language and the way to see the world. The results of their studies came to be known as the "**Sapir-Whorf hypothesis** (萨丕尔-沃尔夫假说)." This hypothesis combines two principles. The first is known as **linguistic determinism** (语言决定论), which states that language determines the way we think. The second follows from this, and is known as **linguistic relativity** (语言相对论), which states that the distinctions encoded in one language are not found in any other language. The hypothesis suggests that since language determines our perception of reality, and since languages are structured differently, different language communities have different views of what is, objectively, the "same" reality: "languages have a tendency to 'impose structure on the real world' by treating some distinctions as crucial, and ignoring others" (Leech, 1974, p. 30; as cited in James, 1980, p. 83).

Whorf illustrated his view by taking examples from several languages, and in particular from **Hopi** (霍皮语), an Amerindian language. In Hopi, there is one word (*masa'ytaka*) for everything that flies except birds—which would include insects, airplanes and pilots. This seems alien to someone used to thinking in English, but, Whorf argues, it is no stranger than English-speakers having one word for many kinds of snow, in contrast to **Eskimo** (爱斯基摩语), where there are different words for falling snow, snow on the ground, snow packed hard like ice, slushy or partly melted snow, and so on. In **Aztec** (阿兹特克), a language spoken by the Aztecs, who lived in Mexico and had an advanced civilization before the conquest of Mexico by the Spanish colonialists in 1519, a single word (with different endings) covers an even greater range of English notions—snow, cold and ice.

Examples such as these made the **Sapir-Whorf hypothesis** (萨丕尔-沃尔夫假说) very plausible; but in its strongest form (language determining its speakers' way of thinking and people from communities whose languages are markedly different from each other would have difficulties understanding each other, as in the example of a **Hopi** [霍皮人] and an English physicist.) it is unlikely to have any adherents now. That there are some conceptual differences between cultures due to language is undeniable, but this is not to say that the differences are so great that mutual comprehension is impossible. One language may take many words to denote what another language says in a single word, but in the end the circuitous or roundabout way of expression (i.e. **analytic expression** [分析式表达]) can make the point, as we have illustrated in the previous section with examples of English and German words for different "brushes."

Similarly, it does not follow that, because a language lacks a word, its speakers cannot then grasp the concept. Several languages have few words for numerals: Australian aboriginal languages, for example, are often restricted to a few general words (such as "all," "many," "few"), and "one" and "two." In such cases, it is sometimes said that the people lack the concept of number—that aborigines "haven't the intelligence to count," as it was once put. But this is not so, as is shown when these speakers learn English as a second language: their ability to count and calculate is quite comparable to that of native English speakers.

However, a weaker form of the **Sapir-Whorf hypothesis** (萨丕尔-沃尔夫假说) is generally accepted. Language may not determine the way we think, but it does influence the way we perceive and remember, and it affects the ease with which we perform mental tasks. Several experiments have shown that people recall things more easily if the things correspond to readily available words or phrases. And people certainly find it easier to make a conceptual distinction if it neatly corresponds to words available in their language (Crystal, 1987, p. 15). Lander (1960) indicates that the monolingual **Zuni** (祖尼人), a tribe of North American Indians living in New Mexico, presented with a small set of different colors and then asked after a brief period to pick out the ones he saw from a much larger collection, will have trouble recognizing the ones for which his language does not have convenient names (Bolinger, 1981, p. 142).

We know that in English an adjective is morphologically marked for three qualitative degrees, e.g. *good, better, best.* The following humor, which is based upon this feature of English grammar, would be impossible in a language in which adjectives are not so marked:

The pernickety English grammar teacher married a man of quality.
"You are the best woman in my life," announced the groom on their wedding night.
"And just who were the other two?" angrily snapped the grammar-conscious bride.

Moser (1997, p. 20), an American professor of English with Beijing Foreign Studies University, made a psycholinguistic experiment in which students at the University of Michigan and Beijing Normal university were given the following question in their respective native languages:

If 1 were greater than 2, and 2 were greater than 3, would 1 be greater than 3?
(如果一比二大,而二又比三大的话,一是不是比三大?)

The results were rather striking. 27 out of 27 American subjects answered "yes" to the question (**100%**), whereas only 23 out of 34 Chinese subjects (about **68%**) answered "yes" to the same question.

Subjects were asked to explain their answers. Virtually all the American subjects answered saying things like "Given the premise, it follows logically" and "This is trivially obvious." Chinese subjects responding "no" or "not necessarily" gave explanations like "The premise is obviously false, and reasoning from a false premise gives a false conclusion," or "Though the structure of the argument is logical, the resulting answer is obviously absurd, and therefore the answer is no." Many Chinese subjects refused to adopt the counterfactual premise, saying things like "1 could never be larger than 2, the question makes no sense."

The responses of these Chinese students had some sense. The question is why the Americans agreed so readily to the absurd premise, whereas Chinese speakers balked at it. One possible explanation is that the result involves the **subjunctive mood** (虚拟语气) in English (If 1 *were* greater than two ... *would* 1 be greater" etc.), which prompts the listener that the premise is false (and thus removed from considerations of practical reality), whereas the Chinese must deduce the intent of the utterance from contextual and pragmatic cues, and are thus encouraged to think more deeply about the realistic implications of the premise. Moser's experiment exemplifies Li Zehou's characterization of the philosophical inclination of the Chinese nation—"pragmatic reason." This example apparently shows again that aspects of language can facilitate or hinder some kinds of thinking (in this case it's that of abstract, logical inference).

American linguist Kaplan (1972) holds the view that the conventions for the organization of thought and argument (i.e. **rhetorical devices** [修辞手段]), are language or culture-specific. He notes that English speakers demonstrate particular skill with six **rhetorical functions** (修辞功能): definition, classification, comparison, contrast, analysis, and synthesis. These would appear to be those most frequently used in scientific discourse, perhaps even constituting the basis of scientific method, suggesting perhaps that it is no historical accident, but a linguistically conditioned necessity that English is the international language of science (James, 1980, p. 121). Kaplan's observation indicates that the fundamental ideas Sapir and Whorf proposed regarding the relationship between language and thought are still inspiring present-day researchers in their explorations into the interaction between language and extralingual reality.

The strong version of **Sapir-Whorf hypothesis** (萨丕尔-沃尔夫假说) views language as the determinant of perceived reality. This view of determinism can, and has been, reversed, into a claim that culture is reflected in language: "the language of a particular society is an integral part of its culture, and … the lexical distinctions drawn by each language will tend to reflect the culturally important features of objects, institutions and activities in the society in which the language operates" (Lyons, 1968, p. 432).

For a specific example we may look at the unusual internal structure of the category of food in the **vocabulary** (词汇) of the **Maricopa** (马利柯帕语), a language of the American Indians native to the desert areas of the southwestern United States. In English and Chinese we distinguish $food_1$ (any substance taken in by people, animals, or plants to maintain life and health) into $food_2$ (the solid kind of $food_1$) and drink, but the Maricopa generic word *camac* "food" includes three categories of edible things which can be easily distinguished since each occurs with a different verb. The first class takes the verb *maum* "to eat"; the second class, the verb *cakaum* "to consume something containing water"; and the third class, the verb *si:m* "to drink." The criterion in the classification is the amount of water food contains. The explanation is very probably that the physical environment of the Maricopa Indians is that of a semi-arid desert with seasonal shortage of water. In aboriginal times such a distinction may have been vitally important to survival (Hickerson, 1980, pp. 119–120).

The **Maricopa** (马利柯帕语) example suggests that the difference between different languages in the degree of specificity and differentiation (or lexicalization) of their **vocabulary** (词汇) may be due to the fact that to designate the continuous and infinite extralingual reality with discrete and practically finite linguistic resources, the reality has to be segmented; and every culture effects the segmentation according to its specific needs or points of emphasis. **Cultural emphases** (文化注重点) determine at least to some extent the properties of the lexical system of a language.

A similar example is that of kinship terminology. In Sect. 4.2.2.3 ("Lexical Fields and Lexical Gaps"), we contrasted the consanguineous **kinship terminology** (亲属称谓术语) in Chinese and English. We noted the remarkable difference between the two, that is, the Chinese kinship terminology is defined against five parameters (generation from ego, linearity/collaterality, gender, seniority/juniority, and paternal/maternal) and is therefore much more complicated than the English one, which involves only three parameters (generation from ego, linearity/

collaterality, and gender). This difference in terminological elaboration is really a reflection of the underlying cultural differences.

According to Haviland (1975, p. 97), the classification of kinship relations generally depends upon:

- how the family is structured,
- what relationships are considered close or distant, and
- sometimes what attitudes to the relationships may be.

We may examine the makeup of Chinese **kinship terminology** (亲属称谓术语) with reference to these three factors.

(1) Traditional Chinese families were nuclear or grand ones, and were in essence patriarchic, i.e. with men having all or most of the power and importance.

(2) The kernel relationship in traditional Chinese family is that between father and son; in most western countries, it is that between husband and wife (Jin, 1984, p. 209). Being a patriarchal society during most part of her history, China sets great store by the relative seniority and juniority among family members, because the father or the eldest male is recognized as the head of the family, and descent and kinship are traced through the male line. This very fact explains why the elder male relatives on the father's side or of one's own generation are lexically distinguished from the younger ones (e.g. 哥哥, 弟弟, 堂兄, 堂弟, 伯伯,叔叔). Besides, as male offsprings were the only legitimate inheritors to family fortune, there arose the necessity to differentiate carefully the paternal and maternal relatives (e.g. 祖父, 外祖父, 侄女, 外甥女).

(3) There are two interesting exceptions to the above-mentioned distinctions: the relative seniority of the husbands of one's father's sisters (姑父) and of the sisters of one's father's father (姑公) are not **lexicalized** (词汇化) in Chinese; neither are the children of one's father's sisters lexically distinguished from those of one's mother's brothers and sisters (both are known in Chinese as *biao* ["表"], or the relationship between the children or grandchildren of a brother and a sister or of sisters). These exceptions have behind them the simple reason that women in patriarchic China were placed in a rather insignificant position in the family structure. (In fact, even today girls are regarded by quite a lot of Chinese people as inferior to boys.) Girls married off were compared to "water poured out of the door" and were assumed to be irrelevant to the descent and prosperity of the family, hence the practice that their husbands and children were not so meticulously labeled as the spouses of the male members of the family and their children.

It is not difficult to perceive here how socio-cultural factors may bear on the degree of differentiation of a language's lexical systems.

Thus we have a two-stage, and perhaps more tenable view of **linguistic determinism** (语言决定论): *first* culture *determines* language, and *then* the language *influences* our view of reality.

The **Sapir-Whorf hypothesis** (萨丕尔-沃尔夫假说) seems to have been a particular source of stimulation for anthropologists. It is they who have investigated **cultural relativity** (文化相对性), and in so doing have shed much light on matters of semantico-lexical relativity (based on James, 1980, pp. 83–84). The two best-known areas of endeavor on the part of anthropologists are the studies of **color categories** (Berlin and Kay, 1969) and kinship terms, which we discussed earlier. The hypothesis is still lending inspirations to anyone who is keen on studying language or communication from the cultural perspective (See Kaplan, 1972).

4.3.2   Translation

A second area where contrastive lexicology has been playing an active role is that of translation. Here again cultural barriers to effective translation have been in the forefront, notably among Bible translators (Nida, 1964 and after; Wonderly, 1968). Wonderly's work, *Bible Translations for Popular Use*, e.g. includes a chapter devoted to lexical problems.

One of the cultural barriers to translation is the differences between **source** and **target languages** (源语) (目标语) in the degree of lexicalization of their culture-specific concepts and notions. To take the example of kinship terms again, the traditional Chinese notion that married daughters are "water poured out" led to the belief that the relationship between the children of brothers (堂房) is internal to the clan; while that between the children of a brother and a sister (姑表/舅表) and that between the children of sisters (姨表) are external to the clan. This belief in turn gave rise to the biologically irrational rule that the children of brothers, who bear the same family name, were forbidden to intermarry whereas the children of a brother and a sister and the children of sisters were allowed to intermarry, despite the fact that genetically members of the two groups are equally closely related to each other by blood: each of them has one fourths of his or her genes coming from the same ancestor. This irrational idea underlies the message conveyed in the following passage from 《红楼梦》 (*The Story of the Stone*), in which Aroma, Baoyu's maid, advises Baoyu's mother to move him out of the garden where Miss Lin (orphaned daughter of Baoyu's paternal aunt) and Miss Xue (daughter of Baoyu's maternal aunt, mistakenly translated as "Miss Bao") live, in case they commit some transgressions:

> 袭人连忙回道:"太太别多心, 并没有这话。这不过是我的小见识; 如今二爷也大了, 里头姑娘们也大了, 况且林姑娘宝姑娘又是两姨姑表姐妹, 虽说是姐妹们, 到底是男女之分, 日夜一处, 起坐不方便, 由不得叫人悬心。" (《红楼梦》)

> "Oh, no, Your Ladyship, please don't suspect that!" said Aroma hurriedly. "That wasn't my meaning at all. It's just that—if you'll allow me to say so—Master Bao and the young ladies are beginning to grow up now, and though they are all cousins, there is the difference of sex between them, which makes it very awkward sometimes when they are all living together, especially in the case of Miss Lin and Miss Bao, ***who aren't even of the same clan***. One can't help feeling uneasy ..." (David Hawkes, Trans. *The Story of the Stone*)

German **translation theorist** (翻译理论研究者) Wilss (1977) discusses problems of cultural and **linguistic relativity** (语言相对论) that accompany the rendition into an **L2** of "individual words that are characteristic of a certain speech-community." He lists such words as *esprit, patrie, charme, Sehensucht,* ("see-mania"), *Ostpolitik* ("East-politics"), etc. (James, 1980, p. 84).

If we examine the English and Chinese languages, we can likewise find many similar "**culture-loaded words** (文化负载词)." How do we translate into Chinese, for example, such typically English expressions as *privacy* ("隐私," "幽静生活," or "私密"?), "gentleman," and "fair play"?

We usually put "gentleman" into Chinese either as "绅士" or "君子," but neither of these two terms conveys the meaning of the original properly. In English, a gentleman is a man who behaves well towards others and who can be trusted to keep his promises and always act honestly. It is claimed that "a gentleman is, rather than does." It is also said that the true criterion for a gentleman is whether he is kind towards people who cannot possibly be of any service to him in any way. The following humorous story may illustrate this:

> Dick was seven years old, and his sister, Jane, was five. One day their mother took them to their aunt's house to play while she went to town to buy some clothes.
>
> The children played for an hour, and then at half past four their aunt took Dick into the kitchen. She gave him a nice cake and a knife and said to him, "Now here's a knife, Dick, cut the cake in half and give one of the pieces to your sister, but remember to do it like a *gentleman.*"
>
> "Like a gentleman?" Dick asked. "How does a *gentleman* do it?"
>
> "He always gives the bigger piece to the other person," answered his aunt at once.
>
> "Oh," said Dick. He thought about it for a few seconds. Then he took the cake to his sister and said to her, "Cut the cake in half, Jane."

In Chinese, a "绅士" was formerly an influential man in local areas. Its closest English equivalent might be "(country) gentry," which is however not a singular noun, but a collective term (cf. 土豪劣绅 "local despots and evil gentry").

The word "君子" was used to refer to an aristocrat or a man of high social position during the Western Zhou dynasty and the Spring and Autumn Period in Chinese history (11th–5th centuries BC). Later it came to mean a man of high moral standard in contradistinction to a mean or morally inferior person. While it is acceptable to turn the phrase "君子协定" into "*gentlemen's* agreement" and "君子之交淡如水" into "The friendship between *gentlemen* appears indifferent but is pure like water," it is flatly misleading or at least confusing to render the expression "君子和而不同" into English as "A *gentleman* (君子 in this context ≈ a man of integrity) gets along with others, but does not necessarily agree with them," or "君子之泽, 五世而斩" (*Mencius*) as "The power and influence of a *gentleman* (君子 in this context ≈ a lord) will not last longer than five generations," or the saying "君子坦荡荡, 小人长戚戚" (*The Analects of Confucius*) as "A *gentleman* (君子 in this context ≈ a noble-hearted man /a superior man) is always calm and contented, while an inferior man is full of anxieties."

As for the phrase "fair play" it is almost impossible to find a Chinese term which may adequately communicate its meaning (the act or fact of abiding by the rules in sports, games, or any other activity; fairness and honor in dealing with competitors).

It was perhaps because of this that Lu Xun (1881–1936), the renowned Chinese writer, chose to transliterate the phrase into Chinese as "费厄泼赖."

Lexical semantics (词汇语义学) is particularly important to **computational linguists** in their development of **machine translation** (**MT**) (机器翻译) systems. In 1954 the Georgetown University of the United States and the IBM jointly performed the first MT experiment (from Russian into English) in the world. Since then linguists, mathematicians, and computer scientists have worked on MT for more than sixty years, but with only limited success. The chief problem they have been faced with is that of meaning (语义). As we mentioned at the beginning of this chapter, meaning is related to **phonology** (音位系统), **grammar** (语法系统) and **textual structure** (语篇结构), but first and foremost, it is related to words and phrases (i.e. the **lexicon** (词库) of a language.

In the first stage of MT research (up to the late 1950s), **lexicon-based systems** were developed which rely heavily on **machine dictionaries**. These systems worked by converting source expressions into **target languages** (目标语表达方式) without much care about their **collocation** (搭配) or **selectional restrictions** (选择性限制) (See Sect. 4.2.3 "Semantic Features" for definition). So if a **source language** (源语) word corresponds to several words in the **target language** (目标语), the machine translation engine simply lists them all for the system operator to choose from. It is conceivable that systems of this architecture could only put out very low-quality target texts.

The second stage of MT research (from the 1960s onward) saw the emergence of **syntax-based systems**, which are superior to the first generation of systems in that they approach the source texts in a structural way. For instance, a special component part of the system would be assigned the task of analyzing polysemous words and selecting a suitable **target language** (目标语表达方式) by reference to the contextual relations it keeps in a sentence instead of just dishing out all the possibilities to the human operator.

In the 1970s, the third generation, **semantics-based**, MT systems began to be researched and developed. Systems of this type take into account the **semantic relations** (语义关系) between words and phrases not only within a sentence, but also across sentences (i.e. in the text), so they are able to turn out more intelligible texts. But the development of such systems depends heavily upon an in-depth study of the meanings of words and sentences. Since **semantics** (语义学) is as yet a difficult and problematic area of study in linguistics, the third generation of MT systems still have a long way to go in its development.

In all of the three generations of MT systems as reviewed above, the study and resolution of problems in **lexical meaning** (词汇意义) has been of pivotal importance. The problems dealt with and the procedures introduced in this chapter regarding the analysis of lexical meaning (**collocation** [搭配], **lexical fields** [词汇场], and the reduction of lexical meaning to a limited number of **semantic features** [语义特征]) have proved to be very useful to the computerized analysis of lexical meaning.

For instance, in **SYSTRAN** (a popular, fairly successful MT system first developed by the Latsec Corporation for the American Air Force in the late 1960s and early 1970s and later taken over by the European Community for further development in the late 1970s and early 1980s), lexico-semantic as well as grammatical information of the **lexemes** (词位) of the source and **target languages** (目标语) are fully analyzed, classified, and then incorporated into one bilingual word dictionary, one bilingual phrasal dictionary, and five sub-dictionaries derived from them (a dictionary of forms used with high frequency, a "Limited Semantics Dictionary" which contains **idioms** [成语] and **compound nouns** [复合名词], a "Conditional Limited Semantics Dictionary" which deals with **collocations** (搭配), and a main dictionary in which **roots** [词根] and **word endings** [词尾部分] are grouped separately). More than twenty semantic labels such as "AGRICULTURE," "AVIATION," "ELECTRIC," "CREATED," "ANALYSIS," etc. are attached to the lexical items in the system's machine dictionaries to specify the subject areas they fall into. In the second stage of its development by the European Community, the semantic labels were improved so that they may be more objective and general. The improved labels include: "DEV" (device, tool, instrument), "CONTR" (container), and "MATER" (materials used in production or operation) (Ke, 1995, pp. 50–51). It is not difficult to see that these labels are exactly names for some broadly distinguished **lexical fields** (词汇场) or **semantic features** (语义特征). They serve to specify the semantic information shared by relevant words and expressions in the languages concerned.

4.3.3 Bilingual Lexicography

Where there are **L2 learners** (二语学习者) and translators, there are **bilingual dictionaries** (双语词典). **Bilingual lexicography** (双语词典学) is the third area in which a practical concern for, if not a theoretical commitment to, contrastive lexicology has been maintained.

A question raised here is what an ideal **bilingual dictionary** (双语词典) should offer its users. Apparently an ideal bilingual dictionary should be based on a solid **CA** of the lexical systems of the two languages concerned and incorporate measures to forestall lexical mistakes that learners and users may commit in the other language. For instance, a "领导" in Chinese should be defined in a Chinese-English dictionary as an *official in charge*, a *leading official*, a *director/manager/superintendent*, or even a *boss* instead of simply a *leader*, because a "领导" in Chinese is rarely, if ever, equivalent to a *leader* in English.

Likewise, "论文" in English is either a *paper* (which refers to any one of the following two kinds of writing: [1] an *academic/scholarly paper*, i.e. a document published in academic journals or presented at academic conferences, containing original research results or reviewing existing research results, [2] a *term paper*, i.e. a lengthy essay a student is required to write on a topic drawn from the subject matter of a course of study) or a *thesis* (also called *dissertation*, which is a document submitted in support of a candidature for a degree or professional qualification, presenting the author's research and findings); or (when you want to use a cover term for all of them) a ***research paper***, which includes *academic paper*, *term paper*, and *thesis*. It is never simply a ***paper***.

Leech (1974, p. 202) draws a distinction between the practical dictionary or "reference-book on the living-room or library shelf" and the theoretical or "inbuilt" dictionary "which every one of us carries around as part of his mental equipment as a speaker of a language" and constitutes his "**semantic competence**." It is the task of lexical **CA**, therefore, to compare linguistic accounts, stated within the same lexicological framework, of the **lexical competence** necessarily possessed by speakers of the two languages concerned. This is a large-scale and arduous undertaking (James, 1980, p. 85). And yet a truly well-written **bilingual dictionary** (双语词典) should be based upon such an undertaking. Actually lexical **CA** to the purpose of providing a sound basis for **bilingual lexicography** (双语词典学) has continually been carried out in many countries, including China. But more work is needed before any truly ideal bilingual dictionary can be developed.

4.4 Questions for Discussion and Research

1. What are the two main divisions of **lexical CA**?
2. What's the difference between a **morpheme** and a **lexeme**?
3. There are very few **derivative affixes** (派生词缀) in the Chinese word stock. Can you identify some Chinese words containing **derivative affixes** and translate these words into English?
4. Is Modern Chinese more **morphologically motivated** than classical Chinese? If so, what do you think may be its cause?
5. Collect from commercial advertisements some foreign trade names and their Chinese translations. Contrast the original names with their Chinese translations and examine what tendency the Chinese names show in terms of **lexical motivation**.
6. Name a few familiar types of **syntagmatic** and **paradigmatic semantic relationships**.
7. Translate the following sentences into Chinese:

   > He *did hard labor* for three years.
   > He *did hard work* for three years.
   > She is *not a little* afraid of snakes.
   > She is *not a bit* afraid of snakes.
   > I have *seen him through*.
   > I have *seen through him*.
   > He is a *medicine man*.
   > He is a *medical man*.

8. What is a **lexical field**? How can we fill up a **lexical gap** in translation?
9. When specified in **semantic features**, *roast* and *bake* in English seem to mean the same thing (see Table 4.4).

Table 4.4 Semantic features of the lexemes in English and German lexical fields of COOKING

	C_1: with water	C_2: with fat	C_3: in oven	C_4: contact with flame	C_5: Gentle
cook$_3$	O	O	O	O	O
boil	+	−	−	+	−
simmer	+	−	−	+	+
fry	−	+	−	+	O
roast	−	−	+	−	O
toast/broil	−	−	−	+	O
bake	−	−	+	−	O
kochen$_1$	O	O	O	O	O
kochen$_2$	+	−	−	+	−
kochen$_3$	+	−	−	+	+
braten	−	O	O	O	O
rösten	−	−	−	+	O
backen	O	O	+	−	O

− with water
− with fat
+ in oven
− contact with flame
O gentle

Do these two words really mean the same thing in English? If not, what other features can we resort to in order to distinguish their meanings?

10. Dr. Eugene Nida, in a lecture delivered to the graduate students of English at Nanjing University, asserts that "**language facilitates thinking, but does not determine thinking.**" Do you agree to his view? Why or why not?

11. The word "君子" was used to refer to an aristocrat or a man of high social position during the Western Zhou dynasty and the Spring and Autumn Period in Chinese history (11th–5th centuries BC). Later it came to mean a man of high moral standard in contradistinction to a mean or morally inferior person. Comment on the English translations of the following Chinese expressions which contain the word "君子":

君子协定 gentlemen's agreement
君子之交淡如水。The friendship between gentlemen appears indifferent, but is pure like water.
君子和而不同。A gentleman gets along with others, but does not necessarily agree with them.
君子之泽, 五世而斩。(《孟子》) The power and influence of a gentleman will not last longer than five generations.
君子坦荡荡, 小人长戚戚。(《论语》) A gentleman is always calm and contented, while an inferior man is full of anxieties.

12. In Table 4.1, English nouns are observed to be much less morphologically motivated than either German or Chinese nouns. What may be the cause of such a discrepancy? Why is it that the English language, which belongs to the same language group (the Germanic group) as German, should be so markedly less motivated in its vocabulary as compared with the latter?

References

Berlin, B., & Kay, P. (1969). *Basic color terms: Their universality and evolution.* Berkeley, CA: University of California Press.

Bolinger, D., & Sears, D. A. (1981). *Aspects of language* (3rd ed.). New York, NY: Harcourt Brace Jovanovich.

Chen, W. [陈文伯]. (1982). 《英语成语和汉语成语》. 北京: 外语教学与研究出版社.

Crystal, D. (Ed.). (1987). *The Cambridge encyclopedia of language.* Cambridge, UK: Cambridge University Press.

Firth, J. R. (1957). *Papers in linguistics 1934–1951.* London, UK: Oxford University Press.

Haviland, W. (1975). *Cultural anthropology.* New York, NY: Holt.

Hickerson, Nancy. (1980). *Linguistic anthropology.* New York, NY: Holt.

James, C. (1980). *Contrastive analysis.* Harlow, UK: Longman Group UK Limited.

Jin, K. [金克木]. (1984). 《比较文化论集》. 北京: 三联书店.

Kaplan, R. (1972). *The anatomy of rhetoric: Prolegomena to a functional theory of rhetoric.* Philadelphia, PA: Center for Curriculum Development.

Ke, P. [柯平]. (1995). 欧美的机器翻译. 《中国翻译》, 1995年第2期, 47–54.

Ke, P. [柯平]. (1996). A socio-semiotic approach to meaning in translation. *Babel, 42*(2), 74–83.

Lander, H. J. (1960). Navaho color categories. *Language, 36,* 368–382.

Leech, G. (1974). *Semantics.* Harmondsworth, UK: Penguin Books.

Lehrer, A. (1969). Semantic cuisine. *JL, 5*(1), 39–55.

Lyons, J. (1968). *Introduction to theoretical linguistics.* Cambridge, UK: Cambridge University Press.

Moser, D. (1997, November). *The semantics of abstract nouns in English: What is lost in the translation into Chinese?* Paper presented at the International Symposium on Translation, Beijing.

Newmark, P. (1988). *A textbook of translation.* London, UK: Prentice Hall.

Nida, E. A. (1964). *Towards a science of translating.* Leiden, The Netherlands: E. J. Brill.

Ullmann, S. (1962, 1983). *Semantics. An introduction to the science of meaning.* Oxford, UK: Basil Blackwell.

Wonderly, W. L. (1968). *Bible translations for popular use.* London, UK: United Bible Societies.

Wilss, W. (1977). *Übersetzungswissenschaft: Probleme und Methoden.* Stuttgart, Germany: Klett.

Xu, Y. [许余龙]. (1992). 《对比语言学概论》. 上海: 上海外语教育出版社.

Chapter 5
Grammatical Contrastive Analysis

Grammatical **CA** is linked to lexical **CA** in that the same **grammatical meanings** (语法意义) may be conveyed by means of either **lexical devices** or **grammatical devices**. For example, while both Modern English and Chinese are quite "analytic" in structure in comparison with such Indo-European languages as German and Russian, Modern English is apparently much less so than Chinese since many of its **grammatical meanings** (语法意义) or **functions** (语法功能) are realized through **inflection** (屈折变化). **Tense** (时态), **voice** (语态), and **aspect** (体) are the most obvious ones. The following passage and its Chinese translation well illustrate this difference.

> Few *follow* the advice of Isabella Beeton, the guru of British cooks in the 19th century, who *decreed* in an early edition of her book that "a good meal, if enjoyed and digested, gives the support necessary for the morning's work."
>
> 十九世纪英国的烹饪大师伊莎贝拉 比顿曾在其著作的一个早期版本中说过: "受用一顿美餐, 能使整个上午工作精力充沛。"这番高见, 现在是很少有人领教了。

In this instance, the meanings of **tense** (时态) is expressed grammatically in English but lexically in Chinese. If the translator fails to notice the contrast in time between the words "follow" and "decreed" in the source text and thence fails to convey it in a lexical way by "adding" such words as "曾," "过," and "现在" in the target text, the meaning of the original would become vague or even skewed, resulting in awkward or confusing translations.

5.1 The Concept of Grammar

Before going into grammatical **CA**, we may stop for a moment to reconsider the notion of grammar. The term "**grammar**" (语法) has at least two quite distinct applications, yielding a specific sense and a general one. The specific sense is the more traditional one, referring to a description of the morphological structure of a language and the way in which linguistic units such as words and phrases are combined to produce sentences in the language. In this sense, grammar is presented

© Peking University Press and Springer Nature Singapore Pte Ltd. 2019
P. Ke, *Contrastive Linguistics*, Peking University Linguistics Research 1,
https://doi.org/10.1007/978-981-13-1385-1_5

as just one branch of the overall structure of language, distinct from **phonology** (音系学) and **semantics** (语义学) (Fig. 5.1).

The general sense of the term, as proposed by Noam Chomsky, covers all aspects of **sentence patterning** (句式形成) While introducing the term "**syntax** (句法)" as the more specific term for **grammar** (语法) in its traditional sense, Chomsky's framework of grammar includes **phonology** (音系学) and **semantics** (语义学) (based on Crystal, 1987, p. 88) (Fig. 5.2):

In this work we employ the term "**grammar** (语法)" basically in its specific sense, subsuming under it two branches: **morphology** (形态学, 词法) and **syntax** (句法).

Morphology (形态学, 词法), as we noted in the previous chapter, comprises two parts, i.e. **inflectional morphology** (屈折形态学) and **derivational morphology** (派生形态学). The essential difference between the two is that the former concerns morphological variations that result from grammatical needs while the latter concerns morphological variations as a means of **word-building** (构词). Since we have dealt with derivational morphology when we discussed lexical **CA** in the previous chapter, what remains for us to consider in this chapter is inflectional morphology and **syntax** (句法).

In classical European languages (**Greek** [希腊语] and **Latin** [拉丁语]), which are characterized by complex changes in word form, **inflectional morphology** (屈折形态学) is a very important part of the **grammar** (语法). With many modern languages (e.g. Modern English), in which **grammatical meanings** (语法意义) are conveyed chiefly through syntactic and lexical means, **syntax** (句法) is much more important than inflectional morphology.

In the following sections we shall first make a short account of **contrastive analysis** (对比分析) on the level of **inflectional morphology** (屈折形态学), and then undertake a more elaborate examination of syntactic **CA** from the vantage points of several major linguistic schools of the present day.

Fig. 5.1 "Grammar" in the framework of traditional linguistics

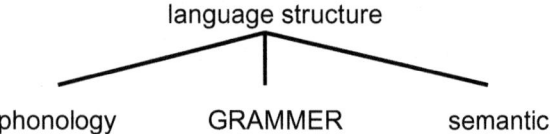

Fig. 5.2 "Grammar" in the framework of transformational grammar (TG)

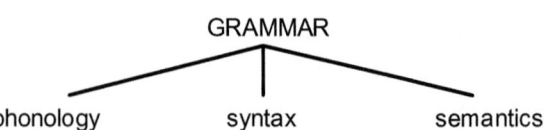

5.2   The Contrastive Analysis of Inflectional Morphology

We may make a distinction between two facets of a morphological variation, i.e. its form and its function. The American linguist Charles Hockett (1916–2000) (1954) proposes three theoretical models for grammatical analysis:

(1) **Item-and-process (IP)**, which stresses the process of variation and is hence regarded as a sort of generative model.
(2) **Item-and-arrangement (IA)**, which best suits the analysis of agglutinating languages (粘着语), whose word-forms may be easily analyzed into a group of **morphemes** (语素).
(3) **Word-and-paradigm (WP)**, which applies most successfully in the analysis of inflectional languages, whose word-forms may not be so easily analyzed into a group of morphemes (Xu, 1992, pp. 162–164).

Formal contrasts of morphological variations may be carried out by employing any appropriate one of these three models. For example, the word "took" (/tʊk/) may be analyzed either on the basis of an IP model as:

1) /tʊk/ = /teɪk/ + (/eɪ/→/ʊ/), which is to be read as: "/tʊk/consists of the present tense form /teɪk/with the medial diphthong /eɪ/replaced by the vowel /ʊ/."

or on the basis of an IA model as:

2) /tʊk/ = /t-k/ + /-ʊ-/, which is to be read as "/tʊk/consists of the discontinuous root /t-k/with /ʊ/inserted to mark past tense."

In the English language, there are eight **inflectional morphemes** (屈折语素). Two are related to **nouns**

(1) the plural number (e.g. *books*) and
(2) "possessive" (genitive) case (e.g. *John's*);

four to **verbs** to mark:

(3) the third person singular (e.g. *shows*),
(4) the past tense (e.g. *showed*),
(5) the present participle (e.g. *showing*), and
(6) the past participle (e.g. *shown*);

and two to **adjectives** to show:

(7) the comparative (e.g. *higher*), and
(8) superlative degrees (e.g. *highest*).

Pronouns, the most heavily inflected parts of speech in English, have different **lexical forms** (not **inflectional morphemes**) to mark distinctions in case:

(1) nominative case (*I*, *we*, *you*, *he*, *she*),
(2) objective case (*me*, *us*, *you*, *him*, *her*), and
(3) possessive case (*my*, *our*, *yours*, *his*, *hers*).

As we can see from the examples cited above, the function of **inflectional morphemes** (屈折语素) is not to transmit **referential meaning** (指称意义), but to convey grammatical information.

Given this fact, **contrastive analysis** (对比分析) on the level of **inflectional morphology** (屈折形态学) is largely a matter of contrasting the morphological and lexical devices different languages employ to transmit **grammatical meanings** (语法意义). These morphological and lexical devices are usually known as "**grammatical categories**" (语法范畴).

5.2.1   Grammatical Categories

In most general terms, we may define **grammatical categories** (语法范畴) as classes or groups of items (including **morphemes** [语素] and lexical items) which fulfill the same or similar **grammatical functions** (语法功能) in a particular language.

In **inflectional languages** (屈折语), such as **Latin** (拉丁语), **Greek** (希腊语), German, French and, to a lesser degree, English, grammatical categories are sometimes also known as **inflectional categories** (屈折范畴).

Familiar grammatical categories or contrasts include *aspect*, *case*, *gender*, *mood*, *number*, *person*, *tense*, and *voice*, which will be considered one by one in the following.

5.2.1.1   Aspect

Aspect (体) indicates how the event described by a verb is viewed, such as whether the action happens once or repeatedly, is completed or still continuing. A typical formal contrast is made between the **perfect(ive)** (完成体) and the **imperfect(ive)** (未完成体) (or "**progressive aspect** [进行体]," as is known in English), e.g.

She *sang*. [action happening once]
She *sings* [action happening repeatedly (e.g. as a job)]
She *has sung*. [action completed]
She's singing. [action continuing]

Chinese has a developed **aspect** (体) system. Like English, it distinguishes the **perfect(ive)** (完成体) from the **progressive aspect** (进行体)":

他理发去了。
He's gone to have his hair cut. [**present perfective aspect**]

他上星期理的发。
He had his hair cut last week. [**past perfective aspect**]

你去理理发吧。理了发就凉快了。
Have a haircut and you'll feel cool. [**future perfective aspect**]

他在理着发。
He's having his hair cut. [**present progressive aspect**]

我进去的时候，他在理着发呢。
He was having his hair cut when I went in. [**past progressive aspect**]

Apart from the perfective and the progressive aspects, the Chinese language has three more aspects that are not known in English:

(1) **Experiencing aspect** (经历体), which, through the attachment of the auxiliary "过" to the verb, indicates that the event or change used to occur, without regard for its outcome, e.g.

你做过什么工作?
What jobs have you done?

(2) **Trial aspect** (尝试体), which expresses the notion of trial by reduplicating the verb or by attaching the auxiliary "– 看 (看)" to the verb, e.g.

这事我们研究研究。
We'll give it our consideration.

这鞋你穿穿看。
You may try this shoe on.

(3) **"One-time" aspect** (一次体), which, by duplicating the verb, shows the briefness or short duration of the action, e.g.

你查一查词典。
Look it up in a dictionary.

他查了查词典。
He looked it up in a dictionary.

5.2.1.2   Case

Case (格) shows the **grammatical functions** (语法功能) of a noun or noun phrase (agency, possession, naming, location, motion towards or from, etc.) in a sentence. Typical formal contrasts in European languages are between:

(1) the **nominative** (主格), which marks a noun or noun phrase as the subject of the verb, and which is known in English as the "**subjective case**" (主格);

(2) the **accusative** (宾格), which marks a noun or noun phrase as the direct object of the verb; for example, in the German sentence *Ursula kaufte einen neuen Tisch* "Ursula bought a new table," the article *ein* and the adjective *neu* in the noun phrase *einen neuen Tisch* have the inflectional ending *-en* to show that the noun phrase is in the accusative case because it is the direct object of the verb;

(3) the **dative** (与格), which marks a noun or noun phrase as the indirect object of the verb; for example, in the German sentence *Sie gab der Katze eine Schale Milch* "She gave the cat a dish (of) milk," the article in the noun phrase *der Katze* has the inflectional ending *-er* to show that the noun phrase is in the dative case because it is the indirect object of the verb (in English, the accusative and the dative are "leveled" under one heading—the **"objective,"** which marks pronouns only);

(4) the **genitive** (属格), which marks a noun or noun phrase as in a possessive relation with another noun or noun phrase; for example, in the German sentence *Dort drüben ist das Haus des Bürgermeisters* "Over there is the house of the mayor /mayor's house," the article and the noun in the noun phrase *des Bürgermeisters* has the inflectional ending *-es* and *-s* respectively to show that they are in the genitive case because they refer to the owner of *das Haus* (in English, the case is called the **"possessive** [所有格]");

(5) the **vocative** (呼格), which marks a noun or noun phrase as being addressed, e.g. "Really *dear*, do you think so?," "*Mr Gates*, listen to me";

(6) the **ablative** (离格, 夺格), which marks a noun or noun phrase as being removed or directed from some place or deprived of something, or indicating source, cause, agency, etc. It is the form of a noun, pronoun, or adjective that you use in some languages when you are talking about who something is done *by*, what something is done *with*, or where something comes *from* (expressed by "by", "with", or "from" in English) (In classical **Latin** [拉丁语], this case is a mingling of the original **ablative**, **instrumental** [工具格] and most of the **locative cases** [方位格] in **Proto-Indo-European** [原始印欧语])

5.2.1.3 Gender

Gender (性), in some languages, is a grammatical distinction in which words such as nouns, articles, adjectives, and pronouns are marked according to a distinction between **masculine** (阳性), **feminine**, and sometimes **neuter** (中性).

The French sentence *Je suis arrivée*, for example, tells us that a woman is speaking apart from the information that she arrived either just now or sometime ago (Cf. *Je suis arrivé*).

5.2.1.4 Mood

Mood (语气) expresses the speaker's or writer's attitude to what is said or written. Typical contrasts are made between the **indicative** (直陈语气) (indicating factuality), the **subjunctive** (虚拟语气) (indicating possibility or uncertainty, its use now being restricted to formulaic phrases or very formal situations), and the **imperative** (祈使语气) (expressing a command or exhortation).

5.2.1.5 Number

Number (数) distinguishes nouns, verbs, adjectives, etc. according to whether they are **singular** or **plural**, and **countable** or **uncountable**.

In Chinese, for example, we may always say "一个面包," but in English one has to say *a loaf of bread* because "bread" is uncountable in the language. According to Lin Yutang (林语堂) (1982, p. 109), the distinction between number and quantity is not made in the Chinese notions of "多" and "少." Thus, one can say in Chinese "僧多粥少," disregarding the fact that monks can be counted while congee cannot. In English, however, one has to say *Many monks, little congee* instead of **More monks, less congee* or **There are more monks than congee.*

5.2.1.6 Person

Person (人称) marks pronouns and, in most languages, corresponding verb forms, according to whether the pronoun represents or includes the person or persons actually speaking or writing ("**first person**"), whether the pronoun represents or includes the person or persons being addressed ("**second person**"), and whether the pronoun represents someone or something other than the speaker/writer or the listener/reader ("**third person**").

5.2.1.7 Tense

Tense (时态) indicates the relationship between the form of a verb and the time of the action or state it describes. Typical contrasts are made between the **present**, the **past (preterite)**, and the **future**.

One thing that distinguishes Chinese verbs from English ones is that English verbs **conjugate** (变位) (i.e. to vary the form of a verb, by which are identified the **voice** [语态], **mood** [语气], **tense** [时态], **number** [数], and **person** [人称]) to mark different tenses whereas Chinese verbs, having no **conjugations** whatsoever, depend upon adverbs and auxiliaries to mark the tense, as we illustrated with the example at the beginning of this chapter.

5.2.1.8 Voice

Voice (语态) expresses the relationship between a verb and the noun phrase(s) which are associated with it. Typical contrasts are made between the **active**, the **passive**, the **middle (reflexive)** (反身语态) (a form of the verb by which its subject is represented as both the agent (doer) and the recipient (object) of the action, that is, as performing some act to or upon oneself, or for one's own advantage, e.g. the classical **Greek** (希腊语) *didaskomai* "I get myself taught"), and the **causative** (使

役语态) (e.g. in Malay: *Dia menjatuhkan gelas itu*, literally, "He cause to fall glass the"—"He dropped the glass").

5.2.2 A Contrastive Study of the Chinese and English Case Systems

In this subsection we shall make a short contrastive study of the Chinese and English **case** (格) systems, with a focus on how the Chinese language employs various devices to mark cases.

As noted above, **case** (格) is a grammatical category that shows the **grammatical function** (语法功能) of a noun or noun phrase (agency, possession, naming, location, motion towards or from, etc.) in a sentence. In most European languages, the form of a noun or noun phrase may change by **inflection** (屈折变化), i.e. to "**decline**" (变格) (to inflect a noun, a pronoun, or an adjective for **number** [数] and **case** [格]), to mark different cases, as what occurs with pronouns (the most heavily inflected parts of speech in English) in Modern English (subjective, objective, and possessive cases: *he*, *him*, *his*, etc.).

However, the notion of **case** (格) is a universal one; other devices must exist in non-European languages to mark this grammatical category. Most linguists studying the Chinese language identify two such devices in Chinese, that is, **word order** (e.g. "狗咬汤姆" vs. "汤姆咬狗") and **prepositions marking various locative cases** (方位格) (e.g. "他们从山下往山头爬").

Starosta (1985; as cited in Xu, 1992), in his model of analysis known as "**Lexicase Grammar**," adds three more, two of which—[**+position**] **nouns as the subject or object of some verbs related to place or time, or as the object of place or time of some prepositions** (e.g. "到处 [+nominative, +place] 都是烟", and "快到开会的时候 [+objective, +time] 了") and **inflectional suffix** (屈折后缀) —may be regarded as plausible additions.

So there are at least four devices to mark case in **Modern Chinese** (现代汉语). These four devices are also employed in English to perform the same **grammatical functions** (语法功能), but there are differences in their usage:

(1) **Word order**, which determines if a noun or noun phrase is in the nominative (**subjective**) **case** (主格) or the **objective case** (宾格). In **nominative languages** (主格语言) (languages such as Russian and English, in which the object of the transitive verb is marked for **case** (格) while the subject of the transitive or intransitive verb is not; the opposite being **ergative languages** [作格语言] (e.g. **Eskimo** [爱斯基摩语] and **Basque** [巴斯克语], wherein the subject of the transitive verb is marked for case while the object of the transitive verb and the subject of the intransitive verb is not), the **nominative case** (主格) and the **objective case** (宾格) largely coincide with the subject and the object in **traditional grammar** (传统语法). Hence the identity of a noun or noun phrase in terms of the nominative and objective cases is basically

determined by its identity as the grammatical subject or object in the clause. Compare:

The dog bit Tommy.
Tommy bit the dog.

Grammatical subjects and objects are relatively easier to identify in English than in Chinese. Starosta holds that in a Chinese clause, the **grammatical subject** is the unmarked noun immediately before the verb while the **grammatical object** is the unmarked noun immediately succeeding the verb. By "**unmarked**" is meant that the noun cannot be the subject or object for pragmatic, stylistic, lexical, or grammatical reasons. For example,

1) 我肉吃,鱼不吃。

   I eat meat, but not fish.
2) 我们下午就动身。

   We shall set off this very afternoon.
3) 他在学校工作。

   He works at a school.

In 1) "肉" and "鱼" cannot be the subject of the verb "吃" because they are both proposed to be the topic of the clause and hence pragmatically marked. In 2) "下午" cannot be the subject of the verb "动身" since it acts as the temporal adverb of the verb and is grammatically marked. And in 3) "学校" cannot be the subject of the verb "工 作" because it forms a locative adverbial together with the preposition "在" that precedes it and is therefore lexically marked.

(2) **Preposition.** As a device to mark various **locative cases** (方位格), prepositions are much more frequently used in English, e.g. *in the room*, *by the window*, *at the conference*, etc. In the Chinese language, prepositions (named "**paraverbs**" or "**coverbs**" by some linguists for their **semantic relationship** (语义关系) to verbs) are used to indicate location, direction, target, etc. In the following sentence

他们从山下往山头爬。
They are climbing from the foot of the hill to the top.

the prepositional phrase "从山下" expresses the starting location of the action while the prepositional phrase "往山头" the target location of the action.

(3) **[+position] noun.** Governed by the verb or preposition, this special category of nouns are used as case markers in the Chinese language. They usually serve as the subject or object of some verbs related to place or time, or as the object of place or time of some prepositions, e.g.

到处 [**+nominative, +place**] 都是烟 。
There's smoke everywhere.

墙上 [**+nominative, +place**] 挂着一幅画。
There is a picture on the wall.

昨天 [**+nominative, +time**] 是国庆节。
It was the National Day yesterday.

三个月 [**+nominative, +time**] 没下雨了。
It hasn't rained for three months.

他们已经到了檀香山 [**+objective, +place**]。
They have arrived at Honolulu.

他们在水里 [**+objective, +place**] 扔球。
They are throwing balls (at each other) in the water.

快到开会的时候 [**+objective, +time**] 了。
It's about time for the meeting.

他到现在 [**+objective, +time**] 还没有回来。
He is still not back yet.

The relationship of place as marked by some of these [**+position**] **nouns** in Chinese have to be expressed by means of prepositions in English, e.g. 城外 "outside the city," 空中 "in the sky."

(4) **inflectional suffix** (屈折后缀) In Starosta's view, there are two types of **suffix** (后缀) in Chinese:

(a) **derivative suffixes** (派生后缀) such as -前 "before, preceding" (e.g. 日前 "a few days ago," 战前 "prewar"), -头 (used with a nominal or attributive **root** [词根], or after a [+position] noun) (e.g. 骨头 "bone," 苦头 "suffering," 里头 "inside; interior"), and -边 (used with a [+position] noun) (e.g. 东边 "in the east, 这边 "here").

(b) **inflectional suffixes** (屈折后缀): **inessive** (内中格) (designating, being in, or pertaining to a case [esp. in Finnish] indicating location or position in or within) suffix -里 "in; inside" (e.g. 心里 "in the heart," 村里 "in the village") and **sublative** (表面接触格) (expressing the destination of the movement: to the surface of something [e.g. *sit down on the ground*], towards the bottomsides or the area under an object, etc.) suffix -上 "above; on" (e.g. 墙上 "on the wall," 事实上 "in fact," 小镇上 "in the small town"), both of which being pronounced with a light **tone** (声调).

In Chinese, the chief distinction between a **derivative suffix** (派生后缀) and an **inflectional one** (屈折后缀) is that the latter is much more productive and explicit in meaning than the former. Compare: 城里 (chéng**lǐ**, < 城 + derivational suffix 里), which means some part of the city, especially the downtown area, and 城里 (chéng**li**, < 城 + inflectional suffix 里), which means "in the city."

Thus we see that as a means of marking the **case** (格), **inflection** (屈折变化) is used in Chinese basically *to indicate the location of a noun*. This is quite different from the situation in English, where case-marking inflections occur only with personal pronouns and mainly serve *to distinguish the subjective, objective, and possessive cases*, e.g. *he/him/his* (Xu, 1992, pp. 192–197).

5.3   Syntactic Contrastive Analysis

Syntax (句法) is the way in which words are arranged to show relationships of meaning within a sentence (and sometimes between sentences). The term comes from *syntaxis*, the **Greek** (希腊语) word for "arrangement" (Crystal, 1987, p. 94).

Classical European languages (e.g. **Greek** [希腊语] and **Latin** [拉丁语]) are characterized by complicated changes in word forms, so **inflectional morphology** (屈折形态学) is quite important in their **grammars** (语法). Most modern languages, however, resort to **word order** and function words for the expression of **grammatical meanings** (语法意义), so they set great store by **syntax** (句法).

Most syntactic studies have been focused on sentence structure, for this is where the most important grammatical relationships are expressed.

In contemporary studies on **syntax** (句法), three major approaches to **CA** are worthy of special attention; these are the **Structural approach** (结构主义路径), the **Transformational Grammarian (TG) approach** (转换语法路径), and the **Case Grammarian approach** (格语法路径), the latter two being known collectively as the **generative approach** (生成语言学路径) in combination with a few other approaches.

Contrastive analysis (对比分析) based upon the structural approach is **surface structure-oriented** (面向表层结构的) while contrastive analysis based upon the generative approaches is **deep structure-oriented** (面向深层结构的).

5.3.1   The Structural Approach (Surface-Structure Contrasts)

Structuralists elaborated on **contrastive analysis** (对比分析), so early studies on syntactic **CA** were mainly based upon the structural model. The earlier volumes of the University of Chicago Contrastive Analysis Series (edited by Ferguson), were based on the structural model. It is the model expounded by Leonard Bloomfield (1887–1949) (1933) and elaborated by Harris (1909–1992) (1963). In fact Harris himself, in an article entitled "Transfer Grammar" (1954), claimed that the model could be used for comparative purposes: "The method outlined here enables us to measure the difference in grammatical structure and to establish what is the maximum difference (or the maximum similarity) between any two language systems."

The analytic technique developed by the structuralists is known as **Immediate Constituent (IC) analysis** (直接成分分析法). The claim is that any grammatical construction which is not "simple" (that is, which does not consist of only one element) can be reduced to pairs of constituents: so a construction like *disgraceful* is analyzed into *disgrace + ful*, while the seemingly identical *ungraceful* reduces to *un + graceful*. In other words, given a construction made up of the parts ABC, it will be analyzable as either AB + C or A + BC. The same procedure applies to larger constructions: thus while *nice old woman* splits into *nice + old woman* (A + BC), *very old woman* has the IC: *very old + woman* (AB + C). The sentence

David is the nicest student who speaks Chinese.

breaks down into the Subject (*David*) and the Predicate (*is the nicest student who speaks Chinese*). The predicate may be further analyzed into two constituents: *is* and *the nicest student who speaks Chinese*, the latter being composed of two constituents: *the nicest student*, and the dependent clause *who speaks Chinese*. The dependent clause is likewise constituted of the Subject (*who*) and the Predicate (*speaks Chinese*). We are then left with the **subject complement** of the main clause—*the nicest student*, which is an ABC construction having the two ICs *the* and *nicest student*. And finally *nicest student* has the two ICs: *nicest* and *student*. The complete analysis of the sentence may be shown in the following IC branching diagram (Fig. 5.3).

In the diagram each horizontal line demarcates a construction, while each pair of vertical lines indicates the two ICs of that construction.

In such an analysis no reference is made to the meaning of a construction or its putative ICs. The whole process of analysis hinges on the notion of **distribution** (分布) or what naturally "goes with" what. For example, the phrase *light house keeper* is capable of two analyses (AB + C or A + BC) and the decision as to which analysis is appropriate is determined by what goes with what, that is, whether we are talking of marine navigation or about domestic help. Take the Hollywood blockbuster *Titanic* for example. The movie tells the tragic story of the great cruiser *Titanic*, which struck an iceberg and sank on her maiden voyage. But if the sea-lane or channel had been well marked with light houses which were kept by competent *light house keepers*, and the ocean liner had followed it, it probably would not have struck the iceberg and sunken. On the other hand, Rose the heroine might have been

Fig. 5.3 The immediate constituent (IC) analysis of a sentence

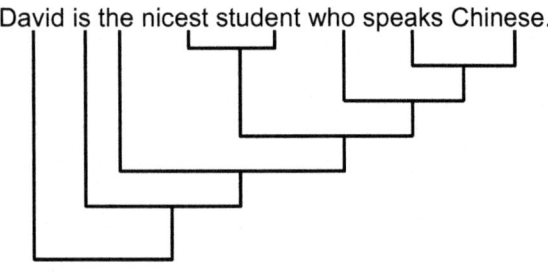

Fig. 5.4 The principle of omissibility in IC analysis

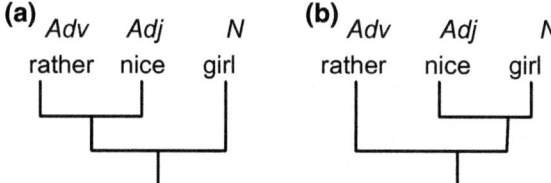

a more pious girl and suggested to her mother that they find some *light house keeper* to help with housekeeping.

Another notion that is used in IC analysis is **omissibility**. The decision for *rather nice girl*, e.g. is made on the basis of **omissibility**: if I omit *nice*, I am left with the **non-construction** *rather girl*, whereas omission of *rather* leaves the grammatical *nice girl*. In other words, the fact that *Adj + NP is* a construction while *Adv + NP is* a non-construction in English suggests that such phrases should be analyzed as (a), instead of as (b) (Fig. 5.4).

This type of analysis is two-dimensional; it presupposes that language is structured on two axes, a horizontal one delineating construction-types, and a vertical one defining sets of possible fillers (ICs) for each position in the construction: the **syntagmatic** (横组合的) and **paradigmatic** (纵聚合的) axes respectively (Lyons, 1968, p. 70). Take the following sentence:

He gave her a lovely *x* yesterday.

The *x* is not specified, but we know that since it is in the environment following a **determiner** (限定词) (*a*) and an adjective (*lovely*), it is going to be a noun. We don't know which noun—no reference is made to meaning—but we can propose a list or "paradigm" which might include *present, watch, dress*, etc. If the adverb were *for her birthday*, we could shorten the list even further by excluding such words as *shock* or *fright*. The principle of **syntagmatic** (横组合的) and **paradigmatic** (纵聚合的) determination of linguistic choices is of course exploited in **L2 teaching** (二语教学) through the substitution table as exemplified in *English 900*, a broadcast English coursebook used by the Voice of America in the 1970s and 1980s.

Fries (1952), when writing an account of English sentence structure, defines **grammar** (语法) in a truly structuralist vein as **"the devices of form and arrangement."** "Arrangement" refers to the relative order of elements in constructions; **formal devices** operating at the level of grammar are of four kinds:

(1) **morphological markers**, such as -*keit* and -*ness* in the words *Sauberkeit* and *cleanliness,* marking these as nouns;
(2) **function words**, such as articles, conjunctions, prepositions, which signal what classes of elements are likely to precede or follow;
(3) **word order**, e.g.

She gave the cat a rat.
She gave the rat a cat.

(4) **suprasegmentals** (超音段; 超音段特征), phonological devices such as **stress** (重音) and **intonation** (语调), which indicate to the hearer whether an utterance (for definition, see Sect. 1.3 "The History and Development of Contrastive Linguistics") is a question or statement, a word is a verb or noun (cf. `conduct: con`duct), or whether a Russian noun is genitive singular or nominative plural (cf. *d`oma: dom`a*, "of house": "houses").

To conduct a **contrastive analysis** (对比分析) on the structural model, we examine how the two languages being contrasted employ these four devices. Usually languages show preferences for the use of some formal devices rather than others—hence the distinction between the so-called "**analytic** (具分析语特征)" and "**synthetic** (具综合语特征)" **languages**.

Also, we are likely to discover that **L1** expresses a certain meaning by one device, while **L2** conveys the same meaning by another device. Thus English uses function words called "articles" (*the* and *a*) to signal the contrast between definite reference and indefinite reference while Russian, like Chinese (cf. Sect. 1.1 "What is Contrastive Linguistics?"), achieves the same contrast through **word order**:

A woman came out of the house: Iz domu viøla *zhenshina.*
The woman came out of the house: *Zhenshina* viøla iz domu.

As we can find here, in Russian, indefinite subject nouns are placed at the end of a sentence while definite ones in the initial position.

5.3.2   The Weaknesses of the Structural Approach

The structural approach to **CA** or studies of language has certain major weaknesses. Consider the following:

1) She is a *beautiful* dancer.
2) The *clever* boy missed the prize.

3) John is *easy* to please.
4) John is *eager* to please.

Each of 1) and 2) contains an ambiguity which is not, unlike that in *light house keeper*, resolvable by drawing an IC boundary, because the notion of "**distribution**" (分布) (i.e. what naturally "goes with" what) does not really help to eliminate the ambiguity:

1) She is a *beautiful* dancer.
   Ambiguity: Is she a *beautiful* girl to behold, or is she an ugly girl perhaps, who nevertheless dances beautifully? Both cases are possible.
2) The *clever* boy missed the prize.
   Ambiguity: Did the boy miss the prize because he was (too) "clever" (that is, his cleverness played a part in his missing it—he might have been, so to speak, "too clever by half," i.e. he perhaps played some trick, attempting to use foul play to get what he wanted, was discovered and fouled out), or was the event merely incidental? In other words, does 2) relate to 2a) or 2b)?

2a) The boy who was clever missed the prize.
2b) The boy, who was clever, missed the prize.

In 2a) we have a restrictive relative clause, in 2b) a non-restrictive clause: no redrawing of IC boundaries in (2) can tell the reader which type of clause—2a) or 2b)—the adjective *clever* before *boy* is related to. So the IC analysis simply does not work here.

In 3) and 4), we have two sentences, each containing an adjective. But the two adjectives are related to different notional subjects. It seems that the selection of either one affects the rest of the sentence grammatically, as the following paraphrases show:

3) John is easy to please = It is easy to please John.

but

4) John is eager to please ≠ *It is eager to please John.

These pairs of sentences show that *identity of position or "**distribution**"* (分布) is no guarantee of identity of function: in 3), *John* stands in an **Object-Verb** relation to *please*; in (4) *John* is in a **Subject-Verb** relation to *please*.

Observations made on the basis of relative position of linguistic items in a sentence merely refer to the **surface structure** (表层结构) of the sentence; observations concerning the functional relations between constituents refer to the **deep structure** (深层结构) (Refer to Sect. 2.3.1 "Surface Structure" for the definitions of "the surface structure" and "the deep structure"). (Based on James, 1980, pp. 36–40) As we now can perceive, the structuralists confine themselves to observations about the surface structure. That very confinement is the root of their problems.

5.3.3 The Generative Approaches

Generative grammars (生成语法) (note the plural number of this term) attempt to define and describe by a set of rules all the grammatical sentences of a language and no ungrammatical ones. This type of **grammar** (语法) is said to **generate**, or produce, grammatical sentences.

There are two categories of **generative grammars** (生成语法), i.e. the **syntax-based Transformational Grammar** (**TG**) or **Transformational-Generative Grammar** (转换生成语法), and the **semantics-based Generative Semantics** (生成语义学), **Case Grammar** (格语法), and **Relational Grammar** (关系语法).

In this section we shall consider **contrastive analysis** (对比分析) conducted on the models of Transformational Grammar and Case Grammar.

5.3.3.1 The Transformational Grammarian Approach (for Deep-Structure Contrasts)

(**Generative**) **Transformational Grammar** (生成转换语法) or **TG** is the most important and influential generative grammar of our times.

As we noted at the beginning of this chapter, **Transformational Grammar** (转换语法) applies the term "**grammar** (语法)" in its broadest sense, assigning to it all aspects of **sentence patterning** (句式形成), including not only **syntax** (句法) but **phonology** (音系学) and **semantics** (语义学) as well.

Grammar (语法) is defined in TG as a mechanism that generates *all and only* grammatical sentences of a language. By "**mechanism**" is meant a set of rules. By "**generate**" is meant the *specification* of the grammaticality of an unlimited number of sentences of a language and the accurate *description* of the internal structure of these sentences (Xu, 1992, p. 179).

Chomsky has been changing his theory over the years.

In the second phase of TG, which is represented by *Aspects of the Theory of Syntax* (1965) and is the most well-known version of TG (the so-called "Standard Theory"), **grammar** (语法) is a tripartition of **syntax, semantics**, and **phonology**.

(1) The **syntactic part** is composed of two components:

(a) The **Base Component**, which includes **Phrase Structure Rules** (also known as "Rewrite Rules") and **Lexicon** (词库), produces ("generates") basic syntactic structures called "**deep structures**" (深层结构). **Phrase Structure Rules** (短语结构规则) (or **Rewrite Rules**), are a set of main rules for analyzing or expanding syntactic constructions into their constituent parts. For example, the rule

- S → NP + AUX + VP

means that a sentence (S) can be analyzed into or rewritten as consisting of a noun phrase (NP), some auxiliary verbs or auxiliaries, and a verb phrase (VP). The rule

- VP → V (+ NP)

means that a verb phrase can be further rewritten as simply a verb or as a verb and a noun phrase.

The **Lexicon** (词库) provides two kinds of information:

(i) the form class or parts of speech of a word, e.g. *N* for nouns, *V* for verbs; and
(ii) the "**grammatical collocation** (语法搭配)" of a word, i.e. what grammatical constructions in which the word may be used, e.g. the English verb *sleep* cannot appear in a Verb-Object construction, i.e. it cannot have an object after it.

The simplified table below shows the **Phrase Structure Rules** (短语结构规则) and the **Lexicon** (词库) which are necessary for the formation of the basic syntactic structure ("**deep structure**" [深层结构]) of the sentence *The dog slept*.

Phrase Structure Rules	Lexicon
1. S → NP + AUX +VP	N → *dog*
2. NP → DET(erminer) +N(oun)	V → *sleep* (-object)
3. AUX → T(ense)	DET → *the*
4. T(ense) → PAST	
5. VP → V(erb)	

A diagram, called "**tree diagram**" (树形图), may be drawn to show how these **Phrase Structure Rules** (短语结构规则) are applied and how the words from the **Lexicon** (词库) are fitted in for a particular sentence (Fig. 5.5).

This simplified diagram shows the basic **deep structure** (深层结构) produced by the base component for the sentence *The dog slept*.

(b) The **Transformational Component**, which changes or "transforms" **deep structures** (深层结构) into "**surface structures**" (表层结构), i.e. actual sentences.

(2) The **semantic part** or component deals with the meaning of sentences. **Deep structures** (深层结构) get semantically represented through the operation of semantic rules.

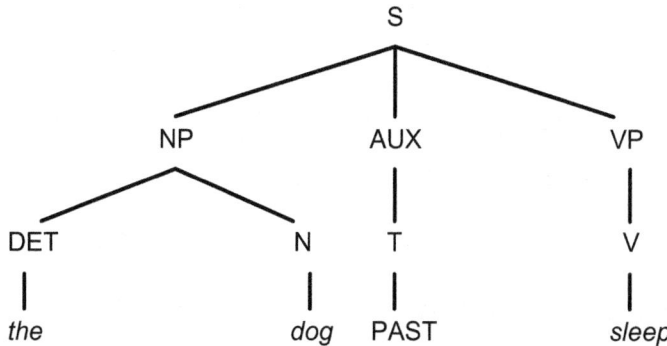

Fig. 5.5 The tree diagram of a sentence formed through the application of phrase structure rules and the selection of words from the Lexicon

(3) The **phonological part** or component gives sentences or **surface structures** (表层结构) a phonetic representation so that they can be pronounced.

Figure 5.6 is a diagram of the grammar.

Chomsky and others later modified the **Aspects Model** because they felt that not only the semantic component but also the transformational and phonological components had some effect on the semantic interpretation of a sentence. The new version of **Transformational Grammar** (转换语法) is known as the "**Extended Standard Theory.**"

As we may readily perceive, the most distinctive feature of TG is that it recognizes a level of **deep structure** (深层结构) and a level of **surface structure** (表层结构), the two being related to each other by a series of transformations. The

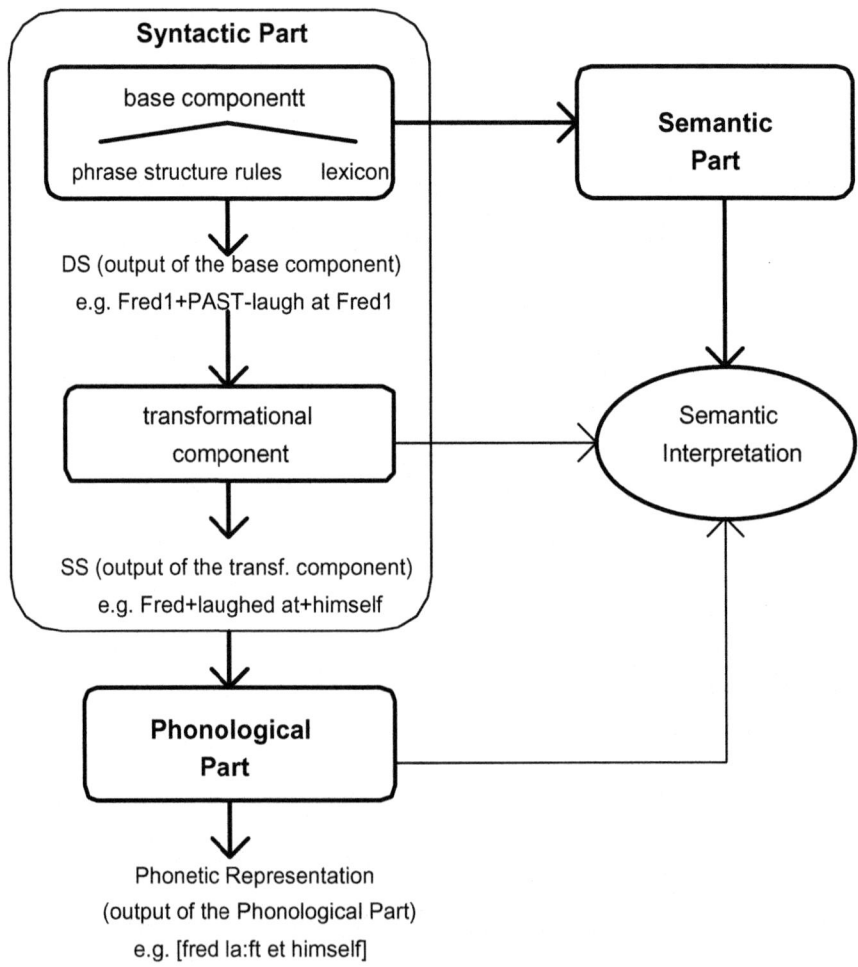

Fig. 5.6 The Standard/Aspect model of transformational grammar

syntactic part of the grammar is "**generative**," while the semantic part is "*interpretative*."

TG possesses some distinctive advantages which make it particularly attractive to **contrastive analysis** (对比分析) on the syntactic level:

(1) **Explicitness of its methodology.** One reason for using **Transformational Grammar** (转换语法) in **contrastive analysis** (对比分析) is the same as that for using it in unilingual description—its explicitness. For each step in deriving **surface structures** (表层结构) from the **deep structures** (深层结构), an explicit rule must be formulated. (Consider the description above of the **Phrase Structure Rules** [短语结构规则] and the **Lexicon** [词库] which are used to form the deep structure of the sentence *The dog slept*.)

(2) **Universality of its basic theoretical constructs** (理论构念). It has been claimed that:

(a) **Deep structures** (深层结构) are "universal" or common to all languages, so we are provided with a common point of departure for **contrastive analysis** (对比分析): the so-called **Universal Base Hypothesis** (see Sect. 5.3.3.2 "Case Grammarian Approach" for explanation);

(b) The **transformations** applied to **deep structures** (深层结构) are taken from a universal stock, which Noam Chomsky calls the "formal universals" (see Sect. 5.3.3.2 "Case Grammarian Approach" for definition), so we have a second criterion or "*tertium comparationis*" (比较参照物) for comparison. Some have gone so far as to claim that a **Transformational Grammar** (转换语法) is a *sine qua non* ("indispensable condition") for **contrastive analysis** (对比分析). For example, König (1970, p. 45) asserts: "Certain differences between English and German can only be observed if a transformational grammar is adopted as theoretical framework for one's statements." So far as the **ideational meaning** (概念意义) or **referential meaning** (指称意义) (the relationship between linguistic signs and the entities in the world which they refer to or describe) of the sentence is concerned, at least, this is a plausible claim.

For example, it is standard TG practice to derive attributive adjectives from predicative adjectives contained in relative clauses. (The relative clause itself is derived from an independent clause.) Three transformations are therefore involved in going from the **deep structure** (深层结构) (DS) to the **surface structure** (表层结构) (SS): (a) **RELATIVIZATION,** (b) **WHIZ-DELETION** and (c) **ADJECTIVE SHIFTING**:

```
DS   I have an apple +        The apple is red →
(a)  I have an apple          which is red →
(b)  I have an apple          red →
(c)  I have a red apple. SS
```

It is possible to postulate exactly the same input and transformational history for analogous German strings:

DS Ich habe einen Apfel.   Der Apfel ist rot →
a)   Ich habe einen Apfel,   der ["which"/ "the"] rot ist →
b)   Ich habe einen Apfel   rot →
c)   Ich habe einen roten Apfel. *SS*

The only differences are that the name we might give to the corresponding transformation b) in the German sentence is not **WHIZ-DELETION**, but perhaps "**DIST-DELETION**"; and in the final German string we must have a transformation to add the masculine accusative case ending *-en* to the attributivised adjective. The analogous French, Spanish or Welsh strings differ from the English and German ones in frequently dispensing with the adjective preposing (adjective shifting) transformation: attributives normally follow the modified noun in these languages: *le moulin rouge, la casa blanca, ty newydd*, etc., hence *J'ai une pomme rouge*. By the same token, those exceptional cases of Noun + Adj. order in English (*the president elect, the heir apparent, the only river navigable...*) can be catered for by dispensing with the adjective preposing rule.

(3) **Providing identical means for resolving syntactic ambiguities in different languages.** An added bonus of TG is that it provides the languages being contrasted with identical means for explaining in an explicit fashion the nature of sentential ambiguities. For example, attributive adjectives can be ambiguous: Chomsky's own example is *The industrious Chinese dominate the economy of South East Asia*. The subject NP is ambiguous in that it can refer either to *all the Chinese* or to just *those Chinese who are industrious*. The ambiguity is simply accounted for by deriving one reading from a **deep structure** (深层结构) with a restrictive relative clause, and the other from one containing a non-restrictive relative clause. The same technique is equally applicable to German:

The industrial Chinese:
The Chinese who are industrious.
The Chinese, who are industrious.

Die arbeitsamen Chinesen:
Die Chinesen, die arbeitsam sind.
Die Chinesen #, die arbeitsam sind.

[The number sign "#" is inserted to indicate the pause observed before spoken non-restrictives since in German it is an orthographic convention to place a comma after the antecedent NP irrespective of whether the clause is restrictive or not]

(4) **Providing a measure of the degree of difference between L1 and L2 constructions**. The TG approach provides the contrastive analyst with some means of measuring the degree of difference between compared constructions in **L1** and **L2**. We have suggested that the **deep structure** (深层结构) is common to all languages, and that languages differ most in their **surface structures** (表层结构). The degrees to which they differ is determined by *where*, in their

derivational histories, the compared constructions begin to diverge. The difference, therefore, between the structural and TG approach in **contrastive analysis** (对比分析) is that instead of looking for **surface-structural correspondence**, the latter looks for **correspondence between transformational rules** (James, 1980, pp. 42–45; author's emphasis).

5.3.3.2   The Case Grammarian Approach (for Deeper-Structure Contrasts)

With the development of **Transformational Grammar** (转换语法), many kinds of transformational rules came to be used, and the **grammar** (语法) became more and more complicated. There were controversies over the status of some of the transformational rules formulated by Noam Chomsky and his followers. And some linguists suspected that the "**deep structure**" (深层结构) was not deep enough. Since the 1960s, several semantics-based models for grammatical analysis have been developed with a view to tracing down to the syntactic structures deeper than that of the "deep structure." One of these fresh, alternative approaches was **Case Grammar** (格语法), which focuses on the semantic roles (or "**case** [格]") played by the elements of a sentence.

It has been proposed (Birnbaum, 1970) that there are two sorts of **deep structure** (深层结构): on the one hand there is what Birnbaum calls "**infrastructure**" which underlies the **surface structure** (表层结构) of a particular language and may be invoked to explain instances of ambiguity and **synonymy** (同义) between pairs of sentences in that language; the other deep structure is called "**profound structure**," and is assumed to be universal. The former, being language-specific, is more complex and diverse than the latter, which is simple in its basicness. The generally believed existence of the latter is the "**universal base hypothesis**," defined by Peters and Ritchie (1969, p. 150) as follows:

> There is a version of the theory of **Transformational Grammar** (转换语法) in which there is a fixed base grammar B which will serve as the base component of a grammar of any natural language.

If this is indeed the case, then this base will be an ideal starting-point for **contrastive analysis** (对比分析). As Di Pietro (1971, p. 3) says: "the assumption that there are universal constraints on language is basic to the implementation of contrastive analysis," since without it, contrastive analysis can be no more than a listing of language idiosyncrasies and a random itemization at best. The existence of some universal set of basic categories will allow the pairing of the respective idiosyncrasies of **L1** and **L2**, since they can be matched by reference to the same underlying category. (Based on James, 1980, pp. 54–55) Even the statement that there is nonoccurrence of a certain surface category in a given language—for example, saying that Chinese has no articles, as we discussed in Sect. 1.1.2 ("Classification")—is vacuous without the recognition of some deep category which is realized by different surface phenomena in different languages. In that specific case, as we exemplified, we need to specify what deep category or "notion" articles express in English and then inquire how the same category or notion is expressed in Chinese before we can make any meaningful statement about the condition of the use of articles in these two languages. The conclusion we could draw, as we found, was that the Chinese **word order** serves at least in part as a vehicle for the expression of the notion of definiteness.

The label "category" or "notion" as used in the above refers to what Di Pietro (1971) calls "**universal constraints**" and Chomsky calls "**language universals**" (语言普遍项). Chomsky distinguishes between the following two types of **language universals**:

(1) "**Formal" universals**, which refer to the type of rule that the **grammars** (语法) of all languages must have. To talk of formal universals is to claim, among other things, that all grammars employ transformations, which are ordered and may be cyclically applied. All languages, e.g. have devices for converting verbals or sentences into adjectives (cf. *singing kettle, kettle that sings*).

(2) "**Substantive" universals**, which are actual elements and constructions in languages. The substantive universals are seen as a common set of linguistic categories such as Noun, Verb, Noun Phrase, Subject, and so on.

As regards formal and substantive universals, it has been demonstrated that:

- all languages have sentences made of expressions of at least two kinds—**nominals** (a linguistic unit which has some but not all characteristics of a noun, e.g. *wounded* in *The wounded were taken by helicopter to hospital*) and **verbals** ([in TG] a word class including verbs and adjectives, e.g. *come* in *John has come*);
- all languages have **adjectival expressions** which modify nominals (e.g. *good* in *good food*) and **adverbial expressions** which modify verbals (e.g. *very* in *very good*); all languages have devices for converting some or all verbals into nominals (e.g. *shrinkage*);
- all languages have devices for the linking of nominals and verbals (e.g. *heaven and earth; sink and swim*);
- all languages have devices to **negativize** and **interrogativize** and turn some sentences into commands and propositions (e.g. *I'm not going, are you? Come on!*);
- all languages have at least two kinds of involvement of verbals with nominals (e.g. *The dog is sleeping; the cat has caught a mouse*); many languages have **dummy elements** as substitutes (e.g.—*John likes to travel.—So do I*); and
- many languages have devices that shift **agent-goal reference**: passives, causatives, etc. (*The mouse was caught*). (Based on Martin, 1964, pp. 354–355)

James (1980, p. 55) highlights the third type of **language universals** (语言普遍项):

(3) **Semantic universals. Semantic relations** (语义关系), i.e. the relationships between action and agent, between action and recipient, between action and result, etc., are universal in all human languages. According to Chomsky (1965, p. 28), the theory of semantic universals "… might assert that each language will contain terms that designate persons or lexical items referring to certain specific kinds of *objects, feelings, behavior*, and so on." The linguist credited

with having developed the theory of a universal semantic base of languages is Fillmore, and his model is known as **Case Grammar** (格语法) (Fillmore, 1968). Case grammar aimed to describe the ubiquitous semantic relationships in languages. Significantly, the most substantial monograph on **contrastive analysis** (对比分析) since Lado's *Linguistics Across Cultures*—Di Pietro's *Language Structures in Contrast* (1971)—adopts Fillmore's framework.

The "**Case Grammar** (格语法)" approach proposes that the "profound" deep structure of any sentence in any language must be of the form (Fig. 5.7).

Specifically, a sentence (S) consists of a **proposition** (P) and its **modality** (模态) (M). Proposition (P) is the "content" of the sentence, while modality (M) embraces such features as negation, **tense** (时态), **mood** (语气), **aspect** (体), and speaker's attitude: these are the features which Noam Chomsky, in the work cited above, loosely refers to as "feelings." P is made up of a lexical verb (cf. Chomsky's "behavior") and one or more nouns, which are differentiated according to case: **Agentive** (施事格), **Objective** (宾格), **Instrumental** (工具格), **Dative** (与格), **Locative** (方位格), and **Factitive** (使役格) (= **Causative** [使役格]). The meanings of the first five cases should be more or less transparent to us. The sixth one, the **Factitive** (使役格), is the case of the object of or entity resulting from the action of the verb. Thus in the following sentences the italic NPs are **surface structure** (表层结构) objects, that in 1) being Objective, while that in 2) is Factitive:

1) John painted *the old kitchen chair* red. (object of the action *paint*—**Objective**)
2) John painted *a controversial portrait of President Barack Obama*. (result of the action *paint*—**Factitive**)

These **case relationships** comprise, as Fillmore (1968, p. 24) puts it:

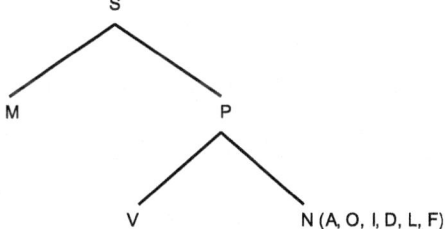

S=sentence
M=modality (aspect [体], mood [语气], negation, tense [时态], speaker/writer's
    attitude, etc.)
P=proposition ("content of the sentence")
V=verb
N=noun(s) differentiated according to case ("情况": Agentive, Objective,
    Instrumental, Dative, Locative, Factitive [causative])

Fig. 5.7 The case grammarian model of syntactic structure

a set of universal, presumably innate, concepts which identify certain types of judgments human beings are capable of making about the events that are going on around them, judgments about such matters as who did it, who it happened to, and what got changed.

So **Case Grammar** (格语法) is a theory of **syntax** (句法) and **semantics** (语义 学) in which nouns in **deep structures** (深层结构) are said to be related to verbs in cases such as agent, object, dative, instrumental, and so on." (Wardhugh 1997, p. 237). In Fillmore's model of case grammar, nouns are "case-specified," or differentiated according to their "cases" or functions in the sentence. Verbs can be classified according to which combinations of **case-specified nouns**—or what Fillmore calls "**case-frames**" they can occur with. Some verbs can occur in more than one case-frame, e.g. *open* in 1)–4):

1) The door *opened*. [**O**]
2) John *opened* the door. [**O + A**]
3) The wind *opened* the door. [**O + I**]
4) John *opened* the door with a chisel. [**O + I + A**]

Notice that in these four sentences only one of the **case-specified NPs** occurs with a preposition: *chisel* in 4) is governed by the preposition *with*. Compare this with *the wind* in 3): this noun is, like *a chisel* in 4), in the **Instrumental case** [工具 格], but, since *the wind* is the (**surface structure** [表层结构]) subject of the sentence the preposition is deleted. It seems that **subjectivization** of a NP in English has the consequence of deleting the case-marking preposition from the noun phrase. In German, by contrast, subject NPs are more likely to retain their prepositions; compare the following:

$100 buys you a nice vacation.
Für ["for"] *$100* können Sie sich einen schönen Urlaub machen.

The German-Polish Treaty begins a new era.
Mit ["with"] *dem deutsch-polnischen Vertrag* beginnt eine neue Ära.

In the same context, Nickel (1971, p. 13) points out that German, since it is able (unlike English) to subjectivize a Locative NP, differentiates between

1) Der Ofen ist warm. [Referring to the touch]
   The stove is warm.

and

2) Im Zimmer ist es warm. [Referring to the atmosphere of the room)
   The room is warm. (Literally, "In the room is it warm.")

The important thing about the German-English sentence pairs here is that, despite their differences in surface-structure, they reduce to the same (deep) case configuration. For example, the German and English sentences in 2) have the same

Fig. 5.8 The same case structure for interlingual translation equivalents

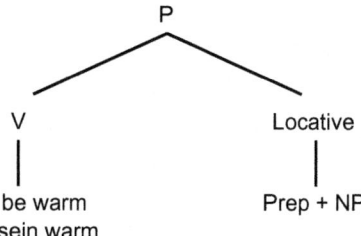

case structure (Fig. 5.8). (In the English sentence, the preposition *in* in the prepositional phrase *in the room* is omitted when the phrase is subjectivized.)

Case Grammar (格语法) would appear to be a model ideally suited to exploitation for purposes of **contrastive analysis** (对比分析) for the following reasons:

(1) Its finite universal array of categories provides us with a common point of departure for any pair of sentences we wish to compare structurally; indeed the fact that a pair of structures of **L1** and **L2**, in spite of their superficial differences, can be traced back to a common single case configuration is a justification for comparing them in the first place, and this **case-structure identity** is the very *tertium comparationis* (比较参照物) that **contrastivists** (对比分析研究者) can rely on.

(2) Secondly, since **surface structure** (表层结构) are derived from deep case configurations by transformations, all the advantages of the transformational approach (as discussed in the previous section), especially the feasibility of tracing sentential derivations through "intermediate structure" apply equally well.

(3) The machinery of deep case configurations is so simple and uninvolved that it lends itself to use by the applied linguist wishing to avoid involvement in the uncertainties of whatever abstract underlying syntactic structure the analyst should postulate for any given **surface structure** (表层结构), as is the case with the syntactic deep structures postulated by **Transformational Grammarians** (转换语法研究者).

On the other hand, however, the theory of **Case Grammar** (格语法) is not devoid of problems. Franz Boas (1858–1942) (1977) draws our attention to two major ones:

(1) How many **cases** (格) is it necessary to postulate?
(2) How can the cases be defined?

In his original theory, Fillmore (1968, p. 24) posited six cases (as we listed above): Agentive, Instrumental, Dative, Objective, Locative and Factitive. As his theory developed, need arose to add more cases. Fillmore himself added the cases of **Experiencer** (经历格), **Source** (来源格), **Goal** (目标格), **Time** (时间格), **Path** (路径格), and **Result** (结果格), while others have suggested the need for **Reciprocal** (相互格) and **Comitative** (伴随格) **cases**, as in the following:

John and Mary are going out tonight.

The subject NP here, consisting of two conjoined proper nouns, implies that John is going with Mary and she *with* him: **comitative**. In the following sentence the action of writing has been reciprocated by each party, so the subject NP may be said to be in the **reciprocal case** (相互格):

Hans und Maria schreiben einander seit Jahren.
(Literally, John and Mary write [to] each other since years.)
John and Mary have been writing (to each other) for years.

The fact that more and more **cases** (格) have to be postulated as the theory develops detracts from its original appeal (for applied linguistics at least), and Fillmore's promise of an inventory of universal **case relationships** "defined once and for all for human languages" (Fillmore 1971, p. 247) seems a little empty.

One solution to the dilemma, for the **contrastivist** (对比分析研究者), might be to relinquish the claim to a *universal* set of **case categories** and satisfy himself with an inventory which is necessary and sufficient for the two languages under contrast. But by so doing, there arises a conflict between the abstractness of these case categories on the one hand, and their specificity (in being valid for only two languages at a time) on the other hand. Assembling an inventory of **cases** (格) for a given pair of languages is certainly open to the charge of being "ad hoc," that is, for a special case only, without general applicability. One way out of the apparent impasse, as suggested by Franz Boas (1858–1942) (1977, p. 25), might be to give up the claim that all cases are unanalysable primitives and represent some of them as consisting of two or more components. (Based on James, 1980, pp. 54–59) That would be something quite resembling the practice of analyzing **phonemes** (音位) into phonological features or **lexemes** (词位) into **semantic features** (语义特征), as we have demonstrated in the previous two chapters. But apparently, further studies remain to be carried out in this direction.

5.4   Questions for Discussion and Research

1. How do you understand the concept of "**grammar**"? In the traditional sense of the term, what branches of study does grammar comprise?
2. What is a **grammatical category**? Name as many grammatical categories in English as you can.
3. **Case** (格) is familiar grammatical category. What grammatical functions does case indicate?
4. According to Lin Yutang (林语堂) (1982, p. 109), the distinction between **number** and **quantity** is not made in the Chinese notions of "多" and "少". Thus, one says in Chinese "僧多粥少," disregarding the fact that monks can be counted while congee cannot. How should the Chinese phrase "僧多粥少" be rendered in English then?

5. What major approaches are there to contrastive analysis on the syntactic level?
6. The analytic technique developed by the structuralists is known as **Immediate Constituent (IC) analysis** (直接成分分析法), whose feasibility hinges on two key notions: **distribution** (what naturally "goes with" what) and **omissibility** (whether the omission of an element from a construction results in a construction or non-construction). Judge the validity of this analytical procedure with reference to the following pair of sentences:

John is easy to please
John is eager to please.

7. In **Transformational(-Generative) Grammar**, grammar is defined as a mechanism that generates **all and only** grammatical sentences of a language. What do "**mechanism**" and "**generate**" mean in this definition?
8. Outline the three parts of grammar and their respective functions in the "**standard theory**" of Transformational Grammar.
9. What are the advantages of using **tree diagrams** to show sentence structures?
10. **Grammatical categories** are classes or groups of items which fulfill the same or similar functions in a particular language. Based on your knowledge of Chinese, English, and other languages, to what extent do you think grammatical categories are universal?

References

Birnbaum, H. (1970). *Problems of typological and genetic linguistics viewed in a generative framework.* The Hague, the Netherlands: Mouton.
Chomsky, N. (1965). *Aspects of the theory of syntax.* Cambridge, MA: MIT Press.
Crystal, D. (Ed.). (1987). *The Cambridge encyclopedia of language.* Cambridge, United Kingdom: Cambridge University Press.
Di Pietro, J. R. (1971). *Language structures in contrast.* Rowley, MA: Newbury House.
Fillmore, C. J. (1968). The case for case. In E. Bach & R. T. Harms (Eds.), *Universals of linguistic theory.* New York, NY: Holt, Rinehart and Winston.
Fries, C. C. (1952). *The structure of English.* London, United Kingdom & New York, NY: Longman.
Harris, Z. S. (1963). *Structural linguistics.* Chicago, IL: University of Chicago Press.
James, C. (1980). *Contrastive analysis.* Harlow, United Kingdom: Longman Group UK Limited.
König, E. (1970). *Transformational grammar and contrastive analysis* (University of Stuttgart PAKS Project Report No. 6), pp. 43–59.
Lyons, J. (1968). *Introduction to theoretical linguistics.* Cambridge, United Kingdom: Cambridge University Press.
Martin, S. (1964). Review of the book Universals of language. *Harvard educational review, 34*(2), 354–355.
Nickel, G. (1971). Contrastive linguistics and foreign language teaching. In G. Nickel (Ed.), *Papers in contrastive linguistics* (pp. 1–16). Cambridge, United Kingdom: Cambridge University Press.

Peters, P. S., & Ritchie, R. W. (1969). A note on the universal base hypothesis. *Journal of linguistics, 5*(1), 150–152.

Starosta, S. (1985). Mandarin case marking: A localistic lexicase analysis. *Journal of Chinese linguistics, 13*(2), 216–266.

Xu, Y. [许余龙]. (1992).《对比语言学概论》. 上海: 上海外语教育出版社.

Chapter 6
Textual Contrastive Analysis

What we have been dealing with thus far is **micro-** or **"code-linguistic" contrastive analysis** (微观对比分析). In this and the next chapters we are going to study **macro-contrastive analysis** (宏观对比分析), which is conducted on the textual and pragmatic levels of language.

The traditional concern of linguistics has been the abstract formal system of the language (called *"langue"* [语言系统], **"Competence** (语言能力)" or **"code** (语码)" respectively by linguists of different persuasions). Linguists claim that to gain access to the code "underlying" a language, it is necessary to disregard much that goes into language. This purging of aspects which are seen either as irrelevant or as complicating factors has been called by Lyons (1970) the **"idealization of data."** One of the ways through which data can be idealized is **decontextualization** (去语境化). A sentence can be decontextualized in two ways, either by being removed from the company of the sentences that precede or follow it in a text, i.e. its **verbal context** (文本语境), or by being separated off from the real-world situation in which it is used, i.e. its **physical** or **situational context** (情景语境).

In the past few decades, however, an increasing interest arose for analyzing the way sentences work in sequence to produce coherent stretches of language.

In fact the search for larger linguistic units and structures has been pursued by scholars from many disciplines. Linguists investigate the features of language that bind sentences together when they are used in sequence. Ethnographers (scientific researchers of different races of people) and sociologists study the structure of social interaction, especially as manifested in the way people enter into dialogue. Anthropologists analyze the structure of myths and folk-tales. Psychologists carry out experiments on the mental processes underlying comprehension. And further contributions have come from those concerned with artificial intelligence, rhetoric, philosophy, and style.

These approaches have a common concern: they stress the need to see language as a dynamic, social, interactive phenomenon—whether between speaker and listener, or between writer and reader. It is argued that meaning is conveyed not by single sentences but by more complex exchanges, in which the participants' beliefs and expectations, the knowledge they share about each other and about the world, and the situation in which they interact, play a crucial part (Crystal, 1987, p. 116).

It was against this intellectual background that macrolinguistics emerged and developed. Sometimes known as "**broad**" or "**human**" **linguistics**, **macrolinguistics** (宏观语言学) takes as its goal the attainment of a scientific understanding of how people use language to communicate with each other or, in Coulthard's terms, of "**situated speech**." (Coulthard, 1977, p. 3) Comparing this with the goal of code linguistics, which is to specify the universal and particular properties of human languages, we may notice that with macrolinguistics the attention has been shifted from **code** (语码) to process: the process of communication. In antithesis to (or complementary to) Noam Chomsky's **Competence** (语言能力), Hymes (1972) proposes that a speaker's **communicative competence** should be the object of linguistic enquiry.

This raises the whole question of how people communicate. Obviously they do so predominantly by means of language, though, to a lesser degree, other signaling devices such as gestures, facial expressions, and other similar paralinguistic devices ("**body language**") also play a part. Since people communicate through language, code linguistics has a major say in any account of the process of verbal communication. Nevertheless, it is not language itself that carries out verbal communication. Knowledge of the **code** (语码) is a necessary condition for verbal communication since all forms of communication involves the use of some code, but it is not a sufficient condition. There are other factors—non-codal, human factors—which affect the success or failure of communication. It is the concern of macrolinguistics to inquire what else is required for successful communication in addition to knowledge of the code (**Competence** [语言能力]). Sometimes we use one word—*sensitivity*—to embrace all these non-codal aspects, but macrolinguistics sets out to investigate and explicitly specify the situational constraints to which speech-events are subject to and the socio-cultural variables which the communicating individual must be able to identify in order to produce appropriate utterances in a communicative event.

To sum up, the following three points characterize **macrolinguistics** (宏观语言学):

(1) focusing on communicative competence rather than "linguistic" competence (in Chomsky's sense of the term)
(2) attempting to describe linguistic events within their extralinguistic settings
(3) searching for units of linguistic organization larger than the single sentence

(Based on James, 1980, pp. 100–102)

6.1 Text and Discourse

A **text** is a piece of structured spoken or written language. It may be of considerable length, e.g. a webpage,, a fairy tale, a sermon, a novel, etc.; or it may consist of only one word, e.g. "DANGER" as a warning sign outside a power substation. One important feature of a text is that a full understanding of it is often impossible without reference to the context in which it occurs (Fig. 6.1).

Discourse (话语) is a general term for instances of language use, i.e. language produced as the result of an act of communication.

According to Van Dijk (1980, p. 29), the difference between **text** and **discourse** (话语) lies in that the former is a theoretical conception related to a language user's **Competence** (语言能力) while the latter is a notion realistically perceived in relation to the user's **Performance**.

We may consider a text from the point of view of its *structure* or *functions* (e.g. warning, instructing, carrying out a transaction, etc.), or both.

On the **structural** or **formal level**, the study of the text addresses the question of how sentences are organized into larger, suprasentential units or texts: this is the field of **text analysis** (文本分析). On the **functional level**, the study of the text concentrates on the ways in which people put language to use: this is the field of **discourse analysis** (话语分析) (Coulthard, 1977).

The terms "**text analysis** (语篇分析)" and "**discourse analysis** (话语分析)" have sometimes been used in a confused way. There seem to be three approaches to the use of these two terms:

(1) Some scholars have suggested that text analysis refers to the European traditions and **discourse analysis** (话语分析) to Anglo-American traditions for doing the same thing.
(2) Others tend to see the two terms as complementary, believing that "**text analysis** (语篇分析)" *starts with linguistic forms and works outwards* to investigate in which contexts they are appropriate, whereas **discourse analysis** (话语分析) *starts with the communicative situations and works inwards* to find the formal linguistic correlates to the situational variables.
(3) Still others use the term "**text analysis** (语篇分析)" to refer to the study of written **discourse** (话语) and the term "**discourse analysis** (话语分析)" to talk about the study of spoken discourse.

Fig. 6.1 Examples of a text

In the present work we shall adopt the second approach, viewing **text analysis** (语篇分析) as concerned with the formal devices used for establishing inter-sentential connections, and units "above" the sentence, and viewing **discourse analysis** (话语分析) as handling considerations of language use. In this chapter we shall be concerned with **contrastive text analysis** (语篇对比分析). **Contrastive discourse analysis** (话语对比分析) will be dealt with in the next chapter ("**Pragmatic Contrastive Analysis** [语用对比分析]").

6.2   The Defining Characteristics of the Text

To call a sequence of sentences a "text" is to imply that the sentences display some degree of mutual dependence between themselves, i.e. they are not just occurring at random. Sometimes the internal structure of a text is immediately apparent, as in the headings of a restaurant menu (e.g. *appetizers, vegetables, meat, poultry, noodles, soup*, etc. which are all items in the **semantic field** [语义场] of "restaurant menu"); sometimes it has to be carefully identified and demonstrated, as in the network of relationships that enter into a literary masterpiece (e.g. *Ulysses*, which, imitating Homer's Odyssey, recounts the passage of Leopold Bloom, a Jewish advertising canvasser, through Dublin in one day, and which establishes a series of parallels between characters and events in Homer's poem and Joyce's novel, such as the correspondence of Leopold Bloom to Odysseus, Molly Bloom to Penelope, and Stephen Dedalus to Telemachus, the son of Odysseus and Penelope; and the correspondence of Bloom's passage through Dublin in a 24-h period in his life to the adventures and ordeals the Greek warrior Odysseus experiences in ten years after the fall of Troy as he struggles to return home and reestablish himself as king of Ithaca). In whichever case, a text is not just a jumble of sentences; rather, it is a meaningful whole: the meaning of a text is more than the sum of the meanings of its constituent parts, just as the meaning of an **idiom** (成语) is different from or larger than the sum of the meanings of all the words it is made up of (cf. "She tried to *break the ice* by suggesting that we all play a game").

What, then, are the essential characteristics of a text?

De Beaugrande and Dressler (1981) proposed seven defining characteristics of a text or, in their terms, seven **standards of textuality**. Any natural text, whatever text type (technical, institutional, or literary) it belongs to, shares these characteristics. They are:

(1) intentionality (the fulfillment of the author's intentions)
(2) acceptability (relevance to the text receiver)
(3) informativity (right amount of information with regard to the reader)
(4) situationality (location in a discrete socio-cultural context in a real time and place)
(5) intertextuality (relationship with other texts which share characteristics with it)
(6) cohesion
(7) coherence.

Failure to comply with any of these seven characteristics makes a piece of spoken or written language non-communicative, hence a "non-text." Of these seven characteristics the most important two are **cohesion** (接应, 接气) and **coherence** (连贯统一).

Cohesion (接应, 接气) and **coherence** (连贯统一) are related to the appropriateness of what one writes or speaks in verbal communication. A well-formed sentence can be appropriate to its context in three ways: it can be

(1) **formally appropriate** in not violating the rules of textual organization,
(2) **functionally appropriate** in that it communicates what its speaker intends (for that purpose, it must conform to the extralinguistic constraints imposed on it), or
(3) **formally as well as functionally inappropriate**.

Formal inappropriacy to linguistic context (i.e. **cotext**) results in **incohesion** (不接应, 不接气) of the text, while **functional inappropriacy** to linguistic context will lead to a breakdown in communication, that is, to **incoherence** (不连贯, 不统一).

Cohesion (接应, 接气) refers to the **structural** and/or **semantic relations** (语义关系) holding between the different elements of a text. This may be the relationship between different sentences or between different parts of a sentence. For example,

A: Will *George* do it?
B: Yes, *he* will.

There is a link between *George* and *he* and also between *will … do it* and *will*. In the sentence:

Paris? I've always wanted to go *there*.

the link (called **anaphora** [复指照应; 前指替代], or use of a word to refer back to or replace a word previously used) is between *Paris* and *there*.

Coherence (连贯统一), just as its **Latin** (拉丁语) root explains, means "sticking together." It refers to the relationships which link the meanings of sentences in a text or the utterances (see Sect. 1.3 "The History and Development of Contrastive Linguistics" for the definition of "utterance") in a **discourse** (话语). The links are usually based on the shared knowledge of the participants in a communicative event, e.g.

A: Could you give me a lift home?
B: Sorry, I'm visiting my sister.

There is no grammatical or lexical link (**cohesive ties**) between A's question and B's reply but the exchange has **coherence** (连贯统一) because both A and B knows that B's sister lives in the opposite direction to A's home.

In English a paragraph is said to have **coherence** (连贯统一) if it is a series of sentences that develop a main idea, that is, with a topic sentence and supporting sentences which relate to it. A sentence is said to be coherent if the subject and object are close to their verb and all modifiers hold hands with what they modify (Don't write, e.g. "Robert Henri felt like Whitman, that America was a land of artistic opportunity," but "Robert Henri, like Whitman, felt that America was a land of artistic opportunity"). All the phrases we use to express the notion that the parts of a composition need to be grouped appropriately—unity, interrelatedness, consistency, focus, tight organization, logic, and congruity—basically refer to coherence (Kolb, 1980, pp. 7–9).

6.3 The Contrastive Analysis of Textual Cohesion

One of the chief tasks of textual analysis (语篇分析) is to identify the linguistic features that cause the sentence sequence to "cohere" or "stick together." The ties that bind a text together are often referred to under the heading of **cohesion** (接应, 接气). Cohesion is utterly important to the identity of a text. This is readily seen if we scramble a text, that is, to make it incohesive, by randomizing the sentences that constitute it:

1) It was at that point that he decided that his countrymen's spiritual sickness was a far more pressing concern than their physical health.
2) What struck Lu Xun were the uncaring expressions on the faces of the Chinese bystanders.
3) The treatment he came to propose was a difficult one: it amounted to nothing less than the remolding of the Chinese personality, and in particular the remolding of his own scholar-gentry.
4) During his second year at Sendai a slide of a Chinese prisoner about to be executed was shown at the end of a class. (Wintle, 1984, p. 242)

The sentences as arranged above do not add up to a text, because the ideas they express appear in an order that does not correspond to the natural real-world order of events and hence do not "make sense" to the reader. To make sense of the passage, we must restore its constituent sentences to their original order of arrangement so that they may make an organic, coherent whole—a text:

4) During his second year at Sendai a slide of a Chinese prisoner about to be executed was shown at the end of a class.
2) What struck Lu Xun were the uncaring expressions on the faces of the Chinese bystanders.
1) It was at that point that he decided that his countrymen's spiritual sickness was a far more pressing concern than their physical health.
3) The treatment he came to propose was a difficult one: it amounted to nothing less than the remolding of the Chinese personality, and in particular the remolding of his own scholar-gentry.

Cohesion (接应, 接气) is understood in both a narrow sense and a broad one.

(1) **Cohesion** (接应, 接气) in its narrower sense (known as "**semantic cohesion**" [语义接应]) is understood to be a situation in which the interpretation (meaning) of one feature in a text is dependent upon another feature elsewhere in the same text. Cohesion in this sense is a *linguistic condition* and is expounded by Halliday and Hasan in *Cohesion in English* (1976), in which they distinguish five **cohesive devices** (接应手段), i.e. **reference** (指代), **substitution** (替代), **ellipsis** (省略), **conjunction** (连接), and **lexical relationships** (词汇关联) (or **lexical cohesion** [词汇接应]).

(2) **Cohesion** (接应, 接气) in its broad sense (known as "**structural cohesion**" (结构接应) is understood to be all the *linguistic relationships* that bind various surface elements in a text together [as demonstrated by de Beaugrande and Dressler in their work *Introduction to Text Linguistics* (1981)]. In line with this understanding, the notion of cohesion should also cover such *structural* connections between sentences in a text as **parallelism** (平行结构), **comparison**, and the **information structure** (信息结构).

In this chapter we take the notion of **cohesion** (接应, 接气) in both its narrow and broad senses and distinguish between **semantic cohesion** (语义接应) and **structural cohesion** (结构接应). In the following we shall first consider the different devices employed by different languages to achieve these two kinds of cohesion.

6.3.1 Semantic Cohesion

Semantic cohesion (语义接应) is achieved through the semantic connections between various forms in a text. Halliday and Hasan (1976) identify five such semantic connections, i.e. **reference, substitution, ellipsis, conjunction,** and **lexical relationships** (or "**lexical cohesion** [词汇接应]").

6.3.1.1 Reference

Language can refer—or make **reference** (指代)—in two ways. When we say *my dog, her cat, American company, Chinese silk, Mrs Thatcher* (or *the former Prime Minister /the Iron Lady /Maggie*), we refer to some entity in the real world or make real-world reference (the last example being a case of the so-called **co-reference** [同指]).

Real-world reference is called **exophoric reference** (文外指代). When we use language to refer to another bit of language, however, we make reference to some elements in the text or make **reference-in-text**. **Reference-in-text** (文内指代) is called **endophoric reference** (文内指代). Consider the following sentence:

1) *Tommy* likes *ice-cream* and *he* always has an appetite for *it*.

Tommy and *ice cream* are two nouns with **exophoric reference** (文外指代), while *he* and *it* have endophoric reference: they refer to "Tommy" and "ice cream" in the cotext, and not directly to real-world entities. Obviously, only **endophoric reference** (文内指代) is related to **cohesion** (接应, 接气) or, more specifically, to **semantic cohesion** (语义接应).

Compare the pronoun *he* in 1) with *he* in 2):

2) Whenever *he* saw an ice cream, *Tommy* would like to taste it.

In this sentence *Tommy* has **exophoric reference** (文外指代) and *he* **endophoric reference** (文内指代). But it is different from 1) in the way in which the pronoun is used to refer to reality: in (1) the pronouns refer back to nouns which have already appeared in the text, while in (2) the pronoun anticipates the full noun *Tommy*. Backward reference is called **anaphoric reference** (前指) while forward or anticipatory reference is known as **cataphoric reference** (后指). The following humor results from the mistaking of a cataphoric-referring pronoun for an anaphoric-referring one:

Co-worker: So you're the father of twins. Who do they look like?"

Excited father: Each other.

The dialogue is humorous because the co-worker uses the *who* as a cataphoric-referring pronoun, expecting the father to tell whether his twins resemble *himself* or *his wife*, but the excited father's mind is so absorbed in his twins that he mistakes the pronoun *who* for an anaphoric-referring one, thinking that the co-worker is referring back to the twins themselves.

Semantically comparable cohesive referents in different languages may have different **functional load** (功能负载量). Take demonstratives for example. A **demonstrative** (指示词) is a *pronoun* or *determiner* which refers to something in terms of whether it is near to or distant from the speaker, such as *this*, *that*, etc. [A **determiner** [限定词] is one of a group of English limiting adjectival words that usually precede descriptive adjectives in a noun phrase and include the articles *the*, *a*, and *an*, and any words that may substitute for them, as *your*, *their*, *some*, and *each*. (Based on **determiner**, 1987)]

In English, **remote demonstratives** (远指示词) (such as *that*) and **remote adverbs** (远指副词) (such as *there*) seem to have a higher functional load than **near demonstratives** (近指示词)(such as *this*) and **near adverbs** (近指副词) (such as *here*). In Chinese the opposite case seems to be true.

The English demonstrative pronoun *this*, e.g. is used to refer to

(1) something that is being, or is about to be, mentioned;
(2) a person or thing that is near the one who speaks or writes; or
(3) some time that is to come soon.

The English demonstrative pronoun *that*, on the other hand, is used to refer to

(1) something that has already been mentioned;
(2) a person or thing that is relatively distant from the one who speaks or writes; or
(3) a situation in the past.

According to some studies (see Xu, 1992, p. 253), the ratio of the absolute frequency of usage of *that* to that of *this* is higher than 2:1 in English while in Chinese the ratio is about 1:2. This suggests that the English **remote demonstrative** (远指示词) *that* has a much greater functional load than the Chinese remote demonstrative "那" and that at least some of the functions performed by *that* in English in referring to something distant would be played in Chinese by the **near demonstrative** (近指示词) "这."

This postulation is substantiated by our observation that the Chinese language does tend to choose **near demonstratives** (近指示词) and **adverbs** (近指副词) in preference to remote ones in both spoken and written texts, as is indicated in the following examples:

"… I assume we are discussing Mrs Bendrix?"
"Not exactly."
"But she passes under *that* name?"
"No, you are getting this quite wrong. She's the wife of a friend of mine."
"And he's sent you?"
"No."
"Perhaps you and the lady are—intimate?"
"No. I've only seen her once since 1944."
"I'm afraid I don't quite understand. This is a watching case, you said."
I hadn't realized till *then* that he had angered me so much. "Can't one love or hate," I broke out at him, "as long as that? Don't make any mistake. I'm just another of your jealous clients, I don't claim to be any different from the rest, but there's been a time lag in my case."

(Graham Greene, The End of the Affair, pp. 21–22)

"… 我想我们是在讨论本德里克斯太太?"
"并非如此。"
"可人家是这么叫她, 对吧?"
"不, 这一点你全搞错了。她是我一个朋友的太太。"
"是你的朋友派你来的?"
"不是。"
"或许你同那位女士很——亲密?"
"不, 1944 年以后我只见过她一次。"
"这我恐怕就不太明白了。你说过的, 这件案子是要派人去盯梢的。"

直到这会儿，我才意识到他让我感到多么的恼火。"一个人是爱是恨，"我冲他发作起来，"都不能那么长久吗？别搞错了，我只是你那些嫉妒的委托人当中的一个，我并没有说自己同其他人有什么不一样，只不过我的案情里有段时间差罢了。"

(柯平, Trans. 《恋情的终结》)

一九八四年重点转入城市改革。经济发展比较快的是一九八四年至一九八八年。这五年，首先是农村改革带来许多新的变化，农作物大幅度增产，农民收入大幅度增加，乡镇企业异军突起。(《邓小平文选》[第三卷]—"在武昌、深圳、珠海、上海等地的谈话要点")

In 1984, the focus shifted to urban areas. The years from 1984 to 1988 witnessed comparatively rapid economic growth. During *those five years*, rural reform brought about many changes: grain output increased substantially, as did the peasants' income, and rural enterprises emerged as a new force. (北京: 外文出版社)

The explanation for this strongly preferred use of "这" in Chinese is perhaps that the Chinese mind has a tendency to bring the distant near when referring to geographically or temporally remote things. The choice of near and **remote demonstratives** (远指示词) and **adverbs** (远指副词) is thus determined more by psychological factors than by real-world time and space, as is the case in English (Xu, 1992, p. 254).

6.3.1.2 Substitution

Substitution (替代) refers to the replacement of a previous expression with a **pro-form** (替代形式) (that is, a form which serves as a substitute for a different element in a sentence). For example,

We invited Mary and John to dinner because we liked *them*.

I've got a pencil. Do you have *one*?

Sometimes an auxiliary may even encode the entire predicate of the preceding sentence, and thereby carry forward the meaning of that predicate, as is shown in the following two examples:

A: Will we get there on time?

B: I think *so*.

Substitution (替代) is used much more frequently in English than in Chinese. On most of the occasions when a **pro-form** (替代形式) would be used in English to replace a previous expression in a text for purposes of **semantic cohesion** (语义接应), the Chinese would reiterate part of the expression and omit the remaining part so as to achieve the same effect. The Chinese versions for the above two dialogs would be:

甲: 我们能准时到达吗？

乙: 我想能(准时到达)。

6.3.1.3 Ellipsis

In **substitution** (替代), **pro-forms** (替代形式) are used to represent full forms occurring elsewhere in the cotext, and a degree of reduction is achieved by their use. **Ellipsis** (省略) takes this process one step further and brings about the total elimination of a segment of text. Its effect is "to create **cohesion** (接应, 接气) by leaving out … what can be taken over from preceding **discourse** (话语)" (Halliday and Hasan, 1976, p. 196). In other words, it leaves something unsaid that is understood or inferable from the context.

Ellipsis (省略) is usually anaphoric in English, but may also be cataphoric. Compare 1) and 2), in both of which the elliptical segments appear in parentheses.

1) A: Have you been to Moscow?
    B: (I have) Never (been to Moscow).

2) Because Alice won't (dust the furniture), Mary has to dust the furniture.

At first sight it might seem paradoxical that the elimination of part of the message should serve to achieve textual cohesion: indeed, one may expect the opposite would happen, i.e. the listener or reader would lose the thread. We might explain the positive effect of ellipsis in terms of the work that the reader or interlocutor has to do. If, in a **conversation** (会话), I ellipt in my contributions segments of text which you, my interlocutor, have made explicit, I thereby show a willingness to accept your explicit contributions as "given," and my not repeating them shows you that I value your contribution as taken for granted (based on James, 1980, pp. 107–108).

A special kind of **ellipsis** (省略) that characterizes Chinese textual organization is that of personal pronouns. Known also as **zero-anaphora ellipsis** (零复指照应省略, 零前指替代省略), ellipsis of this kind is actually a form of personal **reference** (指代) (the term "zero" refers to the fact that the **pro-form** (替代形式) is omitted). For example,

历来野史, 或讪谤君相, 或贬人妻女, [它们] 奸淫凶恶, 不可胜数。

(曹雪芹.《红楼梦》, 第1回)

The trouble is that so many romances contain slanderous anecdotes about sovereigns and ministers or cast aspersions upon other men's wives and daughter so that *they* are packed with sex and violence.

(杨宪益 & 戴乃迭, Trans. *A Dream of Red Mansions*)

贾母一面说, 一面来看宝玉, 只见今日这顿打, 不比往日, [她] 又是心疼, 又是生气, 也抱着哭个不了。

(曹雪芹.《红楼梦》, 第33回)

From the sight that met her eyes she could tell that this had been no ordinary beating. It filled *her* with anguish for the sufferer and fresh anger for the man who had inflicted it, and for a long time *she* clung to the inert form and wept …

(D. Hawkes, Trans. *The Story of the Stone*, Chap. 1)

In the above passage, all the personal pronouns referring anaphorically to "贾母" (the Old Ancestress), which appears only initially in the text, are ellipted.

Zero-anaphora (零复指照应, 零前指替代) can only occur with languages in which the **Subject** and the **Predicate** of a clause are not bound by formal grammatical ties. Since English is a language in which the Subject and the Predicate verb must be in agreement with each other in terms of **person** (人称) and **number** (数), zero-anaphora usually does not apply with its texts, for example,

> My mind however is now made up on the subject, for having received ordination at Easter, I have been so fortunate as to be distinguished by the patronage of the Right Honourable Lady Catherine de Bourgh, widow of Sir Lewis de Bourgh, whose bounty and beneficence has preferred me to the valuable rectory of this parish, where it shall be *my* earnest endeavour to demean myself with grateful respect towards her Ladyship, and be ever ready to perform those rites and ceremonies which are instituted by the Church of England.

(Jane Austen. *Pride and Prejudice*, Chap. 13)

> 不过目前我对此事已经拿定主张，因为我已在复活节那天受了圣职。多蒙故刘易斯·德·包尔公爵的孀妻卡特琳·德·包尔夫人宠礼有加，恩惠并施，提拔我担任该教区的教士，此后 [我] 可以勉尽厥诚，恭侍夫人左右，奉行英国教会所规定的一切仪节，这真是三生有幸。

(王科一, Trans.)

6.3.1.4 Conjunction

What is about to be said may be explicitly related to what has been said before, through such notions as addition, contrast, result, time, etc. For instance,

> This method has been widely adopted. *However*, it is not yet clear that it is the best method.
>
> *Lastly*, could I ask all of you to keep this information a secret.

The use of such formal markers as *and*, *besides* ("**additives**"); *however*, *instead* ("**adversatives**"); *so*, *because* ("**causals**"); *then*, *lastly* ("**temporals**"); *now*, *anyway* ("**continuatives**"), etc. to link sentences and constructions together is known as "**conjunction**" (连接).

Winter (1971) identifies five most frequent categories of "**connectives**" in scientific texts:

(1) **Logical sequence**: *thus, therefore, then, thence, consequently, so …*
(2) **Contrast**: *however, in fact, conversely …*
(3) **Doubt and certainty**: *probably, possibly, indubitably …*
(4) **Non-contrast**: *moreover, likewise, similarly …*
(5) **Expansion**: *for example, in particular …*

These account for 89% of all the connectives in the texts analyzed.

Related to **conjunction** (连接) are two remarkably antithetical linguistic phenomena: hypotaxis and parataxis. **Hypotaxis** (形合 [式连接]) refers to the placement of related clauses, constructions, etc. in a series using connecting words. For example,

I'm high on the work *because* this is the way life is going to be—persuading people.

Parataxis (意合 [式连接]) refers to the placement of related clauses, constructions, etc. in a series without using connecting words, e.g. *Veni, vidi, vici* ("I came, I saw, I conquered") as Julius Caesar, the Roman emperor, wrote in a letter announcing his victory in a campaign near the Black Sea. By analogy to **"zero-anaphora"** (零复指照应, 零前指替代), parataxis may be called **"zero-conjunction (零连接)."**

There is a great difference between the Chinese and western languages with regard to the way successive constructions and clauses are linked up. While **hypotaxis** (形合 [式连接]) is the normal way used by western languages to link up related clauses and constructions, **parataxis** (意合 [式连接]) characterizes most Chinese texts, for instance,

送君千里, 终有一别。

Although you may escort a guest a thousand miles, *yet* must the parting come at last.

太太屋里人多手杂, 别人还可以, 那个主儿的一伙子人见是这屋里的东西, 又该使黑心弄坏了才罢。

(曹雪芹.《红楼梦》, 第37回)

There are so many people in and out of that place—especially You know Who and her lot. *If* they see anything from our room in here, they're sure to find some way of breaking it accidentally-on-purpose, *if* they get half a chance.

(D. Hawkes, Trans. *The Story of the Stone*)

The paratactic property of the textual structure of Chinese allows the readership great freedom in perceiving and interpreting the artistic reality in poems. The poetic space thus created is closer to what we experience in the real world. The Yuan poet Ma Zhiyuan (马致远 1250?–1324?)'s *sanqu* (散曲 or "non-dramatic song," a verse form evolved in the Yuan dynasty, used for lyric songs which were written to express the poet's feelings and observations and which were introduced between parts of the prose dialog in the Yuan drama to express the sentiments of a certain character) "天净沙 · 秋思" is a very typical example:

天净沙 · 秋思	**Tune: Tian Jin Sha**	**Autumn**
马致远		

枯藤老树昏鸦，	Withered vines hanging on old branches,	Crows hovering over rugged old trees
小桥流水人家，	Returning crows croaking at dusk.	wreathed with rotten vine—the day is
古道西风瘦马，	A few houses hidden past a narrow bridge,	about done. Yonder is a tiny bridge
夕阳西下，	And below the bridge a quiet creek	over a sparkling stream, and on the far
断肠人在天涯。	running.	bank, a pretty little village. But the
	Down a worn path, in the west wind,	traveller has to go on down this ancient
	A lean horse comes plodding.	road, the west wind moaning, his bony
	The sun dips down in the west	horse groaning, trudging towards the
	And the lovesick traveller is still at the end	sinking sun, farther and farther away
	of the world.	from home. (翁显良, Trans.)
	(丁祖荫 & Burton Raffel, Trans.)	

天净沙 · 秋思	**Autumn Thoughts**	**Autumn Thoughts**
马致远		

枯藤老树昏鸦，	Dry vine, old tree, crows at dusk.	Withered vines, olden tree, evening crows;
小桥流水人家，	Low bridge, stream running, cottages,	Tiny bridge, flowing brook, hamlet homes;
古道西风瘦马，	Ancient road, west wind, lean nag,	Ancient road, wind from west, bony horse;
夕阳西下，	The sun westering	The sun is setting,
断肠人在天涯。	And one with breaking heart at the sky's	Broken man, far from home, roams and
	edge.	roams.
	(Cyril Birch, Trans.)	(赵甄陶, Trans.)

Both 丁祖荫 and Burton Raffel and 翁显良 introduced many syntactic amplifications into their translations to make the target texts more in agreement with the hypotactic norm of the English language. But their efforts seem to have had only an adverse effect on the poem: compared with Birch's and 赵甄陶's translations, their versions appear to be too logical and hence somewhat confined in the poetic space they would allow.

On the other hand, however, the paratactic feature of the Chinese language quite often causes the meaning of a text or part of a text to be ambiguous. Let us look at an example from *Daodejing* (or *Tao-te-Ching* 《道德经》) by Laozi (or Lao-tzu, c. 6th century BC), a renowned pre-Qin Chinese philosopher and the legendary founder of Taoism:

知不知上不知知病

The **textual structure** (语篇结构), of this well-known aphorism is characteristically paratactic, with no connectives whatsoever. This, combined with the fact that like most ancient Chinese texts it is not punctuated, makes its meaning somewhat indeterminate. Western sinologists and Chinese scholars came up with different interpretations of it according to their own understandings or conjectures:

知不知, 上。不知知, 病。

To know the unknowable, that is elevating.

Not to know the knowable, that is sickness.

(Garus, Trans.)

知不知, 上。不知, 知, 病。

To know when one does not know is best.

To think one knows when one does not know is a dire disease.

(Arthur Waley, Trans.)

知, 不知, 上。不知, 知, 病。

To know, but to be as though not knowing, is the height of wisdom.

Not to know, and yet to affect knowledge, is a vice.

(Lionel Giles, Trans.)

知不知上, 不知知病。

"知道自己不知道, 最好;

不知道, 而自以为自己知道, 就是病。"

(It is best to know that you do not know;

It is a malady to think that you know when you don't.)

(Annotated by 任继愈)

(Cai and Yu, 1997, pp. 175–176)

The observation that Chinese is predominantly paratactic and English largely hypotactic has important implications for the translation between these two languages. In Chinese-English translation, then, translators often need to sort out the various elements of the source message and package the main information into a main clause in the target version, and subordinate to it less important information in the form of subordinate clauses led by formal markers or conjunctions. On the other hand, when working into Chinese, translators should not transfer such function words as conjunctions in the English text indiscriminately into Chinese; otherwise the target text may become rather awkward and unnatural (Fan, 1996, p. 50), as evidenced by the following passage in the first chapter of Graham Greene's novel *The End of the Affair*:

Directly I began to cross the Common I realized I had the wrong umbrella …

which was put into Chinese by most of the junior English majors in a class in Nanjing University as:

*当我刚开始穿越公共草坪的时候, 我发觉我拿错了雨伞。

6.3.1.5 Lexical Relationships ("Lexical Cohesion")

Semantic cohesion (语义接应) may also be achieved by having one lexical item entering into a structural relationship with another, e.g.

The *flowers* were lovely. He liked the *tulips* best.

Foremost among **lexical relationships** (词汇关联) are **synonymy** (同义) and **hyponymy** (上下义).

Since texts have a high probability of opening with a general proposition, or closing with a generalization which has been derived from the specifics of the text, the sentence containing the **superordinate** (上义词) is likely to be the first or the last item in a cohesive passage.

Lexical cohesion (词汇接应) can be achieved by lexical items which summarize complete propositions expressed elsewhere in the text. Note how "bias" and "precautions" in the second sentences of the following two passages refer back to the entire antecedent sentences:

One hundred hours a week were devoted to study and 45 min to football. This *bias* was not wholly popular.

The management have installed closed-circuit television, hired store detectives, and attached padlocks to all portable goods. These *precautions* have reduced shoplifting at Harrod's.

Two things about these two "summative **lexemes** (词位)" should be noted. First, they perform an extra function besides summarizing the antecedent sentence. In the first passage, e.g. *bias* evaluates the content of that sentence, that is, expresses a judgment about the imbalance between work and play in the school. Second, bear in mind that such summative-evaluative words figure prominently also in dialogue: a second speaker can use them to signal, lexically, that he sees the implication of the first speaker's remark, or to express a reaction which was not expected by the first speaker. For example,

A: I don't mind selling a few raffle-tickets.
B: Your *cooperation* is most welcome.

(Based on James, 1980, pp. 104–106)

6.3.2 Structural Cohesion

Structural cohesion (结构接应) refers to all the linguistic relationships that bind various surface elements in a text together. It is cohesion in broad sense of the term and is typically achieved through three devices: **parallelism** (平行结构), comparison, and **information structure** (信息结构).

6.3.2.1   Parallelism

Parallelism (平行结构) means the use of equal forms for elements of equal functions in a text. Sentences in a sequence normally exhibit a variety of different structures: indeed, in training young students to write compositions, teachers stress the need to vary successive sentence-patterns. Yet an experienced writer sometimes reverses the maxim of variety and strings together two or three sentences using **parallel structure** (平行结构): the effect of this is to tie the sentences together conceptually, so that they are read as one cohesive entity of text. Quirk et al. (1972, p. 716) illustrate the notion of parallel structure with the following sentences:

1)   Have you ever seen a pig fly? Have you ever seen a fish walk?
2)   My paintings the visitors admired. My sculptures they disliked.

In 1) we have a sequence of two "rhetorical questions"—they are not normal questions expecting answers, but challenges expressed by interrogative structures. The fact that the speaker or writer produces two such sentences does not mean that he is issuing two challenges: it is *one* challenge, and the two structures are to be read as functionally reiterative: their identity of form reinforces their functional unity.

In 2) the two sentences show the same departure from "normal" **word order** in English: they are both Object-Subject-Verb sequences. It is not unusual for a writer to use *one* O-S-V pattern occasionally in his text, but the sequence of two or more serves a special function: to indicate that the two sentences are to be read as contrastive. We could, in fact, supply a contrastive conjunction *but* or *however* to link the two sentences, but this linking is achieved just as successfully by the very **parallelism** (平行关系) of the two sentence structures. (Based on James, 1980, pp. 108–109)

In the following passage from *Tess*, Hardy employs **parallel structures** (平行结构) to describe a group of village girls:

Some had *beautiful eyes*, others a *beautiful nose*, others a *beautiful mouth and figure*; few, if any, had all.

(Thomas Hardy, *Tess*, p. 50)

她们里面，有的美目流盼，有的鼻准端正，有的樱唇巧笑，有的身材苗条；但众美兼备的，固然不能说没有，却少得很。

(张谷若, Trans.《苔丝》. p. 24)

The use of **parallelism** (平行结构) developed into a literary convention in early Chinese and medieval European literature. For example, the *pianti* (骈体) style, a rhythmical prose style marked by parallelism and ornateness cultivated during the Six dynasties (220–589) in Chinese history, is characterized by parallel sentences and constructions (mostly four-character and six-character ones) and by the counterbalancing of tonal patterns. This style has a strong influence on later writings in Chinese, as we may find in a short passage from a travel note by the Song poet and essayist Ouyang Xiu (欧 阳 修 1007–1072), in the concluding paragraph of an editorial in *Renmin Ribao* (*The People's Daily*), and in the heading of a news story about the 1998 World Cup:

伛偻提携, 往来而不绝者, 滁人游也。

山肴野蔌, 杂然而前陈者, 太守宴也。

(欧阳修.《醉翁亭记》)

两岸合作 振兴中华

新华社评论员

我们注意到台湾国民党当局始终坚持只有一个中国, 反对 "两个中国" 和 "台湾独立" 的正义立场; 对台湾执政人士采取了少许有助海峡两岸局势缓和的步骤, 也觉得欣幸。当前祖国大陆的发展正处在振兴和腾飞的重要时刻, 台湾也面临着摆脱困境力图振作的风云际会。世变日亟, 人谋宜减。恩仇终是同根, 他助莫如自助。夜长梦多, 株守当思落叶; 日新月异, 壁合宁失天成? 理有固然, 义无反顾。尽早统一, 两岸人民将共享安宁富庶, 整个民族亦将与世界各发达国家齐驱并进。盛衰功过, 决于反掌。我们真诚期待国民党当局善自衡量在历史上的地位作用, 辨利害, 悟安危, 识潮流, 顺民心。早在约七十年前, 孙中山先生就说过: "夫事有顺乎天理, 应乎人情, 适乎世界之潮流, 合乎人群之需要, 而为先知先觉者所决志行之, 则断无不成者也, 此古今之革命维新、兴邦建国等事业是也。" (见中华书局《孙中山全集》第六卷228页。) 大哉言乎!能知必能行, 国民党当局诸公其三思之! 归根到底, 今天的急务, 就是毅然决然, 摈除一切不必要的疑虑, 停止一切不切实的空谈, 在新的一年中, 为祖国的和平统一昂首阔步, 勇开新境。这固然是全中国人民全中华民族同声呼唤的幸福, 也显然是国民党当局自身唯一可能的幸福。

(《人民日报》, February 7, 1986)

New Year Wish for Taiwan Reunification

We have noted that the Taiwan Kuomintang authorities always maintain the one-China stand and oppose schemes known as "two Chinas" and "independence of Taiwan"; and we are happy to find that the authorities in Taiwan have, after all, taken a few steps toward easing the tension between the both sides of the Strait. Developments on the mainland at present are at the important point of invigoration and take-off, while Taiwan has the task of extricating itself from a predicament for reinvigoration. The world is changing rapidly, and people should make careful plans. It is better to help yourself than to have others help you. Friend or foe, we both spring from the same roots. Dilatoriness is fraught with dangers, present obstinacy spells future ruin. We must change with rapidly changing circumstances; and is not reunification but a return to the normal and original order of things? Events develop according to their inherent laws, and honour and duty permit no turning back.

The country should be reunified at an earlier date so that the people on both sides of the Strait can live in peace and prosperity forever and the entire Chinese nation advance in step with the developed countries of the world. On your decision hinges success or failure, honour or discredit. It is our sincere hope that the Kuomintang authorities understand their position and role in history well and, balancing advantages and disadvantages and considering their own future, do things that suit the development of events and meet popular demand.

Dr. Sun Yat-sen declared 70 years ago: "persons with foresight always do things that accord with heavenly principles, popular will, the trend of world events and the need of the masses, hence their success in whatever they try to accomplish. This is how all revolutions and reforms and exploits to build up a nation have been carried out since ancient times." How finely said! One can certainly put into practice what one truly knows, and the Kuomintang gentlemen now in power should think this over and over again.

In the final analysis, their pressing task today is to make determined efforts to cast aside all unnecessary doubts and stop all empty talk, and take a bold step in the new year by blazing a new trail for the reunification of the motherland. That will certainly be a blessing for the entire Chinese people and nation, and it is the only way to ensure the well-being of the Kuomintang authorities.

(*China Daily*, February 7, 1986)

今夜不设防   韩国队输得好惨
领先守不住   比利时平得可惜

(《扬子晚报》, June 21, 1998, p. 21)

Parallelism (平行结构) often involves some sort of repetition. The fundamental thing to do is to keep some elements identical or similar and to vary others. In the Second World War, Winston Churchill used to end his famous broadcast speech with the following passage, which gains a rolling momentum through the accumulation of force built up by a long string of sentences that have the same structure "we shall fight":

We shall fight in France, we shall fight on the seas and oceans, we shall fight with growing confidence and growing strength in the air, we shall defend our island, whatever the cost may be, we shall fight on the beaches, we shall fight on the landing grounds, we shall fight in the fields and in the streets, we shall fight in the hills; we shall never surrender …

In the second stanza of his "Flowers in the Morning," Gu Cheng (顾城) (1956–1993), a famous modern Chinese poet and a prominent member of the "Misty Poets (朦胧诗派)," regularly repeats the line "她用花心鸣叫" (she sings with her heart), which helps to bind the successive lines of the stanza together and create an echoic, dreamy effect:

早晨的花

　(一)

所有花都在睡去

风一点点走近篱笆

所有花都在睡去

风一点点走近篱笆

所有花都逐渐在草坡上

睡去, 风一点点走近篱笆

所有花都含着蜜水

所有细碎的叶子

都含着蜜水

(二)

她们用花英鸣叫

她们用花英鸣叫

细细的舌尖上闪着蜜水

她用花心鸣叫

蜂鸟在我耳边轻轻啄着

她用花心鸣叫

风在篱笆附近响着

远处是孩子，是泡沫的喧嚷

她用花心鸣叫

午后的影子又大又轻

她用花心鸣叫

我同时看见

她和近旁的梦幻

6.3.2.2 Comparison

Comparison as located in one sentence is something familiar to us, e.g.

Geographically, Canada is greater than the United States.

But comparison can also be conducted across sentence-boundaries. In such cases, it is not unlike a kind of **antithetical parallelism** (对偶结构) in which opposites are compared. Comparison of this sort makes two or more clauses hang together and meanwhile effectively highlights the message or value judgment carried by one of the clauses:

Art is long; life is short.

Theories are gray; the tree of art is evergreen. (Goethe)

Not that I loved Caesar less, but that I loved Rome more … As he was valiant, I honour him; but as he was ambitious, I slew him. (Shakespeare, *Julius Caesar*)

6.3.2.3 Information Structure

The idea underlying discussions in this subsection is basically that for a text to be cohesive the information structure of successive sentences in it must be related to each other.

Information structure (信息结构) refers to the use of **word order**, **intonation** (语调), **stress** (重音), and other devices to indicate how the message expressed by a sentence is to be understood. In the following we are going first to clarify several key notions related to information structure, notably **Theme** (主位), **Rheme** (述位), **Functional Sentence Perspective** (功能语句观), **Topic** (话题), and **Comment** (议论), and then to make a contrastive study of the **information structure** (信息结构) of English and Chinese with special reference to the notions of **Subject-Prominent language** (主语突出语言) and **Topic-Prominent language** (话题突出语言).

Theme and Rheme

In a text, successive sentences should do two things: they must be informative and, at the same time, be relevant. Being informative involves presenting "new" information to the reader, while being relevant involves associating that "new" information with information that is already known to the reader, i.e. "given" either by the **preceding cotext** (前文) or by the **situational context** (情景语境).

This subtle organization of the information content of the sentences of texts in terms of "given" and "new" determines their "**communicative dynamism**" (James, 1980, p. 109). In other words, how the information is organized in a text may affect its **structural cohesion** (结构接应).

Viewed from the perspective of **information structure** (信息结构), a text contains one or more **units of information** (信息单位). Each unit of information is usually of the length of a clause and, phonologically, it is represented as a separate tone group. Each unit of information must include at least one piece of "given" or known information and will normally also carry some "new" or unknown information. The known information (which is not new to the reader or listener) is known as **Theme** (主位). The unknown information (which is new to the reader or listener) is known as **Rheme** (述位). The tonic stress of a unit of information normally falls on the elements that carry the unknown information (Rheme).

For a text to be structurally cohesive, the information structure of each sentence in it must display some kind of relationship with that of the sentence preceding it.

The linguistic elements occurring at the beginning of a sentence are usually its **Theme** (主位). (In English, the Subject of a sentence is often, but not always, its Theme.) These elements serve as the link between the message given in the previous sentence and the new message presented in the current one. The remaining part of the sentence makes its **Rheme** (述位). (Some linguists regard the Object as the Rheme while the Verb as the Transition between the Theme and Rheme. (See James, 1980, p. 109) A structural arrangement like this makes the transition from the known information to the new information very smooth. Look at the following example:

A: Who switched off the lights?
B: The one who switched off the lights was Mary.

B's reply makes a **unit of information** (信息单位) in the whole text. Its **Theme** (主位) is "the one who switched off the lights" since "(somebody) switched off the lights" is something that has been mentioned in the previous sentence (i.e. A's question) and hence already known to the listener (B). The **Rheme** (述位) of the sentence is "was Mary" since this is the information that A is inquiring about, that is, the information new to him. In this case, the text is structurally cohesive: the second unit of information follows the first one in a natural way.

If, however, B replies to A's question in the following way:

A: Who switched off the lights?
B: What Mary did was switch off the lights.

the text will be structurally incohesive since the **Theme** (主位) of the second sentence "what Mary did" is new, instead of known, information to A (who did not actually bother to ask anything about Mary or what she did), resulting in a sentence whose **theme-rheme** (主述位) structure does not cohere with that of the previous sentence. (In fact, it can only cohere structurally with a sentence which is, however, not there in the context, i.e. "What did Mary do?")

Quite a lot of Chinese students of English and translation, however, are not consciously aware of this principle. The writings of these students are loosely structured textually because what is stated in one sentence is not properly related to the previous one: often something new is brought in as the subject or **theme** (主位) of the new sentence, and yet this subject or theme is not in any way mentioned in (that is, being the **rheme** [述位] of) the previous sentence or sentences. It is not difficult to imagine that the sense of a group of sentences thus strung together would not at all be clear to the reader.

The moral is obvious: when writing in English, Chinese students should always be alert to the **theme-rheme** (主述位) structure of the sentences they set on paper. When a new notion or idea materializes as a sentence under their pen, they should always ask themselves the question: "has this been properly introduced in the rheme part of the previous sentence or sentences?"

Functional Sentence Perspective (FSP)

The type of linguistic analysis concerning the **distribution of information** (信息分布) in sentences in terms of given and new information, as we elaborated above, is popularly known as **Functional Sentence Perspective** (功能语句观) (**FSP**). **FSP** is a theory of information structure developed by the **Prague School** (布拉格学派) of linguists, notably Vilém Mathesius (1882–1945) and Jan Firbas (1921–2000), in the 1950s for the analysis of utterances in terms of their information content, and is still widely used in East European countries.

FSP differs from the traditional grammatical analysis of sentences because the Subject-Predicate distinction traditional grammar makes is not always the same as the **Theme-Rheme** (主述位) contrast. Compare the two groups of sentences below:

1) The term "Cinderella" is derived from the word "cinders" or "ashes."

Cinderella	*slept in cinders.*
Subject	**Predicate**
Theme	**Rheme**

2) The term "Cinderella" is derived from the word "cinders" or "ashes."

In cinders slept	*Cinderella.*
Predicate	**Subject**
Theme (marked)	**Rheme**

"Cinderella" is the grammatical subject in both sentences, but **Theme** (主位) in 1) and **Rheme** (述位) in 2) ("In cinders slept" in 2) is the so-called "**marked Theme** [带标记主位]" in English). We may then distinguish the notions of Theme and Rheme from those of Subject and Predicate in the following way: the former are textual notions while the latter are syntactic notions. They relate respectively to two different levels of linguistic description.

Topic and Comment

Another pair of concepts which are employed in analyzing **information structure** (信息结构) and which are particularly relevant to the **contrastive analysis** of the **textual structures** (语篇结构) of Chinese and English are that of **Topic** (话题) and **Comment** (议论).

Topic (话题) is the part of a sentence which names the person, thing, or idea about which something (**Comment** [议论]) is said.

Not infrequently, the **Topic** and **Comment** (话题-议论) of a sentence in such Western languages as English coincide with its Subject and Predicate. For example,

We	plunged into the stifling smog.
Subject	**Predicate**
Topic	**Comment**

However, as is the case with **Theme** (主位) and **Rheme** (述位), the contrast between **Topic** and **Comment** is conceptually different from that between Subject and Predicate because the former is related to the **information structure** (信息结构) of a sentence while the latter to the syntactic structure of a sentence. The example below well illustrates this difference:[1]

---

[1]There are three types of **adverbial**: adjunct, conjunct, and disjunct. An **adjunct** (附加式状语) is part of the basic structure of the clause or sentence in which it occurs, and modifies the verb. Examples include adverbs of time, place, frequency, degree, and manner.

He died *in an alien country.*
He *frequently* surfs on the Internet.

As for your suggestion,	we	will discuss it at tomorrow's meeting.
Conjunct[1]	Subject	Predicate
Topic	Comment	

In terms of their **information structure** (信息结构), most languages fall into two groups, i.e. Subject-prominent languages and topic-prominent ones.

A **Subject-Prominent language** (主语突出语言) is a language in which the grammatical units of Subject and Predicate are basic to the structure of sentences and in which sentences usually have the Subject-Predicate structure. English is a Subject-Prominent language, since sequences like the following are a usual sentence type in the language:

He	has already been to the new airport.
Subject	**Predicate**

A **Topic-Prominent language** (话题突出语言) is one in which the informational units of **Topic** (话题) and **Comment** (议论) are basic to the structure of a sentence.

Chinese is typically a Topic-Prominent language, since sentences with the **Topic-Comment** (话题-议论) structure are a usual sentence type in it. The information carried in the above English sentence may be represented in Chinese with, say, "新机场" as the topic of the sentence:

新机场	他已经去过了。
The new airport,	*he has already been to.*
Topic	**Comment**

We can observe in the above that in English, the Subject of a sentence is often, but not always, its **Theme** (主位). That implies the possibility of departures from the normal Subject-Predicate or **Theme-Rheme** (主述位) order in an English sentence. Such departures are traditionally referred to as **inversions**. (Inverted order was something quite common in early English, e.g. the line from "Wife of Bath's

---

A **conjunct** (连接式状语) is not part of the basic structure of the clause or sentence in which it occurs. It shows how what is said in the sentence containing the conjunct connects with what is said in another sentence or sentences.

—*All in all*, I shouldn't have come.
—*But* you have.

A **disjunct** (评注式状语) (also called sentence adverb) is an adverb which shows the speaker's attitude to or evaluation of what is said in the rest of the sentence.

Frankly, I don't know exactly why she refused to tell the truth.
He missed the chance, *regrettably*.

Prologue" in Chaucer's *The Canterbury Tales*—"I hate him that my vices telleth me" [谁指点我的错处, 就惹起我的恨].)

Halliday (1970), in his account of what he calls the "textual function of language," introduces the notion of "**marked Theme** (带标记主位)." As we know, **markedness** is a concept used by linguists to refer to departure from the norm. The process by which the normal sequence of **Theme-Rheme** (主述位) in a sentence is reversed and hence a **marked theme** effect achieved is known as **topicalization** (话题化) or **thematic fronting** (or plainly, "Rheme turning Theme"). A sentence structure characterized by thematically fronted rheme is called **topic structure** (话题结构).

There are two ways whereby **topicalization** (话题化) can be effected in English:

(1) **Transposal of Object, Complement, Predicate, or even Adverbial to sentence-initial position**:

   1) *Beer* he'll drink for hours on end. **[transposed Object]**
   2) *Susan* her name is. **[transposed Subject Complement]**
   3) *Sing* I can't very well. **[transposed Predicate]**
   4) *Three times* she's rung me this morning. **[transposed Adverbial]**

(2) **Displacement of tonic stress**. Normally the tonic stress of a clause falls on its rhematic part (as *protested* in this sentence). In *George protested*, however, *protested* is supposed to be given information while *George*, which takes the tonic stress, is the "new" information. By transposing the tonic stress to *George* we mark *George* as the "new" or rhematic element in this sentence. Such suprasegmental devices for marking a **thematically fronted rheme** apply of course only to spoken texts. (Based on James, 1980, p. 110)

But we should note that while syntactic and suprasegmental means may be employed to turn the **Rheme** (述位) or some element in it into **marked Theme** (带标记主位) in an English sentence, the **topicalization** (话题化) achieved thereby is still a "departure" from the norm.

Things are quite different with Chinese, however. As a typical **Topic-Prominent language** (话题突出语言), Chinese displays much greater freedom than English in topicalizing different elements. Some linguists (Xu and Langendoen, 1985, p. 5) note that Chinese has basically six sentence elements:

● Noun Phrase (**NP**)
● Clause (**S**)
● Topicalized Clause (**S'**)
● Verb Phrase (**VP**)
● Prepositional Phrase (**PrepP**), and
● Postpositional Phrase (**PostP**)

Each of these six sentence elements may be topicalized or thematically fronted. For example,

这些话   我不相信。   **[NP]**
These remarks I don't believe.

他会说这些话   我不相信。   **[S]**
That he should be able to make these remarks I don't believe.

这些话他会说   我不相信。   **[S']**
That these remarks he should be able to make I don't believe.

说这些话   我不赞成。   **[VP]**
Making these remarks I do not favor.

在桌子上   他放了几本书。**[Prep P]**
On the desk he put a few books.

桌子上有书，   床上不会有书。**[Post P]**
On the desk there are books; *in bed* there can be no books.

In some typically "Chinese-styled" (Xu and Langendoen, 1985, p. 19) **topic structure** (话题结构), the **Topic** (话题) may be related to the **Comment** (议论) as a whole rather than to one of its constituents. For example,

那回大火   幸亏消防队到的早。
[As to] that terrible fire, fortunately the firemen came soon enough.

这样的社会动荡 中国人经历得太多了。
[As to] such social upheavals, the Chinese people have experienced too many of them.

Contrasting the **topic structure** (话题结构) of Chinese and English sentences, we may notice four major differences between them:

(1) In topicalized English sentences, normally only one element is fronted, but in topicalized Chinese sentences, two elements may be fronted in the meanwhile and their positions are interchangeable. For example,

李先生昨天   我看见了。
Mr Li yesterday I saw.

昨天李先生   我看见了。
Yesterday Mr Li I saw.

The function of the *ba*-construction ("把"字结构) in Chinese is marking the second **Topic** (话题) in a sentence:

熊猫把竹笋   怎么样了？
What did *the panda* do to *the bamboo shoots*?

熊猫把竹笋   吃了。
The panda ate *the bamboo shoots.*

Sometimes, a sentence in Chinese may even have three topics. Chao (赵元任) (1968, pp. 11–12) cites as an example a question his wife asked of him:

你花浇的水　　够不够？
Did you put enough *water on the flowers*?　　(Xu 1992, pp. 242–243)

(2) English **topic structures** (话题结构) mostly occur in declarative sentences while Chinese topic structures may be found in any type of sentence. In fact, topic structure has a high frequency of occurrence in interrogative sentences in the Chinese language. For example,

这花　　　　多少钱一把？
This flower,　　how much is a bunch of it?

烟他已经戒了，你不知道？
He has stopped smoking—you don't know [that]?

(3) In some **topic structures** (话题结构), the **Topic** (话题) and some element in the **Comment** (议论) may contract a kind of cross-reference relationship. That element in the Comment may be an **empty category** (abbreviated to *e*), i.e. a category without any phonetic and graphemic form; or it may be a **lexically realized category**. For example,

王先生　　　我认识 **e**。
Mr Wang,　　I know [*him*].

王先生　　　我认识他。
Mr Wang,　　I know *him.*

王先生　　　我认识这个人。
Mr Wang,　　I know *this man.*

The empty category in topicalized English sentences refers anaphorically to the **Topic** (话题), since, in light of **Transformational Grammar** (转换语法), it is a trace (**wh-trace**) left by the Topic after the transformation of **WH-TRANSPOSITION**:

That shelf,　　he probably put it on [**e** (that shelf)].

In Chinese, the empty category needs not have to back-refer to the **Topic** (话题), but may refer to something else:

那个花园，　　我们已经种上 **e** 了。
That garden,　　we've planted it [with that].

The *e* here does not refer anaphorically to "that garden," but to things planted.

(4) The most important distinction between Chinese **topic structure** (话题结构) and its English counterpart, however, is that thematic fronting is normal **syntax**

(句子结构) in Chinese but something abnormal in English. This may be explicated with the following two observations:

(a) First, **topic structure** (话题结构) is felt by native speakers of English to be markedly abnormal **syntax** (句子结构). As a matter of fact, thematically fronted English sentences, especially **wh-echo questions** can only occur in some specific contexts (e.g. A: "Don't touch my transparencies." B: "Don't touch your ↗ WHAT?"); if used independently, they would be considered ungrammatical (e.g. "这里有什么东西是我不能动的?" ≠ *"Here I should not touch what?"). Each of the following sentences 1)–4), e.g. would only be used where the thematic elements had already been established in the context. Possible antecedents to each would be:

1′) Why not offer him beer if he gets drunk on gin.
1) *Beer* he'll drink for hours on end. **[transposed Object]**

2′) Yes, I remember. That's Susan.
2) *Susan* her name is. **[transposed Subject Complement]**

3′) John, you'll sing at the concert, won't you?
3) *Sing* I can't very well. **[transposed Predicate]**

4′) She'll ring at least three times before she gives up.
4) *Three times* she's rung me this morning. **[transposed Adverbial]**

On the other hand, in both written and spoken texts in Chinese, **topic structure** (话题结构) is regarded as a normal part of the **syntax** (句法), and is used with a much higher frequency than in English. According to Yuen Ren Chao (赵元任), around 50% of sentences in Chinese are in the form of topic structure. And, as exemplified in the following questions, topicalized Chinese sentences may occur without specific contexts.

你最爱看谁的小说?
Literally: You love best whose novels?
谁的小说 你最爱看?
Whose novels do you love best?

(b) Secondly, Subject is indispensable in an English sentence but not so in a Chinese one. Lyons (1977, pp. 504, 507) distinguishes three kinds of Subject:

(i) logical subject (逻辑主语)
(ii) thematic subject (sometimes known as "psychological subject")
(iii) grammatical subject

and points out that the English language demonstrates a positive inclination to make a distinction between thematic subject and grammatical subject. What Lyons terms **"thematic subject"** and **"grammatical subject"** are what we call **"Topic (话题)"** and "Subject" in the present discussion. So what Lyons means and implies is that Topic and Subject are clearly distinguished in English, and that Subject is readily identifiable in any kind of **topic structure** (话题结构). Lyons' argument is evidenced by the fact that topicalized sentences in English can always be restored to forms with the normal **SVO order**. For example,

John he gave nothing, but *George* he gave twenty pounds.

He gave John nothing, but he gave George twenty pounds.

In contrast, the Chinese language does not take (grammatical) Subject so seriously. Subjects of either thematically fronted sentences or sentences with the SVO order are often omitted without affecting the semantic interpretation of the sentence. For example,

(你) 去不去看电影?

Would [you] like to go to see the movie?

电影 (你) 去不去看?

The movie, would [you] like to go to see?

A:　[你] 今天请客都买了些啥?
　　What have [you] bought for today's dinner party?
B:　[我] 买了不少罐头水果。
　　[I] bought a lot of fruit cans.
A:　新鲜水果 [你] 不买, [你] 买这么多罐头的干啥?
　　Why is it that *fresh fruit* [you] didn't buy, but [you] bought so many canned ones?
B:　新鲜的 [我] 买不到, [我] 只好买些听装的充数。
　　Fresh ones [I] could not find; so [I] could not but buy some canned ones to make do with.

On numerous occasions, it would be much more natural for a sentence to go without its Subject than with it. We may readily perceive this in the above **conversation** (会话).

Furthermore, a considerable number of topicalized Chinese sentences cannot be restored to forms with the supposedly normal SVO order, as is the case in English. They do not seem to have any real grammatical subject: only one order—that of **topic structure** (话题结构)—is possible to them. For example,

看戏, 我特别爱看京剧。

As for drama, I'm especially keen on Beijing opera.

他们那帮死脑筋, 我每个人都好好开导了一番。

They blockheads—I gave each of them a good straightening out.

(Jin, 1992, pp. 215–21)

This further evidences that **topic structure** (话题结构) is simply a natural part of normal Chinese syntactic arrangement.

6.3.3 *Different Languages Preferring Different Cohesive Devices*

While every language has at its disposal a set of devices for maintaining textual cohesion, different languages have preferences for certain of these devices and neglect others. The Bible translators are certainly aware of these idiosyncrasies of language. For example, Wonderly (1968, p. 189) points out that while **ellipsis** (省略) is a mark of "good style" for English, there are languages, including the Mayan languages of Central America, for which the exact opposite holds true: repetition is a sign of good style. Consequently, a Mayan translation of Luke's Gospel 15:22 would require a repetition of the verb "put":

Put a ring on his hand and [put] shoes on his feet.

In a similar vein, these languages contrast strikingly with English when it comes to the marking of logical connections between sentences: instead of conjunctions, one finds constructions like the following:

When they got to town they went to the store. Having gone to the store, they bought some candy. After they bought the candy …

Cohesion (接应, 接气) is maintained by repetition of part of each preceding sentence in a grammatically different form. As Wonderly (1968, p. 192) correctly observes: "This is almost the opposite of the use of anaphora (复指照应; 前指替代)(in English) in which the omission of an item and the use of an anaphoric substitute not only avoids repetition but is used as a device to show connectedness" (James, 1980, pp. 113–114).

6.4 The Contrastive Analysis of Textual Coherence

Cohesive links go a long way towards explaining how the sentences of a text hang together, but they do not tell the whole story. It is possible to invent a sentence sequence that is highly cohesive but nonetheless incoherent:

A week has seven *days*. Every *day* I feed my *cat*. Cats have four legs. *The cat is* on the *mat*. *Mat* has three letters.

A text plainly has to be **coherent** (连贯统一) as well as cohesive, in that the concepts and relationships expressed in it should be relevant to each other, thus enabling the reader or listener to make plausible inferences about the underlying meaning.

In different languages, however, the concepts and relationships expressed in a text may be relevant to each other in different ways. One of the aims of **contrastive textual analysis** (语篇对比分析) is to find out the different ways which different languages conventionally use to organize concepts and propositions into an organic whole (i.e. a **text**) in order to convey a specific meaning.

According to Ji (季羡林) (1991), the celebrated Chinese scholar of **Sanskrit** (梵文) literature, different **thinking patterns** underlie various kinds of spiritual (and even material) civilizations in our world. These thinking patterns invariably find expression in various facets of life of the ethnic groups concerned.

One of the areas in which different **thinking patterns** or modes of thought would be mirrored must be the way a language conventionally uses to organize their spoken and written texts.

American linguist Kaplan (1966) made interesting researches into this area and found that the strikingly different thinking patterns of several major ethnic groups in the world caused noticeable differences in the organization of texts produced by members of those groups.

Based on his study of the papers written in English by international students, Kaplan concludes that people with different linguistic and cultural backgrounds tend to think in different modes or patterns, and he illustrates the major thinking patterns graphically in the following diagram (Fig. 6.2):

As may be discerned from the diagram, English texts are characterized by linear organization and development. If we step back for a moment to think of the writings we have read in English, we may readily endorse Kaplan's observation. Typically, English articles, essays, feature stories, or even book-length works tend to start with an introductory paragraph or part, which usually states in an explicit way what the writer is going to be concerned with in the work and, especially in the case of argumentative writings, the basic views of the author as well. The rest part of the

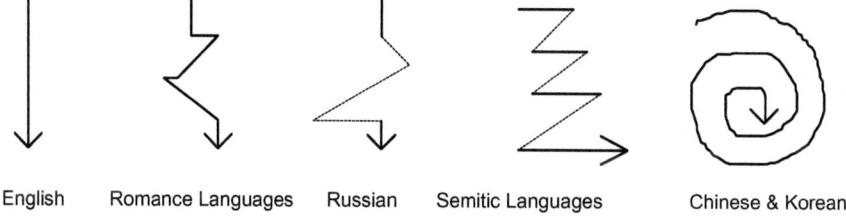

English   Romance Languages   Russian   Semitic Languages   Chinese & Korean

Fig. 6.2 Major thinking patterns displayed by people with different linguistic/cultural backgrounds

work is normally organized around the subject or argument the writer proposed at the very start. The same holds true with the paragraph as well: each paragraph normally has (and often begins with) a topic sentence, which summarizes the basic idea the author tries to put across to the reader through the paragraph. The remaining part of the paragraph would provide evidence to support the thesis as stated in the topic sentence. The whole text appears to be built up along a direct line. The first few lines of Francis Bacon's "Of Studies" may well illustrate this typical structure of English texts:

> Studies serve for delight, for ornament, and for ability. Their chief use for delight, is in privateness and retiring; for ornament, is in discourse; and for ability, is in the judgement and disposition of business. For expert men can execute, and perhaps judge of particulars, one by one; but the general counsels, and plots and marshalling of affairs, come best from those that are learned …

> 读书足以怡情，足以博彩，足以长才。其怡情也，最见于独处幽居之时；其博彩也，最见于高谈阔论之中；其长才也，最见于处世判事之际。练达之士虽能分别处理细事或——判别枝节，然综观统筹、全局策划，则舍好学深思者莫属。

(王佐良, Trans.)

Texts produced by native speakers of Romance and Slavic languages (Russian, Bulgarian, Czech, etc.) are marked by some minor twists and turns in their direction of narration. Régent (1985; as cited in Xu, 1992, p. 263) notes a number of textual disparities between English and French medical writings, the most impressive of which were found with the way medical case histories were written. English case histories were written in linear, chronological order, using exclusively the past tense. French case histories, however, were interspersed with estimations about the prognosis of the disease, using the future tense.

To Anglo-American readers, such twists and turns in the narrative direction of the text may appear to be digressive. The first English edition of Milan Kundera's *Zert* (The Joke, 1969) is a case in point. This novel tells a moving love story but, just like many other works by Kundera, it contains a considerable number of passages which do not seem to be directly linked to the story being told but which subtly reflect the author's thoughts about the general dilemmas in which contemporary men and women find themselves, about the relationship between tradition and modernity, about music and industry, and above all, about the meaning of being. The metaphysical overtones of the work are to a great extent transmitted by the apparent digressions which play an essential role in forming what Kuhiwezak (1990, p. 128) describes as the "**polyphonic**" ("many-voiced") **structure** of the novel. In 1967, one year before the "Prague Spring," the book was first published in Czechoslovakia. In the following two years it was translated into almost all European languages. After the Soviet troops invaded Prague in 1968, the novel was denounced as a pamphlet against socialism and was banned, and Kundera himself was forced to leave his country to live in France.

In 1969, the first English translation of *Zert* by David Hamblyn and Oliver Stallybrass was published by Macdonald & Co. (Publishers) Ltd. in London. But that English version appeared in a mutilated form because the translators and publishers took *The Joke* for a political fantasy that became reality a few weeks after its publication, and thence rewrote it accordingly, cutting, "pasting," and shifting the chapters around, leaving out what they considered the insignificant digressions and repetitions in good faith that this would give the novel a proper chronological order. But by doing that, they not only gave the English readers the wrong impression that "the novel could only have been written in a society where Marxism had been taken seriously," but also destroyed the novel's polyphonic structure, which contributes greatly to the artistic as well as intellectual appeal of the work.

In this case, the misreading of Kundera was due at least partly to the failure on the part of the English publishers to realize that textual patterns are relative instead of universal.

In translating a work of art, therefore, the translator/publisher should not take liberty with the textual structure of the original, deliberately modifying its textual pattern, because in art form is part of the content. In translating chiefly informative texts, however, textual readjustments are allowed and even desirable.

Typical texts generated in Semitic languages (including Arabic and Jewish) are known for their **parallel structure** (平行结构), that is, a balanced or coordinated arrangement of elements such as phrases and clauses. The first few verses of *Genesis* in the Old Testament (which was originally written in Hebrew, a Semitic language) may exemplify this:

> In the beginning God created the heavens and the earth. Now the earth was formless and empty, darkness was over the surface of the deep, and the Spirit of God was hovering over the waters.
>
> And God said, "Let there be light," and there was light. God saw that the light was good, and he separated the light from the darkness. God called the light "day," and the darkness he called "night." And there was evening, and there was morning —the first day.
>
> And God said, "Let there be an expanse between the waters to separate water from water." So God made the expanse and separated the water under the expanse from the water above it. And it was so. God called the expanse "sky." And there was evening, and there was morning—the second day.
>
> And God said, "Let the water under the sky be gathered to one place, and let dry ground appear." And it was so. God called the dry ground "land," and the gathered waters he called "seas." And God saw that it was good.
>
> Then God said, "Let the land produce vegetation: seed-bearing plants and trees on the land that bear fruit with seed in it, according to their various kinds." And it was so. The land produced vegetation: plants bearing fruit with seed in it according to their kinds and trees bearing fruit with seed in it according to their kinds. And God saw that it was good. And there was evening, and there was morning—the third day.
>
> *(Holy Bible: New International Version)*

Texts produced by Chinese and other Eastern peoples (e.g. Korean and Japanese) are characteristically circuitous in their way of expressing ideas. This tendency may be traced back to the early stages of Chinese civilization. In the first stanza of the first poem in *Shijing* (《诗经》, *The Book of Songs* or *The Book of Odes*), we read:

关关雎鸠	Guan! Guan! Cry the fish hawks
在河之洲	on sandbars in the river:
窈窕淑女	a mild-mannered good girl,
君子好逑	fine match for the gentleman.

Here the subject of love between men and women is approached not straight-forwardly, but suggestively, in a roundabout way, by depicting the mating songs of fish hawks.

In the Ming and Qing dynasties (from the late 14th to early 19th centuries), young Chinese scholars had to be capable of writing the so-called "**eight-legged composition** (八股文)" if they wish to pass the **Imperial Civil Service Examinations** (科举考试). The textual organization of this formally rigid style of writing is exactly opposite to that of modern English writing: it prescribes that every article be formed of eight parts or "legs" (破题, 承题, 起讲, 入手, 起股, 中股, 后股 and 束股) and that the writer go through a long string of discoursal formalities by way of preludes to the subject before he could actually come to discuss it. Vestiges of the textual features of the "eight-legged composition" are perceivable even in present-day Chinese prose writings. If a Chinese student of English really wants to write idiomatic English, s/he just cannot afford to ignore the differences between the textual norms of these two languages.

To illustrate the differences between the textual norms of Chinese and English in terms of **coherence** (连贯统一), we may look at two interesting examples. One is related to Hu Shi (1891–1962), a renowned modern Chinese scholar and one of the leading exponents of the **Vernacular Chinese Movement** (白话文运动) (1917–1919). When he was holding the office of the Chinese ambassador to the United States, Hu received one day an invitation for dinner from a lady socialite in New York. In what she imagined to be a gracious, Oriental style, the lady wrote:

O learned sage and distinguished representative of the numerous Chinese nation, pray deign to honor my humble abode with your noble presence at a pouring of libations, to be followed by a modest evening repast, on the forthcoming Friday, June Eighteenth, in this Year of the Pig, at the approximate hour of eight o'clock, Eastern Standard Time. Kindly be assured furthermore, O most illustrious sire, that a favorable reply at your earliest convenience will be received most humbly and gratefully by the undersigned unworthy suppliant.

To reply, the witty Chinese diplomat sent this telegram, which is however typically English in its textual organization: direct and to the point:

CAN DO. HU SHI.

(Kennedy and Kennedy, 1987, p. 507)

The second example is an English essay written by a Chinese college student:

COMPETITION

A new group of students has just enrolled in the University. Can you imagine the moment when they received their notices of admission from various colleges all over the country? One of my middle school classmates, before she got her notice, was anxiety-ridden. She couldn't at all be asleep and she lost her appetite. She felt dizzy all day long and her blood pressure went up. Lying in bed, she said she was dying. Just then, the admission came. She jumped out of bed with joy. All her illness was gone. Was it curious? She was glad because she could at last enjoy the happiness after her painstaking work; she was happy because she was to receive a high education, because winner was she of many rivals.

It is not easy to enroll in college, but it is lucky that the competition for it is open to every youth, which is entirely different from the former system. During the year of 1972-76, there was also competition for enrollment. But it was a competition in power of privilege rather than in power of knowledge. The college students then came from workers, peasants and soldiers who were recommended by their working units without examination. It opened the green light for some of those who abused their privilege. Thus the colleges were the gathering places for students coming from all walks of life, having even different records of formal schooling. How could a teacher teach in such a class? But he could do nothing but to bear everything unfair. It was the time when intellectuals were criticized, when exams and learning were neglected, when our country was in trouble. The meaning of the word competition was distorted. It was humiliating to think about it.

Since the reformation of the educational system in 1977, the situation has completely changed. Every middle school graduate and all young people under the age of 25 get a chance to take a nationwide examination. The competition is tense. Only 7-12 percent can be admitted and their records must be above a certain level. Competition encourages the young to study, increases their passion and interest in science and brings result and victory of the stronger. *But it also is tragic for the weaker.* A young girl who had a strong sense of self respect failed 3 times in competition. She was so depressed and shamed that she committed suicide by drinking DDT.

Competition between pupils has expanded to that between teachers, schools and even parents of those who take part in competition. Every parent hopes his children will be successful, and yet they are afraid that the children will be ruined by endless exercises and hard work. So they are the "King" of the family and are given the best treatment. His mother buys him meat and milk powder, her mother offers her sausage and chocolate, another serves fish and malt. Especially when the exams are drawing near, there is even a "nutrient crisis" in the market.

Competition for college study even worries some very young students. From primary school, one is trying to get good marks so as to enter the best secondary schools where is the first step of the ladder to Qing Hua, the first class university. At an early age, one is told to study harder and harder and forbidden from playing. A lively deer becomes a silent sheep. They are deprived of a teenager's innocence and fun.

This is the case. Though the competition brings about some deleterious effects, I'm afraid the situation may not be changed for the time being. Our country suffered a lot during the ten-year cultural revolution and now we're supplying the lack. Thus high advanced technology requires skilled and expert men, and yet a large population surely makes the competition tight. Not merely through college education, however, one can make achievements. There are many other ways of making contribution. There may also be competitions at every trade and profession. *Where exist human beings, competition exists. But as everybody knows, "where there is a will, there is a way." The enemy of success is self-abandonment. I really hope that the weaker will become stronger. And I believe with the development of the society, time will finally make up the abuse.*

(Guan, 1995, pp. 138–140)

The way this composition is structured is quite typical of many Chinese students' writings. The American teacher who marked this paper, however, frowned upon its narrative structure because it was devoid of the typical quality of an English argumentative essay, i.e. a linear textual organization. The essay starts with a question and an example followed by a review of the historical background of the issue. It is not until in the third paragraph that the reader can find the author's thesis, that is, competition has negative impacts. The next three paragraphs seem to be expanding on and supporting the thesis, but the essay ends with a digression from the thesis, stating that competition occurs everywhere and is inevitable. Without a clear thesis set forth straightforwardly at the beginning and reiterated in the end, the essay struck the American teacher as "eight-legged," incoherent, lacking persuasive power.

To sum up, the **contrastive analysis** (对比分析) of textual **cohesion** (接应, 接气) and **coherence** (连贯统一) is significant in that it can help bilingual workers as well as **L2 learners** (二语学习者) to a better understanding of the differences between **L1** and **L2** in respect of their textual organization and thereby develop **textual competence** to produce more idiomatic texts in **L2**.

American researchers used to sample the English compositions written by Chinese students studying in California and found that they did not contain major flaws in **grammar** (语法) or diction, but shared two serious deficiencies, that is, "**incohesion** (不接应, 不接气)" and "lack of focus" (Guan, 1995, p. 124). The judgment was evidently made from the perspective of English textual organization. The Chinese language has its own way of keeping a text coherent. Only that it employs somewhat different devices to attain that end. But "when in Rome, do as the Romans do." When writing in English or rendering into English something from other languages, or vice versa, one has to respect the cohesive and coherent norms of the language concerned; otherwise what is written or spoken will almost certainly be regarded as awkward or inappropriate.

6.5 Questions for Discussion and Research

1. Textual CA and pragmatic CA are **macro-contrastive analysis** (宏观对比分析) and fall within the domain of **macrolinguistics** (宏观语言学). How does the goal of **macrolinguistics** differ from **microlinguistics**?
2. What **defining features** (i.e. essential characteristics) does a **text** have? What will happen if a piece of spoken or written language fails to comply with any of those defining features?
3. What is **cohesion**? What semantic connections through which is **semantic cohesion** (语义接应) realized? What structural devices through which is **structural cohesion** (结构接应) achieved?

4. Backward reference is called **anaphoric reference** (前指) while forward or anticipatory reference is known as **cataphoric reference** (后指). Analyze the linguistic basis of the following humor from the point of view of **anaphoric reference** and **cataphoric reference**:

Co-worker: So you're the father of twins. Who do they look like?"
Excited father: Each other.

5. The use of formal markers as *and, besides, however, instead*; *so, because, then, lastly, now, anyway*, etc. to link sentences and constructions together is known as **"conjunction"** (连接). Related to **conjunction** (连接) is a remarkable contrast between English and Chinese in their textual structure. While **hypotaxis** (形合 [式连接]) (using connecting words to link up related clauses and constructions) is a norm governing English texts, **parataxis** (意合 [式连接]) (using no connecting words to link up related clauses and constructions) characterizes many Chinese texts. Translate the following sentences into Chinese or English, paying regard to the paratactic feature of Chinese textual structure and the hypotactic feature of English textual structure:

吃水不忘打井人。
前途是光明的, 道路是曲折的。
水能载舟, 亦能覆舟。
天气寒冷, 河水都结冰了。
他不来, 我不走。

"If winter comes, can spring be far behind?" (Shelley)
He had to take a long rest from work.
Urgent business prevented me form coming to class.
We give 10% discount for cash payment.
It is evident that he lied.

6. In textual CA, **information structure** (信息结构) refers to the use of word order, intonation (语调), stress (重音), and other devices to indicate how the message expressed by a sentence is to be understood. Two pairs of key notions related to information structure are **Theme** (主位) versus **Rheme** (述位), and **Topic** (话题) versus **Comment** (议论). Use examples to illustrate these concepts.

7. Is there anything wrong with B's answer to A's question in the following dialog? Analyze the problem from the point of view of **thematic progression**:

A: Who switched off the lights?
B: What Mary did was switch off the lights.

8. The process by which the normal sequence of **Theme-Rheme** (主述位) in a sentence is reversed and hence a **marked Theme** effect achieved is known as **topicalization** (话题化) or **thematic fronting**. A sentence structure characterized by thematically fronted rheme is called **topic structure** (话题结构).

Topicalization is allowed in both English and Chinese and both the two languages have devices for fronting rhemes to form topic structures. However, English is generally asserted to be a **subject-prominent language** (主语突出语言) while Chinese a **topic-prominent language** (话题突出语言)? Explain why this is so.

9. What is textual **coherence** (连贯统一)? Why does a text need to be coherent as well as cohesive?

10. Different languages conventionally use different ways to organize concepts and propositions into an organic whole (i.e. a **text**) to convey a specific meaning. While English texts are characterized by **linear organization and development**, texts produced by Chinese and other Eastern peoples (e.g. Korean and Japanese) are characteristically **circuitous** in their way of expressing ideas. What implications does this fact may have for rendition between and writing in English and Chinese?

11. How is a **text** different from a **discourse**?

12. What essential characteristics does a **text** possess?

References

Cai, X., & Yu, D. [蔡新乐、郁东占]. (1997).《文学翻译的释义学原理》. 开封: 河南大学出版社.

Chao, Y. R. [赵元任]. (1968). *A grammar of spoken Chinese*. Berkeley, CA: University of California Press.

Coulthard, M. (1977). *An introduction to discourse analysis*. London, United Kingdom. & New York, NY: Longman.

Crystal, D. (Ed.). (1987). *The Cambridge encyclopedia of language*. Cambridge, United Kingdom: Cambridge University Press.

de Beaugrande, R., & Dressler, W. (1981). *Introduction to text linguistics*. London, United Kingdom. & New York, NY: Longman.

determiner. (1987). In S. Flexner (Ed.), *Random House Webster's unabridged dictionary* (2nd ed., Chap. 6). New York, NY: Random House Inc.

Fan, H. [范红升]. (1996). 英语形合与汉语意合的特点对翻译的启示.《福建外语》, 1996年第1期, 48–53.

Guan, S. [关世杰]. (1995).《跨文化交流学》. 北京: 北京大学出版社.

Halliday, M. A. K. (1970). Language structure and language function. In J. Lyons (Ed.), *New horizons in linguistics*. Harmondsworth, United Kingdom: Penguin Books.

Halliday, M. A. K., & Hasan, R. (1976). *Cohesion in English*. London, United Kingdom & New York, NY: Longman.

Hymes, D. (1972). On communicative competence. In J. B. Pride & J. Holmes (Eds.), *Sociolinguistics* (pp. 269–293). Harmondsworth, United Kingdom: Penguin Books.

James, C. (1980). *Contrastive analysis*. Harlow, United Kingdom: Longman Group UK Limited.

Ji, X. [季羡林]. (1991). 再论东方文化.《群言》, 1991年第5期, 13–15.

Jin, J. [金积令]. (1992). 英汉语主题结构的对比研究. 载王福祥 编,《对比语言学论文集》. 北京: 外语教学与研究出版社.

Kaplan, Robert. (1966). Cultural thought patterns in intercultural education. *Language Learning, 16*(1 & 2), 1–20.

Kennedy, X. J., & Kennedy, D. (1987). *The Bedford guide for college writers*. New York, NY: St. Martin's.

Kolb, H. H., Jr. (1980). *A writer's guide*. New York, NY: Harcourt Brace Jovanovich Inc.

Kuhiwezak, P. (1990). Translation as appropriation: The case of Milan Kundera's *The Joke*. In S. Bassnett & A. Lefevere (Eds.), *Translation, history and culture* (pp. 118–130). London, United Kingdom: Pinter.

Lyons, J. (1970). *New Horizons in Linguistics*. London, UK: Penguin Books.

Lyons, J. (1977). *Semantics* (Vols. 1–2). Cambridge, United Kingdom: Cambridge University Press.

Quirk, R., Greenbaum, S., Leech, G., & Svartvik, J. (1972). *A grammar of contemporary English*. London, United Kingdom: Longman.

van Dijk, T. A. (1980). *Text and context: Explorations in the semantics and pragmatics of discourse*. London, United Kingdom: Longman.

Winter, E. (1971). Connection in science material. In *Science and technology in a second language*. London, United Kingdom: CILT.

Wintle, J. (Ed.). (1984). *Dictionary of modern culture*. London, United Kingdom; Boston, MA; Melbourne, Australia; and Henley-on-Thames, United Kingdom: Ark Paperbacks.

Wonderly, W. L. (1968). *Bible translations for popular use*. London, United Kingdom: United Bible Societies.

Xu, Y. [许余龙]. (1992). 《对比语言学概论》. 上海: 上海外语教育出版社.

Xu, Y., & Langendoen, D. T. (1985). Topic structure in Chinese. *Language, 61*(1), 1–27.

Chapter 7
Pragmatic Contrastive Analysis

In 1938, Charles Morris (1901–1979) defined semiotics as the use of signs governed by syntactic, semantic, and pragmatic rules. In 1959, Rudolf Carnap (1891–1970) explained that **pragmatics** refers to the relationships between signs and their users. Since then the discipline has been developed with enthusiasm by philosophers and linguists alike (Based on Hickey, 1998, p. 3).

Pragmatics (语用学) or, as it is sometimes known, **pragmalinguistics**, is concerned with how language and **context** interact to achieve the interpretation of a **discourse** (话语) or **text**.

"**Context**" is something very broad, including, for example, "… the intentions of the speaker, the knowledge, beliefs, expectations, or interests of the speaker and his audience, other speech acts that have been performed in the same context, the time of utterance, the truth value of the propositions expressed …" and so on (Stalnaker, 1972, p. 383; as cited in James, 1980, pp. 121–122).

Some linguists put **pragmatics** (语用学) on an equal footing with other branches of linguistics: while **syntax** (句法) studies sentences and **semantics** (语义学) studies propositions, **pragmatics** studies **linguistic acts** and the **contexts** in which they are performed.

In correspondence, **pragmatic contrastive analysis** (语用对比分析) can be carried out along two dimensions: the analysis of speech acts (言语行为分析), and the analysis of conversational interaction.

7.1 Speech Act Theory

Pragmatics has as its theoretical basis the **speech act theory** (言语行为理论) formulated by British philosopher John Austin (1911–1960).

7.1.1 Speech Acts

In his work *How to Do Things with Words* (1962), Austin defines a **speech act** (言语行为) as an utterance (see Sect. 1.3 "The History and Development of Contrastive Linguistics" for definition) or sentence used as a functional unit in an communicative event. It has both **propositional meaning** (命题意义) and **illocutionary force** (which we shall explain in the following).

7.1.1.1 Performatives and Constatives

Austin points out that many utterances do not communicate information, but are equivalent to actions. When someone says "I apologize …," "I promise …," "I will (at a wedding)," or "I name this ship …," the utterance immediately conveys a new psychological or social reality. An apology takes place when someone apologizes, and not before. A ship is named only when the act of naming is complete. In such cases, to say is to perform. Austin calls these utterances **performatives**, seeing them as very different from statements that convey information (**constatives**).

In particular, performatives are neither true or false. If A says "I name this …" B cannot then say "That's not true!" But performatives can be deemed "felicitous" or "infelicitous" according to a set of conditions (see Sect. 7.1.2 "Felicity Conditions" for details).

7.1.1.2 Three Kinds of Speech Acts

(1) In **speech act analysis** (言语行为分析), we study the effect of utterances on the behavior of the speaker and the hearer, using a threefold distinction. First, we recognize the bare fact that a communicative act takes place: this is known as a "locutionary act." A **locutionary act** (表述言语行为) conveys **locutionary** or **propositional meaning** (命题意义) which is the basic **referential meaning** (指称意义) of an utterance made by a "locutor" (speaker).

(2) Secondly, we look at the act that is performed as a result of the speaker making an utterance—the cases where "saying = doing," such as betting, promising, welcoming, and warning: these, known as "illocutionary acts," are the core of any theory of speech acts. An **illocutionary act** (施为言语行为) conveys **illocutionary meaning** (also known as **illocutionary force**).

(3) Thirdly, we look at the particular effect the speaker's utterance has on the listener, who may feel amused, persuaded, warned, etc., as a consequence of the utterance: the bringing about of such effects is known as a "**perlocutionary act**" (成事言语行为).

It is important to realize that the illocutionary force of an utterance and its perlocutionary effect may not coincide. If somebody warns you against a particular course of action, e.g. you may or may not heed his or her warning.

A **speech act** (言语行为) which is performed indirectly is sometimes known as an "**indirect speech act**" (间接言语行为). For example, a visitor may say something like "It's hot in here" as an indirect suggestion to the host to open the window, turn on the air-conditioning, etc. Indirect speech acts are often felt to be more polite ways of performing certain kinds of speech act, such as requests and refusals.

7.1.1.3 Five Basic Types of Illocutionary Acts

There are thousands of possible **illocutionary acts** (施为言语行为), such as requests, orders, complaints, promises, etc. Some research attempts have been made to classify them into several subcategories. Such classifications are difficult, because verb meanings are often not easy to distinguish, and speakers' intentions are not always clear. One influential approach is proposed by Searle (1969), who suggests that there is a nucleus of basic illocutionary acts to which all or most of the others are reducible. Searle sets up five basic types:

(1) **Representatives** (陈述性施为言语行为): The speaker is committed, in varying degrees, to the truth of a proposition (*affirm, believe, conclude, deny, report*, etc.), e.g. "*The department secretary likes Chinese jasmine tea.*"
(2) **Directives** (指示性施为言语行为): The speaker tries to get the hearer to do something (*ask, challenge, command, insist, request*, etc.), e.g. "*Come in, please*"; "*Why don't you take a seat?*"
(3) **Commissives** (承诺性施为言语行为): The speaker is committed, in varying degrees, to a certain course of action (*guarantee, pledge, promise, swear, vow*, etc.), e.g. "*If you don't stop making fighting I'll call the police*"; "*I'll bring you a toy train tomorrow.*"
(4) **Expressives** (表达性施为言语行为): The speaker expresses an attitude about a state of affairs (*apologize, deplore, congratulate, thank, welcome*, etc.), e.g. "*Your garden is so beautiful!*"
(5) **Declarations** (宣示性施为言语行为): The speaker alters the external status or condition of an object or situation solely by making the utterance, e.g. "*I resign*"; "*I baptize*"; "*You're fired*"; "*War is hereby declared.*"

Misunderstanding or deliberate misunderstanding of the nature of the illocutionary force of a speech may produce humorous effects, as is evidenced by the following humor:

"Now, Mr Blank," said a temperance advocate to a candidate for municipal honors, "I want to ask you a question. Do you ever take alcoholic drinks?"

"Before I answer the question," responded the wary candidate, "I want to know whether it is put as an inquiry or as an invitation."

The temperance inquirer puts a question to the candidate from his own position. His remarks may be interpreted in two ways, that is, as performing either of the two

illocutionary acts (施为言语行为) (specifically, **directives**): an inquiry or an invitation; although in this context the right interpretation should be the former. The candidate, however, chooses to bring forth the second interpretation as a counterblow on the originator of the provocative question, hence the humorous effect.

7.1.2 Felicity Conditions

Speech acts (言语行为) are successful only if they satisfy several criteria, known as "felicity conditions." "Felicity" as used here means appropriateness. **Felicity conditions** (恰当性条件) are the conditions which must be fulfilled for a speech act to be satisfactorily performed or actualized.

For example, the **"preparatory" conditions** have to be right: the person performing a particular speech act has to have the authority to do so. This is hardly an issue with such verbs as *apologize, promise*, or *thank*, but it is an important constraint on the use of such verbs as *fine, baptize, arrest*, and *declare war*, where only certain people are qualified to use these utterances.

Then, the speech act has to be *executed in the correct manner*: in certain cases there is a procedure to be followed exactly and completely (e.g. *baptizing*); in others, certain expectations have to be met (e.g. one can only *welcome* with a pleasant demeanor).

In addition, the **"sincerity" conditions** have to be present: the **speech act** (言语行为) must be performed in a sincere manner. Verbs such as *apologize, guarantee*, and *vow* are effective only if speakers mean what they say; *believe* and *affirm* are valid only if the speakers are not lying.

Ordinary people automatically accept these conditions when they communicate, and they depart from them only for very special reasons. For example, the request *Will you shut the door?* is appropriate only if

(1) the door is open,
(2) the speaker has a reason for asking, and
(3) the hearer is in a position to perform the action.

If any of these conditions does not obtain, a special interpretation of the **speech act** (言语行为) has then to apply. It may be intended as a joke, or as a piece of sarcasm. Alternatively, of course, there may be doubt about the speaker's visual acuity, or even sanity (Crystal, 1987, p. 121)!

Felicity conditions (恰当性条件) may be language- or culture-specific. This means that the validity of **speech acts** (言语行为) may be subject to the constraint of linguistic/cultural contexts. For example, in an Islamic country, a husband may get divorced from his wife by declaring orally three times that he divorces her. In Chinese or Anglo-American societies, a husband can never obtain a divorce by just performing the illocutionary act of saying to his wife

I hereby divorce you.

7.2 Conversational Interaction

In the previous section we discussed communication basically as a unilateral process, with information flowing from the speaker to the hearer(s). But communication is just as often bilateral, as is the case in **conversation** (会话). In this section, we shall first study how conversation is structured (its opening, maintaining, and closing), and then inquire into patterns that conversations in general can be traced to. As we go along, we shall consider differences between the typical ways different languages employ to carry on conversations.

7.2.1 The Structural Components of Conversation

Like so many other human activities, conversations have beginnings, middles, and ends; and the ways in which they are opened, maintained, and eventually terminated are something basic to the understanding of how conversations ever take place and are managed.

7.2.1.1 Openings

There is a joke about an English businessman and a beautiful girl who spent a year together shipwrecked on a desert island. On being rescued they were asked how they had got along together. They replied that they had not even spoken to each other, since they had not been introduced! The joke implicates that most people, even without introductions, are able to "break the ice" and strike up a **conversation** (会话) with people they meet by chance.

According to researches on conversational exchanges, we open and close a conversation by means of a fixed repertoire of ritual exchanges which are evidently dependent on cultural definition and can be expected to vary quite markedly from society to society (Goffmann, 1976, p. 266). If this is so, there should be ample scope for **contrastive analysis** (对比分析) in this area.

Pragmatists suggest that openings and closings are negotiated by "ritual" exchanges. This suggestion is reminiscent of a class of verbal formulae which some early sociologists of language identified and named "phatic communion" or "phatic communication." **Phatic communion** or **phatic communication** (寒暄) consists of "choices from a limited set of stereotyped phrases of greeting, parting, commonplace remarks about the weather, and small talk" (Laver, 1975, p. 218).

According to Laver, **phatic communion** or **phatic communication** (寒暄) is **indexical** or **deictic**, i.e. it refers to "factors narrowly specific to the time and place of the utterance" (Laver, 1975, p. 222) and can therefore involve either time or place deixis.

Time reference is divisible into the present, the past and the future, and so are phatic expressions with **time deixis**:

Past: Nasty storm last night.
Present: What a beautiful time of year it is!
Future: D'you think we shall get rain tonight?

Place-deixis is two-termed, according to whether the place referred to is "here" or "there"; but of course, "there" will in any case be viewed from the perspective of "here":

Nice hotel this.
What a boring play.
They served afternoon tea at the other hotel.

Some exploratory **contrastive analysis** (对比分析) work on conversation openings in English and German has been done by House (1977). There is evidence of a difference in the structuring of conversation-openings in these two closely related languages. The pattern of **talk exchanges** (话题交换) typical of openings is (1) or (2) in English, but (3) or (4) in German:

English:

(1) X: Greeting
     Y: Greeting + Inquiry after X's health
     X: Answering inquiry + Inquiry after Y's health

(2) X: Greeting
     Y: Greeting
     X: Inquiry after Y's health
     Y: Answering inquiry + Inquiry after X's health

German:

(3) X: Greeting: - Hallo. (嘿！)
     Y: Greeting + Inquiry after X's health: - Hallo. Wie geht es Ihnen?
                                            (嘿！你好吗？)

     X: Answer Inquiry: - Danke, gut. (谢谢，挺好的。)

(4) X: Greeting + Inquiry after Y's health
     Y: Greeting + Answering inquiry

The major contrasts are:

(1) **Opening** is an exchange typically consisting of 3-4 turns (话轮) (see the following sub-section for definition) in English and of 2-3 turns in German, and
(2) Germans may dispense with the reciprocation of an inquiry about health: neither (3) nor (4) has this reciprocation. Why should this be so? It may be explained in terms of the German viewing this health-inquiry as nothing more than a formula, a bit of etiquette which need only be observed once by one speaker. (Based on James, 1980, pp. 131–134)

7.2.1.2 The Maintaining of a Conversation

The essence of **conversation** (会话), at least in Anglo-Saxon culture, is that "at least and not more than one party talks at a time." This is not hard to understand for, if nobody talks, there will be no conversation and, if more than one party talks at the same time, what happens would be more like a quarrel than a conversation.

The person talking is said to have the **turn** (话轮), and conversations are organized round the alternation of turns. A **turn** (话轮) is an opportunity or right for each party in a **conversation** (会话) to talk in regular order. It is any one of the following three kinds:

(1) opening (发话)
(2) response (回话)
(3) closing (收尾) (Xu, 1992, p. 299)

Turns (话轮) are organized into moves. A **move** (话步) is a talk-task that the speaker and the hearer are co-operating over, having reached some tacit agreement on the goal of their talk. It may consist of just one turn or a pair of turns (called "**adjacency pairs** [邻接话轮对]"). For example, the following utterance of a teacher

That's right, Tommy, and can you give us some examples?

consists of two **moves** (话步):

(1) *That's right, Tommy*, which gives the teacher's reaction to something Tommy just said, and
(2) *Can you give us some examples?* which attempts to elicit another response from Tommy.

Moves (话步) are organized into exchanges or **talk exchanges** (话题交换). A **talk exchange** is a relatively complete interaction. It consists of one or more **moves** (话步) plus a closing. Exchanges are organized into **conversations** (会话). So we have the following scale of units of **discourse** (话语):

Conversation (会话 < one or more talk exchanges)

　　↑

Talk exchange (话题交换 < one or more moves [话步] + a closing)

　　↑

Move (话步 < adjacent pairs [i.e. pairs of turns])

　　↑

turn (话轮)

In each **adjacency pair** (邻接话轮对), the first part is said to have "transition-relevance" to the second, and the second part is always a response to the first. It is participants' skill in recognizing first-parts to respond to, and having second-parts to respond with, that keeps **conversations** (会话) moving. Familiar examples of adjacency pairs include: Greeting-Greeting, Question-Answer, Statement-Agreement, Complaint-Apology, Complement-Denial, Invitation-Acceptance/Refusal, Offer-Decline, and so on. For example,

A: Who ate the cake?
B: It wasn't me!

Adjacency pairing (邻接话轮结对) has to do with talk-response rather than with response-in-action. Let us consider what different linguistic communities see as the first-part and the second-part in a Complement-Denial adjacency pair. Manes and Wolfson (1981) find that the complimentary language daily used by Americans is quite fixed in its pattern. 85% of the 686 cases analyzed involve merely three patterns:

(1)   **NP is/looks (really) ADJ**, e.g.   *Your house is beautiful.*
(2)   **I (really) like/love NP**, e.g.   *I really like your house.*
(3)   **PRON is (really) (a) ADJ NP**, e.g.   *This is really a great house.*

The verbs *like* and *love* account for 86% of all the verbs used.

If we examine the case in Chinese, we would find that Chinese **complimentary moves** seldom contain the pattern "我喜欢你(们)的 ……" (I like/love your …) as in:

*?我喜欢你们的房子。
I love your house.

A widespread strategy in the American culture to respond to a compliment is to invoke machinery to demonstrate one's modesty. There are three ways of doing this:

(1) **Scaled-down agreement**:

  A: I've been given a scholarship to Oxford.
  B: That's absolutely bloomin' fantastic!
  A: It's quite pleasing.

  A: My, you've lost a hell of a lot of weight.
  B: Just an ounce or two

(2) **Reassignment to a third party**:

  A: You're the best pastry-cook in town, Vera.
  B: It's that new Kenwood mixer.

  A: You've got a lovely house.
  B: My wife found it

(3) **Return the compliment: tit for tat**:

  A: That was a fantastic party.
  B: You were the life and soul of it

The Chinese, when complimented, would usually contradict (at least ostensibly) the compliment by saying something like:

哪里, 哪里!
No, no! /I'm flattered.

您过奖了!
I'm flattered.

One way in which **conversation** (会话) is kept moving is by participants' continually making valid contributions, that is, contributions seen as valid by the culture involved. In addition, there are certain conventions (of a linguistic type) which are "used to lubricate **discourse** (话语) already initiated." These conventions are called "**gambits** (开场白)."

In conversational analysis, a **gambit** (开场白) is an **opening move** in a talk, discussion, etc. It is usually a remark intended to open a conversation. It may be used to show whether the speaker's contribution to the conversation adds new information, develops something said by a previous speaker, expresses an opinion, agreement, etc. so that a discourse already initiated may be "lubricated." For example, gambits which signal that the speaker is going to express an opinion include: "To my mind...," "In my view...," and "The way I look at it...".

Two familiar **gambits** (开场白) are the "pick-up" and the "downtoner."

(1) The **pick-up** occurs when the hearer repeats part of what has been said to him, as:

X: I wonder whether you've finished servicing my *Ford Escort*.
Y: *Ford Escort*, Sir: Well, let's just see

This **gambit** (开场白) serves a number of functions. First, it is a time-gaining device, used by someone short of a ready answer. In the above conversation, if Y is a clerk, he can be looking up the information he needs in a timetable or things like that while uttering his pick-up. It is used not only to save one's own face, but at the same time to show respect: the question must not be ignored, even if I have no ready answer. My pseudo-contribution does at least signal that I don't find his question outlandish—in fact, it can look as if I was expecting this question. For this reason the pick-up is referred to as a **Theme-Rheme** (主述位) device.

(2) The **downtoner** is the classic case of Robin Lakoff's first maxim of politeness: *don't impose* (see Sect. 7.2.2.2 "Rules of politeness" for detailed explanation). As the name suggests, its function is to attenuate the force of the **speech act** (言语行为) it happens to accompany, so as to make it less blunt and abrasive or, in other words, more acceptable to the hearer. It may, in English, either precede or follow the central speech act, but normally precedes it:

I think I'm right in saying that X = Y.
Correct me if I'm mistaken but X = Y.

X = Y *unless I'm mistaken*.
X = Y *or I'm imagining things*

It goes without saying that **conversations** (会话) can fail if they are not managed properly. Basically, they can fail in two ways:

(1) The participants can realize that they are not achieving their communicative goals, and so they abandon the conversation (会话); or
(2) One of the participants can cease to contribute, in which case either a mono-logue results or there is complete abandonment.

To have "communicative competence" is to be able to activate strategies for avoiding such failures, and while such breakdown may even occur among native speakers, it is more likely to occur when one of the conversationalists is a learner.

Let us look at an example. An Englishman visiting a German restaurant, or a German an English one, will want to place an order. Two ways available to the German for performing this **speech act** (言语行为) are exemplified in:

1) Herr Ober, wir hätten gern zwei Bier bitte.
2) Bringen Sie uns zwei Bier bitte.

These realizations of order are declarative and imperative respectively. Both would be unlikely in this setting in English:

? Waiter, we'd like two beers please.

? Bring us two beers please.

In an English restaurant an interrogative would be used:

Could we have two beers please?

Would you bring us two beers please?

The English order is less direct than the German, and, since it leaves the waiter's options open, is more "polite." To transfer the German realizations to an English setting, and vice versa, would lead to **pragmatic infelicity**. Communication might fail, since the German might be ignored by the English waiter to chastise his arrogance, while the German waiter would ignore the English customer because the latter's signals cannot compete with those of the Germans present (Based on James, 1980, pp. 136–139).

7.2.1.3 Closings

Phatic communion or **phatic communication** (寒暄), as defined above, is used also to terminate **conversations** (会话) amicably. Of course one can intend to, or by accident dispense with the etiquette, whereupon one will be viewed as socially awkward or tactless, or one's partner will be led to believe that he has upset one. One thing is sure: conversations terminated without phatic communion will not be easy to resume on some future occasion. The function of polite closing is to ensure easy resumption. Laver (1975) identifies six strategies employed in closings in English:

(1) **Giving one's reasons for terminating the encounter**. These, if **indexical**, may be either **self-oriented** or **other-oriented**.

Well, I'll really have to get on my way.
Now, I mustn't keep you any longer.

Note that the second expression here invokes quite clearly Robin Lakoff's **maxim of non-imposition**.

(2) **Assessing the quality of the encounter**. Presumably one can make a favorable or a critical assessment:

> It's been nice talking to you.
> Well, I don't think all this has got us far.

(3) **Expressing concern for the other person's welfare when you will no longer be with him**:

> Take care now.
> Mind how you go.

(4) **Referring to future resumption of encounter**. Some languages have fixed forms of farewell that refer to future encounters:

> *auf Wiedersehen*
> *au revoir*
> *do svidaniya*, etc.

These are, however, not so much signals that one wishes to terminate, but symbols that termination has been agreed and even accomplished. English is more literal in this respect, using such forms as

> See you next week then, *or*
>
> Can we fix a date for next time?

and people may flick through their diaries or organizers to reinforce the signal.

(5) **Referring to a mutual acquaintance**, where that acquaintance is closer to the hearer than to the speaker: i.e. the expression is other-oriented. Thus one says such things as:

> Give my regards to Mary (Hearer's wife).
> Say hello to the kids.

(6) **Using terms of direct address increasingly**: this has the effect of reassuring one's addressee, lest he should interpret one's desire to close the **conversation** (会话) as a rejection. In a sense, it is compensatory. It also tells him that, although business is necessarily impersonal, one has not lost sight of him on a personal level (James, 1980, pp. 134–135).

These six devices were identified as being conventionally employed in the English language. We may ask the question whether other language-cultures (Chinese, for example) use some other devices for closing a conversation or, in other words, to what extent these devices for closing a conversation are universal.

Another question that may follow is that, if different devices are customarily employed in different language communities, what cautions sensitive intercultural communicators should take when trying to bring a conversation to a close. These questions may form part of a meaningful topic on **contrastive discourse** that merits further investigation.

7.2.2 Principles of Conversational Organization

Conversations (会话) are exchanges of acts, not just exchanges of words, although they are certainly exchanges of words too. However, we may well ask how we can make such exchanges without achieving some prior agreement concerning the very principles of exchange. According to philosophers like Paul Grice (1913–1988), we are able to converse with one another because we recognize common goals in conversation and specific ways of achieving these goals.

In any **conversation** (会话), only certain kinds of "**move**" are possible at any particular time because of the constraints that operate to govern **talk exchanges** (话题交换) (see Sect. 7.2.1.2 "The maintaining of a conversation" for explanations of "move" and "talk exchange"). These constraints, which limit the speaker as to what he/she can say and the listener as to what he/she can infer, are summarized under two headings: Paul Grice's **Principle of Cooperation** and Robin Lakoff's **Rules of Politeness**.

7.2.2.1 The Cooperative Principle (Be Clear)

Paul Grice maintains that the overriding principle in **conversation** (会话) is what he calls the "**Cooperative Principle**":

> Make your conversational contribution such as is required, at the stage at which it occurs, by the accepted purpose or direction of the **talk exchange** (话题交换) in which you are engaged. (Grice, 1975, p. 45)

Conversational Maxims

Grice lists four **conversational maxims** that follow from the **Cooperative Principle**, i.e. the maxims of quantity, quality, relation, and manner:

(1) **Quantity**: Contribute to the conversation (会话) by giving as much information as is needed.
(2) **Quality**: Speak only what one believes to be true or what one has evidence for.
(3) **Relevance**: Be to the point and say things that are relevant.
(4) **Manner**: Avoid obscurity of expression and ambiguity, and be brief and orderly.

Grice (1975, p. 47) points out that the four maxims do not apply to **conversation** (会话) alone:

It may be worth noting that the specific expectations or presumptions connected with at least some of the foregoing maxims have their analogs in the sphere of transactions that are not **talk exchanges** (话题交换). In the following is listed briefly one such analog for each conversational category.

(1) **Quantity**. If you are assisting me to mend a car, I expect your contribution to be neither more nor less than is required; if, for example, at a particular stage I need four screws, I expect you to hand me four, rather than two or six.
(2) **Quality**. I expect your contributions to be genuine and not spurious. If I need sugar as an ingredient in the cake you are assisting me to make, I do not expect you to hand me salt; if I need a spoon, I do not expect a trick spoon made of rubber.
(3) **Relevance**. I expect a partner's contribution to be appropriate to immediate needs at each stage of the transaction; if I am mixing ingredients for a cake, I do not expect to be handed a good book, or even an oven cloth (though this might be an appropriate contribution at a later stage).
(4) **Manner**. I expect a partner to make it clear what contribution he is making, and to execute his performance with reasonable dispatch.

Conversational Implicature

Of course, everyday speech often occurs in less than ideal circumstances and speakers do not always follow the maxims Paul Grice has described, and, as a result, they may **implicate** something rather different from what they actually state.

The striking thing about the aforementioned **conversational maxims**, which differentiates them from **rules of grammar** (语法规则), for example, is that speakers flout them much of the time: indeed, a **conversation** (会话) that observes them consistently would be a very dull affair! When hearers notice these infringements they continue to assume that the speaker is making infringements for a good reason: the speaker intends the hearer to notice faults and draw conclusions. These conclusions are described by Grice as "conversational implicatures."

Conversational implicature (会话含义), also known as **implicature** (含义), is meaning implied by a speaker who infringes upon the **conversational maxims** but whose hearers, still assuming that he complies with them, are capable of deducing what he is talking about. In the following conversation between two university professors, Professor B apparently made infringements on the **maxim of relevance** by not providing Professor A with relevant information:

A: How do you find Tom's thesis?
B: It was a good printer that he used

But Professor A could perceive what Professor B meant to express (the **impli-cature** [含义] of his remarks), that is, Tom's thesis was too awful to be worth discussing. We may also consider the following two sentences, which may serve as examples of implicating:

1) The police came in and everyone swallowed their cigarettes.
2) You're the cream in my coffee.

1) is informative by flouting the **maxim of quantity**, while 2) is so by flouting the **maxim of quality**.

Now, to take 1), why should people swallow cigarettes just because the police came? One reason for swallowing something is to conceal it, and one reason for concealing something (from the police) is that it is illegal. What kinds of cigarettes are illegal in our society? Those containing marijuana. The **implicature** (含义) generated by 1) is that the cigarettes contain pot.

To interpret 2) as not breaking the **maxim of quality**, the hearer must assume that the speaker is trying to convey something other than the literal meaning of the sentence. Since cream is something which is not only a natural accompaniment to coffee, but a perfect accompaniment, the speaker is perhaps saying that the hearer possesses similar attributes. He is therefore paying the hearer a great compliment.

To interpret the **implicature** (含义) intended, the hearer must share the cultural assumptions of the speaker: in the case of 2), each must agree that coffee is deli-cious with cream. In a coffee-less culture, the equivalent of 2) might well be "You are the lemon in my tea" (James, 1980, pp. 128–129).

Many jokes work by breaking **conversational maxims** so as to generate **im-plicatures** (含义). The following are some interesting examples:

> The richest man in town died, and everybody was curious to know who would benefit. Agnes Thornberry, the town busybody, made a point of running into the lawyer who had handled business matters for the deceased.
>
> "Harry," she said bluntly, "you know Mr Chumley better than most of us. Tell me, how much money did he leave?"
>
> "All of it, Agnes," the lawyer said without hesitation, "All of it."

In this joke, the meddlesome lady was eager to find out how much money the richest man in town had left. The lawyer's reply to her inquiry was nothing more than a sarcastic equivocation, lacking sufficient information for satisfying her idle curiosity. The humorous effect resulted from the lawyer's infringement of the **maxim of quantity**.

> A young girl entered a hospital to see her boyfriend. She walked boldly up to a woman whom she took to be a nurse there. "May I see Mr Jackson, please?" she said politely.
>
> "Certainly," said the woman. "By the way, may I ask who you are?"

"I'm his sister," calmly replied the girl.

"Well, well!" chuckled the woman. "I'm so glad to meet you, honey. I'm his mother."

This heart-warming humor owes its effect to the young girl's shyness which caused her to break the **maxim of quality**.

Mistress: "Now, Matilda, I want you to show us what you can do tonight. We have a few very special friends coming for a musical evening."

Maid: "Well, ma'am, I ain't done no singin' to speak of for years, but if you all insist upon it, you can put me down for 'The Holy City'."

The mistress wanted the maid to serve the guests well at the musical party, but the maid mistook her mistress' instruction for a suggestion that she made an exhibition of her skills in music. By doing that, she evidently broke the **maxim of relevance** for **conversation** (会话).

One high-ranking official once responded to a subordinate's request for a raise by saying: "Because of the fluctuational predisposition of your position's productive capacity as juxtaposed to government standards, it would be momentarily injudicious to advocate an increment."

The staff person said, "I don't get it."

The official responded, "That's right."

In this **conversation** (会话), the official used pompous and obscure language to avoid giving a direct answer to the staff member's request for a raise. The humorous effect comes from this deliberate infringement of the **maxim of manner**. (Lü, 1988, pp. 53–56)

7.2.2.2 The Rules of Politeness (Be Polite)

Robin Lakoff (1973) reduces Paul Grice's maxims to two: **Be clear** and **Be polite**. For her these two rules are sufficient for the purpose of measuring a speaker's **"pragmatic competence."** The clarity requirement is accounted for by Grice's four **conversational maxims**, so Lakoff concentrates on the **Rules of Politeness**, of which there are three:

(1) Don't impose on your hearer.
(2) Give the hearer options.
(3) Make the hearer feel good: be friendly.

Rule 1: Don't Impose on Your Hearer

The first rule of politeness has to do with minding one's own business, that is, not intruding on the hearer's privacy or embarrassing the hearer with the citation of "unmentionables": for in the western culture private affairs and unmentionables are "non-free goods." If one must intrude, one seeks permission while doing so:

May I ask what this car cost you?

What did you pay for it, *if I may ask*?

For "free" goods, we may cite those things that are of public knowledge, for mentioning of which asking permission is unnecessary and downright odd:

*May I ask how much 12 + 74 make?

English has two ways of referring to unmentionables without giving offense: either the technical term or an euphemism is used:

Prisoners *defecated* on the floor of the cell.

Prisoners *did their toilet* on the floor of the cell.

("Prisoners *shit* on the floor of the cell" is taboo.)

There is obvious contrastive analytical scope in this area. We need to know what different cultures consider unmentionables, since this is a relativistic notion. Then it would be useful to know whether other cultures have available means for referring to unmentionables other than technical terms and euphemisms; and in what circumstances these avoidance expressions are used.

Sex and defecation are the most obvious taboo areas that spring to mind. Take the translation of Buddhist scriptures as an example. Generally speaking, Indians are indifferent about sexual matters. They are plain-spoken in describing sexual affairs and accept a description so far as it is that of an objective nature. German scholars, among the modern Europeans, usually translated literally the sexual explanations mentioned in Indian literatures. On the contrary, English scholars in many cases used the **Latin** (拉丁语) or euphemistic explanation instead of the literal translation. Chinese translators of sutras resembled the English gentlemen in equivocating about expressions involving sex, because educated Chinese, influenced by Confucianism, regard sex as a taboo even in writing. A Pali sutra text mentions that one of the defilements connected with drinking stimulants is that "those who drink liquor are apt to display their sexual organs." The Chinese translator turned this phrase into "those who drink liquor are apt to become angry" (Nakamura, 1981, p. 261).

This puritan attitude toward sex is still perceivable now and then in the translations published in present-day China. The translators of an essay carried in a well-known bilingual English-learning magazine published in Beijing, for example, rendered the phrase "Hollywood's great *sex object* of the 1980s" as "Hollywood's great *comedian* of the 1980s" (*The World of English*, No. 2 [1985], 40–41).

Rule 2: Give the Hearer Options

The second rule of politeness, calling for the giving of options to the hearer, is related to the rule of non-imposition: if you let the other person make his own decisions he cannot complain that you are imposing your will on him.

Rule 3: Make the Hearer Feel Good: Be Friendly

The third rule of politeness involves establishing rapport, camaraderie, a sense of equality or respect, etc. between the speaker and the hearer. This rule has converse realizations according to the real relative statuses of the speaker and the hearer. If the speaker is of higher or equal status to his addressee, the use of "familiar" or "solidarity" forms of address on his part will put the addressee at ease. But if the speaker's status is lower than that of his addressee he must not use these familiar forms, lest he be seen as "taking liberties": he will have to use forms which are deferential or polite.

The contrastive dimension of this rule will involve initially some documentation of what the linguistic markers of "**power and solidarity**" are in **L1** and **L2** respectively. Some languages, like Thai and Japanese, seem to reflect a very status-conscious social order and offer several grades of **deference marking**. Chinese and most European languages (except English) have at least a two-term second-person pronoun system to differentiate "polite" and "familiar" address. But the fact that English lacks this dualism in the second-person pronouns does not mean that it never makes such distinctions: it does, by other means. Such second-person forms of address like *Sir, Your Grace, Your Honor, Your Excellency* are clearly **status-marking**, e.g.

> I had only turned on my reading lamp and he came towards it, peering short-sightedly; he couldn't make me out in the shadows. He said, "Mr Bendrix, *Sir?*"
>
> (Graham Greene, *The End of the Affair*. p. 36)

> 我刚把台灯打开, 他便朝台灯走过来, 同时因为眼睛近视而费力地张望着。我站在暗处, 他看不清我。他问: "您是本德里克斯先生吗?"
>
> (柯平, Trans. 《恋情的终结》)

At the other end of the scale English freely generates familiar forms of address such as *Billy, Teddy, mate, my friend, old boy*, etc. What would be informative in the process of familiarization in two languages could make an interesting topic of **contrastive analysis** (对比分析). **Contrastivists** (对比分析研究者) may study the process of familiarization in two languages, including the stages involved, their linguistic marking, and the speed of familiarization (Based on James, 1980, pp. 129–131).

One thing in which Chinese and English display differences with regard to Robin Lakoff's third rule of politeness is the way forms of address are used to address one's relatives of the same generation. While it is quite normal to address such relatives directly by their names in English, the practice is usually regarded as disrespectful in Chinese. The Chinese are accustomed to addressing their brothers, sisters, or cousins in terms of relative seniority. As this is not a convention in English, such forms of address usually have to be replaced with functionally equivalent English terms in Chinese-English translation, e.g.

"四妹, 时间不早了, 要逛动物园, 就得赶快走。" 四小姐蕙芳正靠在一棵杨柳树上用手帕擦眼睛。"九哥!——他是不是想跳水呢?神气是很象的"

(茅盾. 《子夜》)

"*Huei-fang*!" he called. "It's getting late, We'll have to get a move on if you want to see the zoo."

Huei-fang was leaning against a willow, dabbing her eyes with a handkerchief.

"*Chih-sheng*, was he going to throw himself into the pond? He looked as if he was."

(许孟雄 & A.C. Barnes, Trans. *Midnight*)

Lakoff's three **Rules of Politeness** are regarded by many cultures (including Anglo-American and Chinese ones) as quite sensible and important to the success of conversational interactions, but there are cultures in which other qualities may be valued over politeness in verbal communication. The Dutch people, e.g. tend to think that straightforwardness, directness, and equality are more essential attributes of a successful conversation (this at least partially explains why the English word "Dutch" or "Dutchman" carries the derogatory associations of "raw" or "rudeness"). Culturally insensitive English-Dutch translators may overlook the real meanings of a "polite" English utterance and hence cause misunderstandings on the part of Dutch recipients, e.g.

ANGLO-DUTCH TRANSLATION GUIDE

WHAT THE BRITISH SAY	WHAT THE BRITISH MEAN	WHAT THE DUTCH UNDERSTAND
With all due respect ...	I think you are wrong.	He is listening to me.
Perhaps you would think about ... I would suggest ...	This is an order. Do it or be prepared to justify yourself.	Think about this idea and do it if you like.
Oh, by the way ...	The following criticism of the purpose of the discussion is ...	This is not very important.
I was a bit disappointed that ...	I am very upset and angry that ...	It doesn't really matter.
Very interesting ...	I don't like it.	They are impressed.
Could you consider some other options?	Your idea is not a good one.	They have not yet decided.

(see Dekker, 2015)

The **contrastive analysis** (对比分析) of conversational organization and norms in **L1** and **L2** is indispensable to the command of **L2**. It is generally recognized that children learning their mother tongue acquire linguistic competence and sociocultural competence concurrently since part of the knowledge of a language is that of how the language is actually used in daily life to fulfill different kinds of communicative tasks. To cultivate **L2 learners**' (二语学习者) ability to effect appropriate as well as meaningful communication with **L2** speakers, **L2 teaching** (二语教学) programs should include material aimed at developing learners' communicative competence. Such material will no doubt draw heavily upon the findings yielded by **contrastive pragmatics**.

7.3 Questions for Discussion and Research

1. What is **pragmatics**? What are the two major dimensions along which **contrastive pragmatics** may be made?
2. What is meant by **phatic communion**? Contrast ways English speakers and Chinese speakers conventionally use to open and close conversations.
3. Why is B's response odd in each of the following two conversations?

   > A: Good morning!
   > B: What's so good about morning?
   > A: [to a friend who just arrived from a trip] 路上辛苦了!
   > B: [the friend] 你怎么知道我辛苦不辛苦?

4. Can **L1 discourse conventions** transferred to **L2** performance lead to breakdown in communication? If so, give some examples.
5. Contrast the way **compliments** are paid and **modesty** shown in English and Chinese.
6. **Implicature** is meaning implied by a speaker who infringes upon the **conversational maxims** but whose hearers still assume that he complies with them and are capable of deducing what he is talking about. What does the hearer need to possess in order to deduce or interpret correctly the implicatures intended by the speaker?
7. Contrast the **linguistic marking of familiarization** in Chinese and English.

References

Crystal, D. (Ed.). (1987). *The Cambridge encyclopedia of language*. Cambridge, United Kingdom: Cambridge University Press.

Dekker, S. (2015, February 15). No hugs please; I'm Dutch! *LinkedIn*. Retrieved Febraury 18, 2015, from: http://www.linkedin.com/pulse/hugs-please-im-dutch-sacha-dekker?midToken=

AQFalAHsVXGqIw&trk=eml-b2_content_ecosystem_digest-recommended_articles-193-null&fromEmail=fromEmail&ut=1aNjRdO4n9c6E1.

Goffmann, E. (1976). Replies and responses. *Language in Society, 5,* 257–313.

Grice, H. P. (1975). Logic and conversation. In P. Cole & J. L. Morgan (Eds.), *Syntax and semantics. Vol. III: Speech acts* (pp. 41–58). New York, NY: Academic Press.

Hickey, L. (Ed.). (1998). *The pragmatics of translation.* Clevedon, United Kingdom: Multilingual Matters.

House, J. (1977). *Interaktionsnormen in deutschen und englischen Alltagsdialogen.* Paper Presented at the GAL Conference, University of Mainz, Germany.

James, C. (1980). *Contrastive analysis.* Harlow, United Kingdom: Longman Group UK Limited.

Lakoff, R. (1973). *The logic of politeness; or minding your p's and q's.* Papers from the 9th Regional Meeting (pp. 292–305). Chicago, IL: Chicago Linguistics Society.

Laver, J. (1975). Communicative functions of phatic communion. In A. Kendon, R. M. Harris, & M. R. Key (Eds.), *Organisation of behavior in face-to-face interaction.* The Hague, The Netherlands: Mouton.

Lü, G. [吕光旦]. (1988). 英语幽默的语用分析. 《外国语》, 1988 年第1期, 53–56.

Manes, J., & Wolfson, N. (1981). The compliment formula. In F. Coulmas (Ed.), *Conversational routine* (pp. 115–132). The Hague, The Netherlands: Mouton.

Nakamura, H. [中村元]. (1981). *Ways of thinking of eastern peoples* (Philip Wiener, Rev., Trans. and Ed.). Honolulu, HI: The University of Hawaii Press.

Searle, J. (1969). *Speech acts: An essay in the philosophy of language.* Cambridge, United Kingdom: Cambridge University Press.

Stalnaker, R. C. (1972). Pragmatics. In D. Davidson & G. Harman (Eds.), *Semantics of natural language* (pp. 380–397). Dordrecht, The Netherlands: Reidel.

Xu, Y. [许余龙]. (1992). 《对比语言学概论》. 上海: 上海外语教育出版社.

Uncited References

Bach, E. (1962). The order of elements in a transformational grammar of German. *Language, 38,* 263–269.

Boas, H. U. (1977). Some remarks on case grammars as bases for contrastive analysis. *PSiCL, 7,* 21–32.

Cao, X. [曹雪芹]. (1979).《红楼梦》. 4卷本. 北京: 人民文学出版社.

Cao, X. (1978, 1980). *A dream of red mansions* (杨宪益、戴乃迭 译) (Vols. 1–3). Beijing: Foreign Languages Press (Original work published 1792).

Cao, X. (1973–1980). *The story of the stone* (David Hawkes & John Minford, Trans.) (Vols. 1–4). Harmondsworth, United Kingdom: Penguin Books (Original work published 1792).

Li, D. [董黎 编译]. (1992).《英语幽默集萃》. 北京: 外语教学与研究出版社.

Ellis, H. C. (1965). *The transfer of learning.* New York, NY: Macmillan.

Ferguson, C. A. (1971). Absence of copula and the notion of simplicity. In D. Hymes (Ed.), *Pidginization and creolization of languages* (pp. 141–150). Cambridge, United Kingdom: Cambridge University Press.

Fillmore, C. J. (1963). The problem of embedding transformations in a grammar. *Word, 19,* 208–231.

Fisiak, J. (Ed.). (1980). *Theoretical issues in contrastive linguistics.* Amsterdam, the Netherlands: John Benjamins B.V.

Fisiak, J. (Ed.). (1984). *Contrastive linguistics: Prospects and problems.* Berlin, Germany: Mouton.

Siyi, F. [傅似逸 编著]. (1999).《英汉实用书信手册》. 北京: 北京大学出版社.

Greene, Graham. (1962). *The end of the affair.* Harmondsworth, United Kingdom: Penguin Books.

Zhuzhang, G., & Qingsheng, L. [郭著章、李庆生 编著]. (1996).《英汉互译实用教程》(修订版). 武汉: 武汉大学出版社.

Harris, Z. S. (1954). Transfer grammar. *IJAL, 20*(4), 259–270.

Hartmann, R. R. K. (Ed.). (1973). *German linguistics: Papers from the Nottingham BAAL Seminar.* Tübingen, Germany: Langenscheidt.

The Holy Bible: New international version. (The Committee on Bible Translation, International Bible Society, Trans.) (1982). London, United Kingdom; Sydney & Auckland, New Zealand; Toronto, Canada: Hodder & Stoughton. (1st edn. published 1979).

Hu, Y. [胡裕树 主编]. (1981).《现代汉语》(第3版). 上海: 上海教育出版社.

James, Carl. (1971). The exculpation of contrastive linguistics. In G. Nickel (Ed.), *Papers in contrastive linguistics* (pp. 53–68). Cambridge, United Kingdom: Cambridge University Press.

© Peking University Press and Springer Nature Singapore Pte Ltd. 2019
P. Ke, *Contrastive Linguistics*, Peking University Linguistics Research 1,
https://doi.org/10.1007/978-981-13-1385-1

James, C. (1972). Foreign language learning by dialect expansion. In *Papers from the International Symposium on Applied Contrastive Linguistics* (pp. 1–11). Cornelsen-Velhagen & Klasing.

James, Carl. (1981). The transfer of communicative competence. In J. Fisiak (Ed.), *Contrastive linguistics and the language teacher* (pp. 57–69). Oxford, United Kingdom: Pergamon Press.

Jespersen, Otto. (1947). *Language: Its nature, development and origin.* Crows Nest, Australia: Allen and Unwin.

Jones, S. W. (1824). *Discourses delivered before the Asiatic Society: And miscellaneous papers, on the religion, poetry, literature, etc., of the nations of India.* Printed for C. S. Arnold.

Karlgren, B. (1949). *The Chinese language.* New York: Ronald University Press.

Kasper. G. (1977). *Pragmatische Defizite im Englischen deutscher Lerner.* In Paper presented at the GAL Conference, University of Mainz, Germany.

Ke, P. (1995/1996).《英汉与汉英翻译》. 台北: 书林出版有限公司.

König, E. (1972). Major and minor differences between languages. In *Papers from the International Symposium on Applied Contrastive Linguistics* (pp. 51–56). Cornelsen-Velhagen & Klasing.

Krzeszowski, T. P. (1974). *Contrastive generative grammar: Theoretical foundations.* Lodz, Poland: Lodz University Press.

Kundera, Milan. (1983). *The joke.* London, United Kingdom: Faber and Faber.

Kundera, M. (1991).《玩笑》(景凯旋 译). 北京: 作家出版社.

Lado, R. (1968). *Contrastive linguistics in a mentalistic theory of language learning, CURT, No. 21..* Washington, DC: Georgetown University Press.

Li, R. [李瑞华]. (1996).《英汉语言文化对比研究》. 上海: 上海外语教育出版社.

Lü, S. [吕叔湘 编著]. (1980a).《中诗英译比录》. 上海: 上海外语教育出版社.

Mao, D. [茅盾]. (1983).《子夜》. 北京: 人民文学出版社.

Mukattash, L. (1977). *Problematic areas in English syntax for Jordanian students.* Amman, Jordan: University of Amman.

Newmark, Peter. (1982). *Approaches to translation.* Oxford, United Kingdom: Pergamon Press.

Nida, E. A., & Taber, C. R. (1969). *The theory and practice of translation.* Leiden, the Netherlands: E. J. Brill.

Nida, E. A., & Reyburn, W. (1981). *Meaning across cultures.* American Society of Missiology Series, No. 4. New York, NY: Orbis Books.

Nida, E. A., & de Waard, J. (1987). *From one language to another.* New York, NY: Thomas Nelson Publishers.

Nida, E. A. (1993). *Language, culture, and translating.* 上海: 上海外语教育出版社.

Oller, J. W. (1971). Difficulty and predictability. In *PCCLLU Papers* (pp. 79–98). University of Hawaii, HI.

Richards, J. C. (Ed.). (1974). *Error analysis: Perspectives on second language acquisition, London, United Kingdom and New York.* NY: Longman.

Richards, J. C., Platt, J., & Platt, H. (Eds.). (1985). *Longman dictionary of language teaching and applied linguistics.* Harlow, United Kingdom: Longman Group UK Limited.

Searle, John. (1976). A classification of illocutionary acts. *Language in society, 5,* 1–23.

Selinker, L. (1972). Interlanguage. *IRAL, 10*(3).

Skinner, B. F. (1957). *Verbal behavior.* Acton, MA: Copley Publishing Group.

Stockwell, R. P., & Bowen, J. D. (1965). *The sounds of English and Spanish.* Chicago, IL: University of Chicago Press.

Wang, R., & Li, D. [汪榕培、李冬 编著]. (1983).《实用英语词汇学》. 沈阳: 辽宁人民出版社.

Wang, Z. [王佐良]. (1989).《翻译: 思考与试笔》. 北京: 外语教学与研究出版社.

Wardhaug, H. (1986). *An introduction to sociolinguistics.* Oxford: Basil Blackwell.

Wardhaugh, Ronald. (1994). *Introduction to linguistics.* Toronto: McGraw-Hill Book Company.

Yanchang, D., & Runqing, L. [邓炎昌、刘润清]. (1989). *Language and culture.* (《语言与文化》) 北京: 外语教学与研究出版社.

Zhan, B. [詹蓓]. (2001). 译名与文化——从 "可口可乐" 谈起.《中国翻译》, 2001 年第 1 期, 59–60.

Index

© Peking University Press and Springer Nature Singapore Pte Ltd. 2019

P. Ke, *Contrastive Linguistics*, Peking University Linguistics Research 1,

https://doi.org/10.1007/978-981-13-1385-1

Printed by Printforce, the Netherlands

—